acoustical aspects of woodwind instruments

acoustical aspects of woodwind instruments / c.j.nederveen

Northern Illinois University Press   DeKalb   1998

revised edition

© 1998 by Northern Illinois University Press
Published by the Northern Illinois University Press,
DeKalb, Illinois   60115
Manufactured in the United States
using acid-free paper
All Rights Reserved

Library of Congress Cataloging-in-Publication Data
Nederveen, Cornelis Johannes.
Acoustical aspects of woodwind instruments / C.J.
Nederveen—2nd ed.
    p.   cm.
Includes bibliographical references and index.
       ISBN 0-87580-577-9 (alk. paper)
       1. Woodwind instruments—Construction.
2. Woodwind instruments—Tuning. 3. Music—
Acoustics and physics. I. Title.
ML931.N43   1998
788.2'192—dc21 98-3054
          CIP
          MN

contents

preface to the revised edition

The first part of the revised edition is a reprint of the 1969 edition. Apart from corrections of printing errors, nothing has been changed in this part. Added have been an addendum devoted to new developments, a new reference list, a list of symbols and a subject index. In the new text, references to the literature in the original book, listed on pages 98–102, are given in square brackets: []; references to new literature are given with the author's name and the publication year in parentheses: ().

In the past 25 years, the knowledge on the functioning of musical instruments has increased substantially. Theoretical insight, advances in measurement instrumentation and digital computing have contributed. However, it is still not possible to design a woodwind instrument on the drawing board, and maybe that stage will never be reached. Many questions have been answered, but many remain awaiting a solution. Perhaps this work will inspire others to look for new solutions.

I would like to acknowledge contacts and discussions with Ingolf Bork, Michael Bernard, Murray Campbell, John Coltman, Jean-Pierre Dalmont, Bruce Denardo, Neville Fletcher, Joël Gilbert, Uwe Hansen, Peter Hoekje, Mico Hirschberg, Douglas Keefe, Jean Kergomard, Thomas Rossing and William Strong. Their opinions and unpublished investigations helped me to shape my ideas on woodwinds. I am especially grateful to Joël Gilbert, Mico Hirschberg, Thomas Rossing and Guus Schwippert for their many helpful comments on the manuscript.

foreword

Physicists are strange people who do not rest before everthing is "understood", which to them means: "formulated in mathematical relations and equations". Musical instruments obey fundamental acoustical laws, and it is understandable therefore that many prominent acousticians — such as von Helmholtz, Rayleigh and Bouasse — have studied various aspects of instruments' behavior, and not without success.

An important aim of investigations into a musical instrument is to explain its pitch when sounded, a subject already inaugurated by Pythagoras, though in a somewhat mystical manner. Were this problem solved for all instruments, a significant step in the direction of scientific design would have been taken. In instrument-making today, rule-of-thumb or trial-and-error methods are far too often the ruling factor.

In my opinion, the author of this book — which served also as a thesis for the Ph.D. degree — has been successful in giving a physical and mathematical description of many, if not all, mechanisms governing the tuning of woodwind instruments. He has thus made an important contribution towards the qualitative and quantitative explanation of their behaviour. His results constitute a powerful tool both for correcting tuning errors in existing instruments and for creating new designs.

It is my sincere hope that the author will be successful in bringing a little closer together musicians, instrument-designers and physicists.

Prof.dr. C.W. Kosten
Delft Institute of Technology

preface to the 1969 edition

Woodwind instruments are a pleasure to look at, to listen to and to play on. For me, they have also been a pleasure to investigate, since from early in my life they have held a great fascination. As a student of physics at the Delft Institute of Technology, I tried to construct a clarinet according to my own design but failed to make it acoustically satisfactory. This encouraged me to look into the acoustics of woodwind instruments, and I soon found myself researching into woodwind instruments as a sideline to "serious" research. Some of the earlier results were published, but the investigations were completed and rounded off later when they took on the form of a doctor's thesis. I have many pleasant reminiscenses to the discussions with my "promotor", Prof.Dr. C.W. Kosten, and with Ir. D.W. van Wulfften Palthe, of the Acoustics Department of the Delft Institute of Technology. They very scrutinously read the manuscript and improved its contents and presentation substantially.

The present study presents theoretical and mathematical fundamentals of air oscillation in woodwind instruments and offers calculations on bore and holes. The contents should be of interest to the instrument-maker and to the scientifically trained musician. However, since each chapter is provided with a recapitulation, non-mathematically trained readers can become acquainted with many of the results and they should ultimately be able to perform many of the calculations themselves.

Many of the diagrams and formulae have stories attached to them, stories of informal and inspiring contacts with various colorful people of all shades between science and art. To many of them I owe much, such as practical co-operation with the measurements on their instruments such as blowing them and establishing their dimensions. I would like especially to mention Miss A.D. Blink, Dr. A. de Bruijn, Drs. J. van Ham, Mr. E. Mesman, Dr. P.J. Napjus, Miss M. van Spanje, Mr. E.J. Spelberg and Mr. F.P. van Velden. The instrument maker Schenkelaars (Eindhoven) and the music store Hackert (Rotterdam) lended brand-new instruments. Will Jansen and his collection of bassoons was an excellent source of data.

I am pleased to acknowledge the partial support of the Organization for Industrial Research T.N.O.

acoustical aspects of woodwind instruments

chapter 1
introduction

*De wetenschap te ontdoen van
romantiek is de romantiek van
de wetenschap.* *

11. On music and musical instruments

Music may be described as consisting of an
intricacy of air vibrations produced by musical
instruments. Music is an art which needs to be
appreciated in the main subjectively and emo-
tionally. Although it is no easy matter to
specify objective standards for this appreciation,
it becomes necessary when any measurements, so
common to science, are to be made. There is a
lack of knowledge as to how air vibrations are
transformed by the ear into signals for the brain.
and still more unexplored are the criteria used
by the brain for appreciating the incoming musical
message. Though the opinions of various listeners
may be alike in many instances, it is not easy to
find factors governing appreciation.

An important link in the production of music is
the musical instrument. Opinions tend to diverge
more on the quality of music than on that of an
individual instrument; and the beauty of the tone-
colour of an instrument appears to be more difficult
to decide on than on the purity of the tuning.
We observe clearly that the more emotional is the
topic, the less unanimous is the vote. Science is
of little help, because the more emotional a subject the more difficult is a scientific approach.
Although large-scale computers are nowadays used
for composing music, it is the human composer
that still makes the decisions on the quality of

* *'It is removing the romantic from science that
makes science romantic'.*

the results. Rating the beauty of the sound of an
instrument, without simply listening to it, is
still in its infancy. Certain things are known.
Two factors are important [103, 108, 109] namely:
the way the note starts (its transient phenomenon),
and the structure of harmonics when the transient
phenomenon has damped out.

It is necessary to mention here the essential
difference between "note" and "tone", though in
daily use this difference is not always observed.
A tone is a vibration purely sinusoidal in time.
Each air vibration, and therefore also every note,
can be analysed in a number of tones. The frequencies of the tones forming a note mostly are in the
ratio of simple integers, so 1 : 2 : 3 : 4 and so
on. The lowest tone is called the fundamental, the
others overtones. Groups of tones of which the frequencies are in the proportion of integers are
called harmonics. Notes produced by musical instruments may contain non-harmonic overtones, but these
tend to be weak. In practice, the note which is
played by the musician receives its name from its
fundamental. The frequency of the fundamental is
the measure by which tuning is judged. It seems
feasible to start investigations on musical instruments at the point where notes are approximated
by their fundamental tones, and only later to expand
the investigations to the tone colour, where overtones and transient phenomena become important.

In wind instruments an enclosed volume of air
oscillates and radiates sound to the listener.
The oscillations are excited and maintained by the
player, who blows air into the instrument in one
or other way. By manipulation of the lips and
modification of blowing pressure, a discrete row
of notes of various pitch can be produced: the so-
called natural tones. These closely resemble a
row of harmonics. Their mutual distance on the
tonal scale, however, is too large to be sufficient
for music, and there should be means

for making notes in between. This is achieved by changing the length of the tube in some way or another, so that another row of natural tones is generated. This change in length is realized either by adding tube-pieces using valves or by piercing the tube-walls with holes and so effectively shortening the length. These two different methods give a natural division into valve-instruments and hole-instruments. Historically, the material used for valve-instruments was brass and for hole-instruments wood. Wind instruments are still classed according to traditional pipe materials, although many woodwinds are today made from metal.

Brass wind instruments are excited by pressing air from the vibrating lips into the tube. Woodwind instruments are excited in a variety of ways. The serpent, which is gone out of use, is blown in the same way as valve instruments. The flute is excited by blowing a thin jet of air against the edge of a hole near the top of the instrument. In the clarinet and saxophone a single reed (an elastic wooden plate) is fixed onto an opening at the top of the instrument, leaving a narrow chink through which air is blown into the tube (Fig. 11.1). The oboe and bassoon are blown with a double reed. This consists of two slightly curved wooden plates, which are placed one on top of the other, leaving an oval, lens-shaped entrance to the tube (Fig. 11.2). In brass and reed instruments all the player's air is blown into the instrument, in the flute and flue organ pipe the air passes almost entirely outside the tube.

The shape of the inner diameter of woodwind in-

Fig. 11.1. Embouchure with single reed.

Fig. 11.2. Embouchure with double reed (bassoon).

struments, called the bore, is approximately either cylindrical or conical; at the extreme ends of the tube rather large deviations may be found.

Woodwind instruments have been developed empirically. Originally very primitive, their evolution has been strongly dependent on the development of mechanisms for the closing of holes. Music kept closely apace with advances in instruments, and composers have turned these immediately into account. At present, there are no spectacular developments in the woodwind section, old designs still being refined today.

The earliest woodwind instruments consisted of a single tube with six fingerholes (Fig. 11.3).

1500

1700

1800

1850

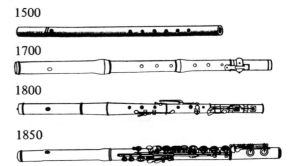

Fig. 11.3. Stages in the development of the flute.

Lifting the fingers one by one, starting at the bottom*, a diatonic scale was produced covering

* Although most flue organ pipes are blown from below, flutes from the left and bassoons from behind, we will, for brevity, call the side where the instrument is blown the upper side, or occasionally, the left hand side. The other end is the bottom or the right hand side.

approximately one octave. By overblowing, the scale could be extended by one octave to higher frequencies. The clarinet is the only instrument which behaves differently: it overblows at the fifth of the octave instead of at an octave. When required (which was not often), semitones were produced by partial coverage of the hole or by closing one or more holes just beneath the highest open hole (cross-fingering). As results were not satisfactory, extra semitone-keys were mounted during the 17th and 18th century; these were actuated by free fingers. The result was a rather impractical system of fingering with marked impurities. In the beginning of the 19th century Boehm devised an ingenious key mechanism for the flute, radically changing the bore and the position and size of the holes. His first flutes, still with a conical bore, date from 1832; his final design, based on a cylindrical bore, was introduced around 1847 [26, 104]. This design is still in general use and is essentially unaltered. It inspired Klosé to develop a key mechanism for the clarinet (around 1843) which is called Boehm-system and which has gradually gained recognition as the best and mechanically simplest system (Fig. 11.4).

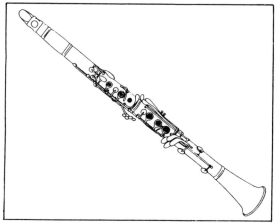

Fig. 11.4. Contemporary Boehm-clarinet.

Unfortunately, two other popular instruments, the oboe and the bassoon, have not as yet been improved in such a radical way. Apart from the fact that blowing double reeds is difficult, these instruments are provided with a very intricate mechanism difficult to handle (especially the bassoon) and incorporating many adjusting screws (especially the oboe). Yet in the 19th century many improvements were realized e.g. by Heckel for the bassoon and by Triébert for the oboe. For these we refer the reader to some excellent books on woodwind instruments [14, 15, 100, 104].

Systematic scientific investigation of musical instruments was not begun before the end of the 19th century. We may mention Von Helmholtz [50] and Rayleigh [98]. The three books of Bouasse [28, 29] form a kind of link between the oldest and the newest publications. Das [43] and Backus [6] studied the action of the clarinet reed, Mercer [77, 78], Cremer and Ising [41] and Coltman [38] of the blowing mechanisms of flutes and flue organ pipes. Boehm was the first to attempt calculations of hole positions [26]. A firm theoretical basis to these calculations was given later by Bouasse [29], Richardson [102] and Benade [17]. The present author has extended this method to a tube with many holes, applying it to clarinets and oboes [92, 93]. In the present study these methods are expanded and refined so that virtually every existing woodwind instrument is now open to a desk-calculation of its system of holes.

Because empirically designed instruments are fairly satisfactory, there has always been a lack of commercial interest in instrument research. The number of papers on musical acoustics has not kept pace with the growth of other fields of acoustics. Moreover, a musical instrument often is said to be a work of art inaccessible to scientific research, although several publications suggest

4

otherwise [52, 53, 54]. These recent investigations have increased knowledge in matters of tuning and tone-quality of musical instruments, knowledge that can replace mere trial-and-error by scientific calculations. Up to now, however, there have been no spectacular results and this may explain the reserve of musicians and instrument makers towards research. This reserve is paramount when drastic changes are proposed, e.g. the note-script (Klavarscribo), the fingering (Jankó's wholetone-keyboard for piano*, Boehm-clarinet and Boehm-oboe).

The conservatism of the artist — which we would not expect — is the better understood if we realize that a musical instrument tends to become an extension of the player's body and incorporates all natural reflexes pertaining to such a situation. This causes the musician, once adapted to the idiosyncrasies of his instrument, to be reluctant to risk his technique (and therefore his living) with revolutionary experiments. The same applies to the production of music with another character: it is difficult to write poetry in a foreign language.

This attitude of the musician influences that of the instrument-maker. Moreover, many of these firms are small and traditional, having no contact with the pure scientist. As there is a tendency towards production on a larger scale (some popular instruments are already almost mass-produced) it can be expected that methods pertaining to such productions will lead to instruments of reasonable quality at a reasonable cost. It cannot be forecast yet whether this will mean an increase or a decrease in the overall quality of musical instruments.

* *In this keyboard black and white keys succeed each other, black as well as white keys forming a full-tone scale.*

12. Aim of the investigations

The aim of the investigations was to find a method for calculating the right position and size of the holes of a woodwind instrument. This can be useful for designing a new instrument or changing an existing one. It may also be expected to be of use when holes are to be moved or when extra holes are to be added (for trills, etc.), or when impure notes have to be corrected.

In order to achieve this aim a study was made of a number of existing woodwind instruments in the rôle of acoustic oscillators. Using laws of acoustics, equations were derived from which the desired frequencies could be calculated. This was done for a number of instruments in current use, some of them of good quality. All necessary data on bore and holes were obtained by careful measurements. Mechanical properties of reeds, if present, were included. With all these data, resonance-frequencies were calculated for the various possible hole-closures as specified in so-called fingering charts, from which the finger positions can be read for every note.

The results found are compared with the nominal frequencies according to the fingering chart; the deviation of the calculated from the nominal frequency is specified for every note and plotted in a diagram.

The deviations thus calculated were compared with the deviations occurring when the instrument is actually blown. Since the player has some control over the frequency these blowing experiments were repeated a number of times so as to reduce chance results. The musician was instructed not to correct tuning errors of the instrument proper, though a certain amount of correction was unavoidable.

The comparison of calculated and measured deviations is the subject of the last chapter; Chapters 2 and 3 discuss how to derive the equations for future calculations. In the next two sections, this method will be briefly reviewed; this review is preceded by an introduction to some basic acoustics.

13. General acoustic concepts

Any study of tuning is concerned with calculating the frequency of vibrations. The number of (complete) vibrations per second is expressed in hertz (Hz); and the frequency is determined by the interaction of two properties of matter, namely inertia and elasticity.

An instructive example of this interaction is a mechanical oscillator consisting of a helical spring, clamped at its upper end and provided with a mass at its lower end (Fig. 13.1). The compliance C is

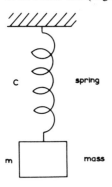

Fig. 13.1. Mechanical oscillator containing elastic and inertia element

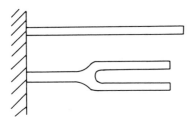

Fig. 13.2. Examples of vibrating systems with distributed mass and compliance: bar (top), tuning fork (bottom).

defined as the elongation of the spring, expressed in meter, when it is stretched by the unit of force, the newton (N). The mass m is expressed in kg. When the mass is given a small displacement from equilibrium and then released, it begins vibrating around the equilibrium with a frequency f determined by

$$f = \frac{\omega}{2\pi} = \frac{1}{2\pi} \sqrt{\frac{1}{mC}} . \qquad (13.1)$$

This formula shows that increasing m and/or C results in a lowering of frequency, a fact confirmed by practice.

In the previous example compliance and mass were clearly separated. They are said to be lumped. In many instances, however, these two properties are distributed along the whole vibrating system. This is the case with a bar clamped at one end or with the well-known tuning-fork (Fig. 13.2). A calculation of the frequency is possible for the bar, but already impossible for the tuning-fork.

Every vibration of every realistic oscillator appears to be damped more or less, due for example to friction with the surroundings or to internal damping (vibrational energy transformed into heat). An example of such a damped oscillator is obtained when a mass-spring-oscillator is provided with a plate, attached to the mass, which is suspended in a viscous oil (Fig. 13.3). The deviation of the mass from equilibrium, x, as a function of time t, of the system having a mass m, a resistance r and a compliance C is governed by the second order differential equation

$$m \frac{d^2x}{dt^2} + r \frac{dx}{dt} + \frac{x}{C} = 0. \qquad (13.2)$$

For small values of r the solution is a vibration that is nearly sinusoidal and gradually decreases in amplitude, with a frequency close to that of the undamped case. At larger damping the frequency differs more.

The mechanical oscillator with m, r and C has an analogue in the electrical circuit consisting of an inductance L, a resistance R and a capacitor C in series (Fig. 13.4).

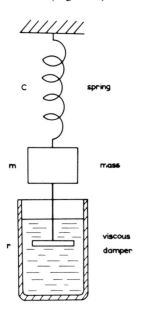

Fig. 13.3. Mass-and-spring oscillator with viscous damper.

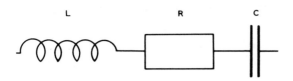

Fig. 13.4. Electrical analogue of the damped mechanical oscillator of Fig. 13.3.

We now focus our attention on oscillating air. An example of a system where mass and compliance are practically lumped is an empty bottle with a shallow neck (Fig. 13.5). This bottle can

be blown to produce a note. The volume of the bottle acts as compliance and the dimensions of the neck determine the acoustic mass. The natural frequency can be changed by partly covering the opening or by partly filling the bottle with water.

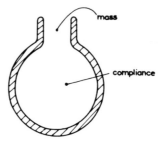

Fig. 13.5. Example of air oscillator with lumped mass and compliance.

Wind musical instruments are examples of vibrating systems where mass and compliance are distributed along the whole vibrating volume. Wind instruments are mostly long and slender tubes, folded when they are very long, and blown at one side (to avoid confusion we choose this to be the top or the left end). The simplest wind in-

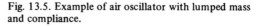
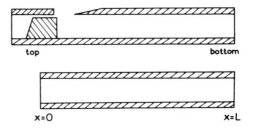

Fig. 13.6. Essentials of a flue organ pipe (top), and its simplest acoustic approximation (bottom).

strument appears to be the open, cylindrical flue organ pipe, as schematically drawn in Fig. 13.6, top; it resembles a flute or recorder without holes. At the left air is blown across the opening. For a calculation of the natural frequency the excitation mechanism may be neglected to a first approximation, so that the simplest form of this organ pipe is a purely cylindrical tube, open at both ends (Fig. 13.6, bottom). Investigations have revealed how the air in the tube moves. At both open ends it periodically moves in and out of the tube. Inside the tube one or more places can be found where the air is at rest and where air flows to and from both sides; pressure fluctuations therefore take place here. Considering this, we distinguish the so-called nodes and the antinodes or loops. In a node the air is at rest, in an antinode there is a maximum of movement. More precisely these places are called displacement-node and displacement-antinode because these notions may also be related to pressure fluctuations and then nodes and antinodes interchange position. In the lowest vibrational mode of an open tube, the fundamental, we find one displacement-node only and it is located in the middle of the cylinder. Apparently the compression properties of the air are manifest here. The mass properties of the air are found at the open ends of the tube.

For a calculation of the frequency, equations must be derived. In this section, damping is neglected for simplicity. For the case considered here, a plane wave in a cylindrical tube, the equation of motion and the equation of continuity are [40, 66, 87, 98]

$$- \partial p / \partial x = \rho \ \partial u / \partial t, \qquad (13.3)$$
$$- \partial p / \partial t = K \ \partial u / \partial x, \qquad (13.4)$$

where p = sound pressure, the pressure above atmospheric pressure,
x = place coordinate,
ρ = density of air,
u = particle velocity (positive in positive x-direction),
K = bulk modulus of air.

After elimination of u we get the wave equation

$$\partial^2 p / \partial t^2 = (K / \rho) \ \partial^2 p / \partial x^2. \qquad (13.5)$$

A solution which satisfies this equation is of the type

$$p = \sin \omega (t - x / c), \qquad (13.6)$$

which shows the character of the waves. They are harmonic as a function of time and are progressive in the positive x-direction with the velocity of sound c:

$$c = (K / \rho)^{1/2} \approx 340 \text{ m/s}. \qquad (13.7)$$

The waveform according to eq.(13.6) is repeated when the argument of the sine increases with 2π. From the time-dependent term it follows that the frequency f, the number of repetitions per second, equals $\omega / 2\pi$. From the position-dependency it follows that a repetition occurs at a distance λ, called the wavelength, determined by $\omega \lambda / c = 2\pi$, from which we find the relationship

$$\lambda \times f = c. \qquad (13.8)$$

Adding a wave travelling in the opposite direction, two constants A and B, and using complex notation a more general solution takes on the form

$$p = (A \sin kx + B \cos kx) \exp j\omega t, \qquad (13.9)$$

where $k = \omega / c$ is called the wave number. Introducing $B/A = \tan \psi$, where ψ may be complex, the sound pressure can be rewritten as follows:

$$p = \hat{p} \sin (kx + \psi) \exp j\omega t, \qquad (13.10)$$

where $\hat{p}$ is a complex constant. Inserting this into eq.(13.3) and using eq.(13.7), the particle velocity is obtained:

$$u = \frac{-\hat{p}}{j\rho c} \cos(kx + \psi) \exp j\omega t \qquad (13.11)$$

8

A useful quantity when dealing with oscillations in tubes is the volume velocity U which is found by multiplication of the particle velocity u with the area of the cross-section S,

$$U = S \times u. \qquad (13.12)$$

Equally useful are characteristic quantities for the ratio of p to U. For this purpose we define the acoustic impedance Z and the acoustic admittance Y as follows:

$$Z = p/U, \quad Y = U/p. \qquad (13.13)$$

Substituting eqs (13.10), (13.11) and (13.12) into (13.13) we obtain the impedance as a function of the position x in the tube:

$$Z = \frac{1}{Y} = \frac{-j\rho c}{S} \tan(kx + \psi). \qquad (13.14)$$

At the left hand side (Fig. 13.6), say at $x = 0$, the tube ends in free space, which implies that the pressure here is always equal to the atmospheric, so that always $p = 0$. This means that the impedance is zero here, i.e. $\psi = 0$. At the other (open) end, $x = L$, the impedance is zero too, so that a condition for the wave number is found

$$\tan kL = 0. \qquad (13.15)$$

Solutions to this are

$$kL = m\pi, \ m \text{ integer.} \qquad (13.16)$$

From eqs (13.8) and (13.16) it follows that in the fundamental mode, $m = 1$, half a wavelength fits in the tube; for the first overtone, $m = 2$, a full wavelength; *et cetera*. The frequencies of the vibrational modes appear to be in the ratios of whole numbers. In other words, we have now derived what was already mentioned in Section 11. On the keyboard of a piano, shown in Fig. 13.7, crosses in-

Fig. 13.7. Piano keyboard. Notes marked with crosses indicate a group of natural tones which can be extracted from a cylindrical tube open at both ends.

dicate the fundamental C_3 and its overtones*.

In a displacement node, $U = 0$, so it follows from eq. (13.13) that here the impedance goes to infinity. In an antinode the impedance is zero. The positions of the nodes and antinodes for the first three vibrational modes are sketched in Fig. 13.8.

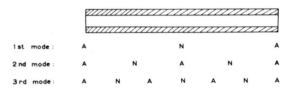

Fig. 13.8. Positions of displacement nodes (N) and antinodes (A) for the first three modes of a two-sided open cylinder.

Besides the so-called "open" organ pipe, as sketched in Fig. 13.6 there also exist the "closed" organ pipe. Such a pipe is closed at the non-blown end. The acoustical behaviour of the closed pipe is different from that of the open pipe. We can transform an open pipe into a closed one by inserting a wall at the position of a node (Fig. 13.8). Then there will be no change in the fundamental

* *We prefer to use the notation system for notes as proposed by Young [11, 114] and as included in the American Standard Acoustical Terminology, S1.1-1960 (see Fig. 13.7). This notation is more systematic and scientifically convenient than the widely used Helmholz' notation with its dashes and small and capital print.*

frequency since no movement of air took place at this spot. That part of the pipe containing vibrating air is half as long as that of the open pipe: a closed organ pipe is shorter for the same fundamental frequency than an open organ pipe. This can be shown from a calculation. The impedance for a closed end at $x = L$ is infinite, yielding $\psi = \pi/2$, so eq. (13.14) becomes

$$\cot kL = 0, \qquad (13.17)$$

giving

$$kL = m\pi, m = \tfrac{1}{2}, 1\tfrac{1}{2}, 2\tfrac{1}{2}, 3\tfrac{1}{2}, \text{ and so on.} \qquad (13.18)$$

From this follows a different row of overtones, viz. according to 1 : 3 : 5 : 7, so odd harmonics, with a fundamental twice as low as that of an organ pipe of the same length.

Another cylindrical instrument overblowing in odd harmonics is the clarinet. As the non-blown side of the instrument is open, the other end (where a reed is found) must necessarily be in effect closed. As the reed opens periodically to let in air, this will only be approximately true, as will be shown in Chapter 2.

Next to the cylindrical instruments there are a number of instruments, such as saxophones, oboe and bassoon, with a bore following the course of a cone, truncated for about one tenth of its entire length. These instruments are blown at the narrow end of the bore with a single or double reed. Just as with the clarinet we expect a node near the reed. But although this appears to be the case, the instruments overblow in the octave like the flute. The frequency is calculated from eq. (13.16) where L is equal to the sum of the geometrical length of the tube and the truncated piece of the cone. To illustrate this, in Fig. 13.9 two tubes which resonate in the same frequency are shown. They are an open-open cylindrical flute and a closed-open conical tube. These two tubes vibrate

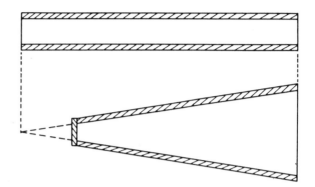

Fig. 13.9. Flute and conical reed instrument on the same scale, vibrating in the same frequencies.

in the same fundamental and they possess the same series of overtones. This property of the reed-blown cone does not seem to be generally known [99].

Finally there exist conical flutes, open at both ends, which are blown at the widest end of the cone. This type of instrument will appear to behave in almost the same way as the cylindrical tube of the same length.

It must be stressed, that all considerations given here are approximate. For a more accurate calculation it is necessary to consider everything more closely and to include end-corrections and deviations from ideal bore and ideal behaviour. It is also necessary to include losses of vibrational energy when the air passes in friction with the walls, and also losses due to energy radiating through the holes and open end into the atmosphere. This energy-radiation is very important, because it is that part of the instrument's sound which reaches the listener. The losses have to be compensated for by continually blowing the instrument. In flutes and organ pipes this is achieved by a jet of air streaming along the edge of a hole in the instrument. Pressure fluctuations in the inside of the instrument cause the jet to fluctuate in such a way that air flows into the instrument in the right phase to maintain the vibrations. In reed instruments the reed bends outwards due to increasing pressure inside the instrument; as the reed bends outwards the area of the chink-like passage is increased. Then there is an increase in pressurized air flow from the player's mouth, which sustains the sound-pressure in the tube.

14. Survey of the calculation method

We wish to determine the natural frequency of a hypothetical or existing woodwind instrument only from its dimensions and the mechanical properties of reeds. In the first place some simplyfying assumptions have to be made concerning the geometry and properties of the walls and of the movement of air particles. These assumptions are:

1. The air in the tube performs longitudinal vibrations.

2. The cross-dimensions of the tube are small with respect to the wavelength.

3. The bore of the tube resembles either a pure cylinder or a pure cone.

4. The tube wall is sufficiently stiff and heavy not to vibrate.

5. The tube wall has a sufficiently large heat conductivity and heat capacity to remain at constant temperature.

6. The change in particle velocity from zero at the wall to a nearly constant value throughout the cross-section of the tube takes place in a layer at the wall which is very small with respect to the diameter of the tube.

Besides these assumptions, the real geometry of a woodwind instrument is described in a simplified way, since the tube with the side-holes is considered to be a combination of tube-pieces arranged in series and parallel. Where pipe ends discharge into the surroundings they are "terminated" with a radiation impedance. It appears to be possible to calculate the natural frequency of this intricate pipe-combination, as will be shown in the next section.

Then we may replace this pipe-combination by a so-called substitution-tube without holes, with the same bore as the main tube and with the same frequency. This tube is useful to the theorist considering corrections due to

a) excitation mechanism,
b) boundary-layer effects at the wall,
c) deviations from the ideal bore.

The influence on resonance frequency of the substitution-tube is calculated for each of these corrections independently of the others, and their joint influence is found by simple addition. Then, returning to the real tube, it is assumed that their effect on the real tube is the same as on the substitution-tube. The influence of the corrections is substantial. A change, mostly a lowering, of a semitone is not unusual.

a) The excitation mechanism

In the flute, the frequency appears to be slightly dependent on the velocity of the jet of air which is blown across the edge. Besides that, the player may cover a larger or smaller part of the embouchure hole to alter the effective length of the air column. Both effects provide the player with means to adjust the pitch.

A closer inspection of reed action reveals that the air injected through the chink is not exactly in phase with the pressure at the top of the instrument. In the first place the combination of reed and lip has a finite damping, secondly the movement of the reed itself causes a movement of air in the tube. Both effects lower the frequency. The magnitude of this lowering can be more or less controlled by the player by varying the position of his lip, so that a slight but essential control is maintained during playing.

The efficiency of the excitation, i.e. that part of the product of mouth-pressure and air-flow which is converted into sound in the instrument, varies widely; it can be as low as 0.1 % [30].

b) Boundary-layer effects at the wall

The velocity of sound in the tube is slightly different from that in free space because of the action of friction and heat exchange of the air with the wall. In practice this causes a damping and a change in the frequency.

c) Deviations from the ideal bore

The bore is never purely cylindrical or conical. Deviations from this ideal bore can be important for compensation of certain defects of the tuning. Besides that, the closed holes form a row of niches in the main tube. The effects of these two factors on the tuning can be calculated reasonably well.

15. Principles of hole calculation

As hole calculation is the kernel of these investigations, its principles are presented here as an introduction to the detailed study in Chapter 3. The method can be used for every hole-instrument with only slight variations necessary.

For reasons of clarity we will explain it here for a cylindrical flute. We start with a single hole and thereafter expand the method to any desired number of holes.

In Fig. 15.1 are sketched the two situations before and after opening of a single hole in a cylindrical tube. In the situation "closed" the cylindrical hole is supposed to be closed with a piston which precisely fits onto the main tube yielding a perfect cylinder. The tube is excited at E. The cross-sectional areas of main tube and hole are S_1 and S_H respectively. The distances from the centre of the hole to the pipe-ends are L_L and L_R respectively, where L_R is much smaller than L_L, i.e. the hole is located very close to the open end. The length of the hole is denoted by L_H.

As a rule a tube is considered as having a length which is much longer than the diameter. This does not apply to the hole nor perhaps to the piece L_R. We therefore make some preliminary remarks about determining the three lengths L_L, L_R and L_H. For a very narrow tube it is sufficiently accurate to assume that the terminating impedance of an open end is zero and to neglect the so-called end-correction which is the common

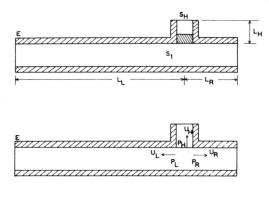

Fig. 15.1. Situation with closed and open hole in a cylindrical tube.

way of dealing with a non-zero terminating impedance. In many wind instruments however, the side holes are rather short and wide so that end-corrections are necessary, making the acoustical length much larger than the geometrical. A similar problem arises at the excitation end, where finite length corrections may have to be included. Later on, these problems will be considered anew; at this moment it is assumed that the acoustical length can be determined and understood as somewhat larger than the geometrical length.

If the piston closes the hole, the wave number of the resonances can be calculated from eq. (13.16)

$$k(L_L + L_R) = m\pi, \ m = \text{integer}. \qquad (15.1)$$

When the piston is removed, the open end of the tube is effectively shifted to the left. It will not be situated exactly at the position of the open hole, as the tube-pieces in parallel offer more "resistance" to the air flow outwards than a tube sawn off at the location of the hole. We have to use the acoustic laws of Kirchhoff for the branched pipe. When the diameter is small with respect to the wavelength, the pressures at the three tube-entrances are equal:

$$p_L = p_R = p_H. \qquad (15.2)$$

From the law of continuity of flow, the sum of the three volume velocities entering the tubes must be zero:

$$U_L + U_R + U_H = 0. \qquad (15.3)$$

From these two equations it follows that the sum of the acoustic admittances must be zero. Inserting expressions for these admittances derived with the aid of eq.(13.14) one obtains:

$$\frac{S_1}{\tan kL_L} + \frac{S_1}{\tan kL_R} + \frac{S_H}{\tan kL_H} = 0. \qquad (15.4)$$

At first view, this expression does not seem very friendly towards attempts at calculating k, since k is found at three places under the argument of a goniometric function. But simplifications are possible. Both L_R and L_H are small with respect to the wavelength, so that kL_R and $kL_H \ll 1$. In that case the tangent of the argument may be replaced by the argument itself. The sum of the 2nd and 3rd term of eq.(15.4) then becomes large and positive, and therefore the first term must be large and negative. This implies that $\tan kL_L$ is small and negative. The said function is only small and negative if kL_L is close to and smaller than $m\pi, m$ integer. But then the tangent may be expanded in a power series around these points and all terms but the first may be dropped. The simplified eq.(15.4) now looks as follows:

$$\frac{S_1}{L_L - m\pi/k} + \frac{S_1}{L_R} + \frac{S_H}{L_H} = 0. \qquad (15.5)$$

Herewith the wave number k is determined.

The length L_S of the substitution-tube (introduced in Section 14) for this case can be calculated from $kL_S = m\pi$, where k has the same value as in eq.(15.5). Apparently the length of the substitution-tube is equal to $L_S = L_L + L_x$, where L_x is found by substitution of the last expression into eq.(15.5):

$$S_1/L_x = S_1/L_R + S_H/L_H. \qquad (15.6)$$

This could be seen immediately when the following is considered. If the cylinder is sawn off at the hole, the two admittances of the tube L_H and L_R are removed. To keep the natural frequency the same, L_L must be increased by a tube-piece L_x with an admittance equal to the sum of the two removed admittances.

The whole procedure fails when kL_R and kL_H are not sufficiently small and a closer observation of these quantities therefore is justified. When the frequency shift occasioned by an open hole is a semitone, the substitution-tube L_S is about 6% shorter than the tube with closed hole. L_R varies between 6 and 15% of the tube-length so that kL_R in the fundamental mode varies between 0.18 and 0.45. We observe that at this highest value, the tangent differs from the argument by 7%. At the first overtone, this is around 40%. We expect the procedure to fail here, and this indeed confirms with practical experience.

Writing eq.(15.6) as follows

$$\frac{S_H}{L_H} = \frac{S_1 (L_R - L_x)}{L_x L_R} \ , \qquad (15.7)$$

we observe that S_H/L_H decreases when L_R increases, since $L_R - L_x$ is a constant for a prescribed substitution tube. In other words: when kL_R is as large as 0.45 the hole is very long and narrow (L_H large, S_H small). Such holes do exist in woodwind instruments and the notes produced with these holes are known for their impu-

rities when overblown. For most holes, however, kL_R is not so large and the condition (15.6) is sufficiently accurate for at least two modes.

Assuming the first hole to be determined, we proceed with the problem of a second hole, as illustrated in Fig. 15.2. For the moment the second hole is stopped with a piston. The tube with one open hole can be replaced by a tube of length $L_L + L_x$ which sounds the same note. According to eq.(15.6), L_x is independent of frequency. This is confirmed by experience, though for exceptional situations, since the instrument yields a perfect octave when overblown. It is logical, therefore, to assume that the procedure may be used for determining k of the instrument with two holes open, since the shift here is much less than one octave. We start with the substitution-tube for an instrument with one hole opened. Its length is known. Applying the same system of computation we find a new substitution-tube with a new value for k, viz. that of the instrument with the two holes opened. As long as the instrument can be overblown in the pure octave, which normally is the case in practice, the system must be considered applicable.

It will be clear by now that every succeeding hole can be tackled in the same way. It even is not necessary to investigate every preceding hole, when it is specified what frequency results at the closing of the hole. Knowing this frequency, it is possible to find the length L_x pertaining to that hole. We can even accept a slight frequency dependence in L_x, because the frequency does not change much when the closed hole is opened. This method is very convenient as every hole can be considered independently of the others. We only need to know the frequencies for closed and opened hole and this is exactly what is specified in fingering charts.

Questions may arise if, with the increased

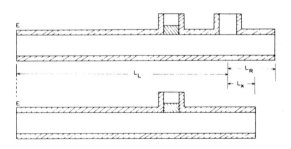

Fig. 15.2. Situation for a tube with two holes, one of which is stopped with a piston. Top: the real tube. Bottom: the substitution tube for the real tube.

number of open holes, a frequency dependence can grow in L_x because the tube length containing the many open holes is by no means short with respect to the wavelength. Benade [17], however, has shown that such a long perforated tube can be treated as acoustically very short, since only the top of it is acoustically relevant. He calculated the impedance of an infinite row of evenly spaced holes of fixed size; it was found that the system behaves as a high-pass filter below cut-off, so that no waves propagate in the open-hole section of the bore. An experimental proof can be obtained by closing the lowest holes. As long as two higher holes are open a frequency shift can hardly be heard by opening or closing such low holes. Another argument is obtained from overblowing the instrument. If the substitution-tube were frequency-dependent it would be different for two registers, and it would be impossible to tune purely both fundamental and first overtone. In practice only a few — though very annoying — situations are found in which the tuning between two registers is disturbed. This is found e.g. with cross-fingerings. The following chapters will show that there is no simple cure for these impurities.

16. Recapitulation

After a survey of some elementary acoustics and of phenomena found in vibrating bodies and vibrating air, it was shown how the frequency of air vibrations in the tube is dependent on the length of the tube. The phenomenon of overblowing was mentioned, i.e. from a tube a number of tones of various pitch can be extracted without changing the positions of the fingers. The sequence of these so-called harmonics appeared to be different for tubes open at two sides, and for those open at one end and closed at the other side. The

anomalous behaviour of a conical tube blown with a reed was mentioned.

When a hole is opened, the effect is to shorten the vibrating column of air, causing the tone to increase in pitch. A formula was derived to calculate the proper position of the hole: a simple algebraic equation, easy to apply. In practice, however, the note is lower than the calculated one, sometimes up to a semitone. A more detailed study of the properties of woodwinds will yield an explanation of this discrepancy. It will appear to be due to the excitation of air into the pipe, the energy lost through friction at the tube-walls and through radiation to the outside, and the irregularities of the bore.

chapter 2
the excitation mechanism of woodwinds

21. Introduction

Oscillations of air in the tube of a wind instrument tend to lose energy due to friction and heat exchange with the walls and to radiation at openings in the tube (Fig. 21.1). These losses must be compensated for by further excitation by the musician.

The energy balance of a woodwind instrument and the properties of the excitation mechanism are studied in this chapter. The considerations refer to a woodwind without holes, either real or fictitious, the latter a substitution tube resonating in the same frequency. In Chapter 3 it will be shown how to apply this to a real instrument with holes and how to calculate accurately the resonance frequency for an instrument with a number of opened holes or how to calculate the hole positions for specified resonance frequencies.

In Sections 22 and 23 the sound velocity in cylindrical and conical tubes will be determined as will its dependency on temperature and boundary-layer effects. How the resonance frequency of a flute is found, taking into account effects of radiation and excitation, is given in Section 24. In a separate Section 25, the reed action is investigated and described mathematically; the results are applied to clarinet, saxophone, oboe and bassoon in later sections.

22. Longitudinal waves in cylindrical tubes

To derive equations for waves in cylindrical tubes a number of suppositions have to be made. First, the losses in the medium are supposed to

be negligible with respect to those at the walls, which can be justified easily [69]. Secondly, the walls are assumed to be stiff and heavy and of good heat conductivity and heat capacity, so that they are mechanically and thermally in complete rest.

The losses taking place at the tube walls are distinguished in viscous and thermal losses. Viscous losses are due to the fact that air has a finite viscosity, so that the particle velocity of the air gradually goes to zero when we approach the walls. Thermal losses take place because the walls are practically of constant temperature whereas the temperature in the gas fluctuates due to the (mainly) adiabatic pressure fluctuations. These temperature fluctuations diminish near the wall because heat periodically flows into and out of the wall.

The closer we are to the walls, the more both influences are felt. In woodwind instruments the situation is such that the influence of the wall is felt only in a rather thin boundary layer. Outside this boundary layer the particle velocity is practically constant across the whole cross-section, and changes of state are nearly adiabatic. The thickness of this boundary layer (the formula given here pertains to the viscous boundary layer) is $(\eta/\omega\rho)^{1/2}$ [40, 66]. With a viscosity of $\eta = 18 \times 10^{-6}$ N s/m², a density of $\rho = 1.2$ kg/m³ and a frequency of 1000 Hz this thickness is 0.05 mm. Diameters of musical instruments always considerably exceed this value (the smallest observed diameter at the top of the oboe is 2.5 mm) so that the notion of a boundary layer is justified. This means a tremendous simplification for the mathematics.

The effect of the boundary layer on the air oscillations is accounted for by providing the equations of motion and continuity as they are valid in free space with (complex) damping terms

Fig. 21.1. Energy balance of a wind musical instrument.

which describe the action at the wall. We may express this otherwise. The particle velocity is assumed to be constant over the cross-section of the tube and the damping influence of the wall is assumed to be spread out across the whole cross-section. In this view the problem is reduced from three-dimensional to one-dimensional. The way how to perform this reduction can be found in the source-literature, and the results can be immediately applied for the present case. Some of the symbols were explained in Section 13. New symbols are

a = tube radius,
η = viscosity of air,
γ = ratio of specific heats,
λ = thermal conductivity (not to be confused with wavelength λ),
C_p = heat capacity at constant pressure.

The equation of motion and continuity for sinusoidal motion are [40, 67, 120]*

$$-\partial p/\partial x = \rho_w\, \partial u/\partial t, \text{ where } \rho_w = \rho[1 + (1-j)\,\alpha_v'], \tag{22.1}$$

$$-\partial p/\partial t = K_w\, \partial u/\partial x, \text{where } K_w = K[1 - (1-j)\,\alpha_t'], \tag{22.2}$$

in which α_v' and α_t' are real quantities, which is indicated by a dash:

$$\alpha_v' = \frac{1}{a}\sqrt{\frac{2\eta}{\omega\rho}}\,, \quad \alpha_t' = \frac{1}{a}(\gamma-1)\sqrt{\frac{2\lambda}{\omega\rho C_p}}\,. \tag{22.3}$$

As could be expected the viscosity influences the density, the thermal conductivity the bulk modulus.

The mathematical handling of the formulae is in many respects identical to that in the loss-free case,

---

* *In the list of symbols in reference 120, on page 30, 5th line from bottom, the symbol C_p should be C_v.*

except that all quantities are corrected for the boundary-layer effects. The quantities are the density, the bulk modulus, the velocity of sound $c_w = (K_w/\rho_w)^{\frac{1}{2}}$ and the wave number $k_w = \omega/c_w = \omega(\rho_w/K_w)^{\frac{1}{2}}$.

Because of the important role the wave number plays, its relative change due to the wall presence is indicated by a separate symbol α:

$$k_w = k(1+\alpha) = k[1 + (1-j)\alpha'], \tag{22.4}$$

$$\alpha' = \tfrac{1}{2}(\alpha_v' + \alpha_t'). \tag{22.5}$$

Some authors use the resonator quality Q:

$$Q = \frac{1}{2\alpha'} = \frac{1}{\alpha_v' + \alpha_t'}\,. \tag{22.6}$$

The general solution of the wave equation for sinusoidal motion, corrected for boundary layer effects is similar to that of eq.(13.10), corrected correspondingly:

$$p = \hat{p}\sin(k_w x + \psi)\exp j\omega t. \tag{22.7}$$

In the same way the corrected acoustical impedance is similar to the expression of eq.(13.14)

$$Z = \frac{-j\rho_w c_w}{S}\tan(k_w x + \psi). \tag{22.8}$$

Unless specified otherwise, the positive direction will be to the right, i.e. down the tube from the point of excitation; the impedance is also taken looking down to the right.

Measurements have been published [44, 106, 111] which prove a satisfactory agreement with this theory for tubes with very smooth walls. However, the walls of wind instruments are far from smooth. Moreover, the holes, which are closed by fingers or by pads, are an even more serious deviation from the ideally smooth wall. According to Coltman [38], the losses are dependent on amplitude; Backus [7] found losses to be dependent on a superimposed steady air flow. Measurements of the damping by Backus [6] for a clarinet showed values for α about 60% higher than predicted by theory. Benade [16] reports an increase of 70% in damping for a plastic tube provided with holes, closed with masking tape. We therefore choose to increase α' with 60% to account for wall roughness and holes. Then, using this correction, and moreover taking [44]

$$\eta = 17.1\,(1+0.00288T)\,10^{-6}\ N\,s/m^2 ,$$
$$K = 1.402 \times 101400\ N/m^2 ,$$
$$\lambda = 0.0223\,(1+0.0028T)W/m\ ^\circ C,$$
$$\gamma = 1.402,$$
$$C_p = 1010\ J/kg\ ^\circ C,$$
$$T = 25\,^\circ C,$$

we get

$$\alpha' = 0.33 \times 10^{-3}\,k^{-\frac12}a^{-1} ,$$
$$\alpha_t/\alpha_v' = 0.46. \tag{22.9}$$

All quantities depend on temperature and composition of the gas. The temperature of the gas blown into the instrument is somewhere in between room and blood temperature; the gas is saturated with water vapour and contains $2\frac12\%$ CO_2 [36]. Denoting by

c_0 = velocity of sound of "standard" air (at $0\,^\circ C$ and without CO_2 and H_2O),

h_0, h_v = number of degrees of freedom of standard air and additional gas, respectively, where $\gamma = 1+2/h$,

ρ_0, ρ_v = densities of standard air and additional gas respectively,

r_v = fractional pressure of additional gas,

the velocity of sound c of a gas in which small amounts of additional gas are added is calculated [60] from

$$c/c_0 = 1 + T/546$$
$$+ \sum_v \tfrac12 r_v\ [1-\rho_v/\rho-2(h_v-h_0)/h_0(2+h_0)]. \tag{22.10}*$$

The density ρ of the gas mixture is given by

$$\rho/\rho_0 = 1-T/273 + \Sigma r_v\,(\rho_v/\rho_0-1). \tag{22.11}$$

Taking $h_0 = 5$, $h_{CO_2} = h_{H_2O} = 6$, $\rho_0 = 1.293$, $\rho_{H_2O} = 0.815$, $c_0 = 331.5$ m/s [49a], $\rho_{CO_2} = 1.98$ kg/m^3 (at $0\,^\circ C$), eqs (22.10) and (22.11) become

$$\left.\begin{array}{l} c/c_0 = 1 + T/546 + 0.15\,r_{H_2O} - 0.30 r_{CO_2}, \\ \rho/\rho_0 = 1 - T/273 - 0.37\,r_{H_2O} + 0.54 r_{CO_2}. \end{array}\right\} \tag{22.12}$$

In Fig. 22.1 the velocity of sound is plotted as a function of temperature, where at each temperature $r_{CO_2} = 2\frac12\%$ and r_{H_2O} is such that at any temperature the air is saturated with water vapour. As can be seen from the additional scale, where the influence on the tuning of the temperature is calculated, a temperature difference of $10\,^\circ C$ corresponds with one third of a semitone, which is considerable and in general difficult to compensate for by lip manipulations. In a room, and after some time of playing, some mean temperature in the instrument is reached, which will depend on room temperature, type of instrument and player. Coltman [36] measured a mean temperature of $28\,^\circ C$ in a flute, Meyer of $25.6\,^\circ C$ in an oboe [80]. A bassoon probably will attain a lower mean

* *This equation can be brought in a more elegant form when $\gamma_v \approx \gamma$. Introducing the ratios of specific heat we then find:*
$$1-2(h_v-h_0)/h_0(2+h_0) =$$
$$= \gamma_v/\gamma_0 - (\gamma_v-\gamma_0)^2/\gamma_0(\gamma_v-1) \approx \gamma_v/\gamma_0. \tag{22.10a}$$
This simplification is sometimes used [94].

18

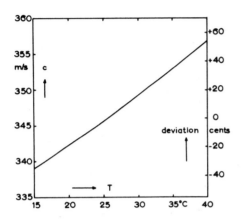

Fig. 22.1. Velocity of sound in free space as a function of temperature for air saturated with water vapour and containing 2.5 % CO_2. On an additional scale the deviation in the tuning with respect to the adopted value at 25.5°C is plotted.

Fig. 22.2. Schematic cylindrical wind instrument. Excitation at E.

temperature than a piccolo. For simplicity, we neglect all these effects and assume the same temperature for all instruments, viz. 25.5°C. With this,

$$\left.\begin{array}{l} c = 346 \text{ m/s}, \\ \rho = 1.175 \text{ kg/m}^3, \\ \rho c = 406 \text{ kg/m}^2\text{s}. \end{array}\right\} \tag{22.13}$$

The temperature of the air entering the instrument may be close to 37°C, but it rapidly cools when it travels down the instrument. The velocity of sound, therefore, is higher in the top than in the bottom of the instrument. Benade calculated the influence of a temperature difference of top

and bottom of 12°C on the tuning [19]. He found that the fundamental can be flattened up to 10 cents, whereas the first overtone can be sharpened the same amount.

To derive equations for resonance frequencies of cylindrical tubes we start from the expression for the impedance, eq. (22.8), in which two unknowns appear, viz. k_w and ψ. They can be solved by imposing the two boundary conditions, one at the point of excitation, say at $x = -l$, and one at the open end, say at $x = 0$. All wind instruments considered here are provided with an open end, where the impedance equals the radiation impedance [65, 66, 71, 87]:

$$Z_{rad} = \frac{j\rho c}{S}(\xi ka - j\theta), \tag{22.14}$$

The radius a of the open end is small with respect to the wavelength. For most open ends, ξ and θ are quantities in between those for a cylinder with infinite flange: $\xi = 0.821$, $\theta = \frac{1}{2}k^2a^2$ and those for a cylinder without flange: $\xi = 0.613$, $\theta = \frac{1}{4}k^2a^2$. In any case, $|\xi ka - j\theta| \ll 1$. Inserting eq. (22.14) into eq. (22.8), setting $x = 0$, we find the condition

$$\tan \psi = -\frac{\rho c}{\rho_w c_w}(\xi ka - j\theta). \tag{22.15}$$

Since this is (see above) a small quantity, $\tan \psi$ may be set equal to ψ. Leaving out the suffix w in ρ and in c does not introduce any great error in a quantity which is a correction itself. So with a very good approximation:

$$\psi = -(\xi ka - j\theta). \tag{22.16}$$

At the embouchure-end, $x = -l$, the impedance becomes

$$Z_E = \frac{j\rho_w c_w}{S}\tan(k_w l - \psi). \tag{22.17}$$

The magnitude of Z_E is determined by the properties of the excitation which will receive attention later. It appears that

$$|Z_E| \ll \rho c/S, \text{ for flute embouchure,} \quad (22.18)$$

$$|Z_E| \gg \rho c/S, \text{ for reed embouchure.} \quad (22.19)$$

For cylindrical instruments of the flute type, this means that $|\tan(k_w l - \psi)| \ll 1$, so that the tangent can be expanded in a power series around $m\pi$, m integer, and only the first term needs to be retained. Application to eq.(22.17) now leads to the following expression

$$\frac{Z_E}{j\rho_w c_w/S} = k_w l - \psi - m\pi, \ m \text{ integer.} \quad (22.20)$$

When the actual value of Z_E is substituted, the wave number can in principle be solved. $Z_E/\rho_w c_w$ can be split in real and imaginary parts in the following way

$$Z_E S/j\rho_w c_w = Z_E'(1 + j\delta_E)S/j\rho c, \quad (22.21)$$

where Z_E' and δ_E are real quantities. Using this, eq.(22.20) can be separated in imaginary and real parts, inserting k_w and ψ according to eqs (22.4) and (22.16):

$$Z_E' = (\alpha'kl + \theta)\rho c/S, \quad (22.22)$$

$$kl + \alpha'kl + \xi ka - \delta_E(\alpha'kl + \theta) = m\pi,$$
$$m = 1, 2, 3, \text{ etc.} \quad (22.23)$$

For a flute tube with radius 9.5 mm, resonating at 600 Hz, $\theta = \frac{1}{2}k^2 a^2 = 0.002$, which is small compared with $\alpha'kl = 0.06$. This implies that the real part of the impedance, Z_E', is solely dependent on the boundary layer effects at the walls. Apparently, see eq. (22.23), the frequency is determined by the tube length corrected with terms due to the boundary layer, the phase angle at the excit-

ation and an end-correction. We return to this in following sections.

In the same way, for a cylindrical instrument of clarinet type, $|\tan(k_w l - \psi)| \gg 1$, so that we expand around $\pi/2$, $3\pi/2$ etc., giving

$$\frac{Z_E}{j\rho_w c_w/S} = \frac{-1}{k_w l - \psi - m\pi}, m = \text{integer} -\tfrac{1}{2}. \ (22.24)$$

This yields a solution for the wave number when Z_E is given. Setting

$$\frac{Z_E S}{j\rho_w c_w} = \frac{S}{j\rho c Y_E'(1-j\delta)}, \quad (22.25)$$

where Y_E' and δ are real quantities, eq.(22.24) becomes

$$\frac{j\rho c}{S} Y_E'(1-j\delta) = -(k_w l - \psi - m\pi),$$
$$m = \tfrac{1}{2}, 1\tfrac{1}{2}, 2\tfrac{1}{2}, \text{etc.} \quad (22.26)$$

Inserting k_w and ψ according to eqs (22.4) and (22.16) and separating imaginary and real parts:

$$Y_E' = (\alpha'kl + \theta)S/\rho c, \quad (22.27)$$

$$kl + \alpha'kl + \xi ka + \delta(\alpha'kl + \theta) = m\pi,$$
$$m = \tfrac{1}{2}, 1\tfrac{1}{2}, 2\tfrac{1}{2}, \text{etc.} \quad (22.28)$$

Here too the impedance is determined mainly by wall losses and hardly at all by radiation losses. In the same way as for instruments of the flute type, a frequency shift is determined by wall effects and radiation as well as by an imaginary part of the impedance characterized by δ.

23. Longitudinal waves in conical tubes

The bore of conical woodwind instruments resembles a truncated cone. Two types of conical instruments are distinguished, viz. those blown with reeds and those blown across a lipped hole. In the first case the instrument is blown at the narrow end of the cone; the truncation of the cone is about 0.1 of the total geometrical length of the tube. When the instrument is excited by blowing across a hole, as is the flute, this hole is located at the wide end of the cone; the truncated part is larger than the length of the instrument.

The cones of woodwind instruments have little flare. Half of the top angle of the cone varies between 0.005 and 0.04 rad. Therefore it is not unreasonable to consider the wave as spreading uniformly over a cross-section of the tube as it travels outwards. Then the displacement of the gas molecules all over the surface perpendicular to the axis of the horn will be the same and displacement, pressure etc., will be functions of time and distance along the tube only. The difference between spherical wavefronts with their origin at the apex of the cone and plane wavefronts is neglected; both ways of description will be used indiscriminately.

The acoustical behaviour of a conical flute differs from that of a conical reed instrument; this will first be shown from the wave equation for undamped waves. The distance to the apex of the cone (which, it should be recalled, lies outside the tube) is denoted by r. The equations of motion and continuity for quasi-plane waves in a conical tube are [87]

$$-\frac{\partial p}{\partial r} = \rho \frac{\partial u}{\partial t}, \tag{23.1}$$

$$-\frac{\partial p}{\partial t} = \frac{K}{r^2} \frac{\partial (ur^2)}{\partial r}. \tag{23.2}$$

Eliminating u between these two equations and introducing the dimensionless quantity

$$w = kr, \tag{23.3}$$

the wave equation for harmonic phenomena becomes

$$\frac{d^2 p}{dw^2} + \frac{2}{w} \frac{dp}{dw} + p = 0. \tag{23.4}$$

The general solution of this equation can be written as follows

$$p = \frac{A}{w} \sin (w + \psi), \tag{23.5}$$

with two (complex) constants A and ψ. The particle velocity u is found when this solution is substituted in eq.(23.1). The admittance Y can, then, be calculated as $Y = uS/p$:

$$Y = \frac{S(r)}{j\rho c} \left[\frac{1}{w} - \cot (w + \psi) \right] \tag{23.6}$$

This is valid for a cone expanding to the right, which we will call a *positive* cone. For a so-called *negative* cone – which contracts to the right, as in conical flutes – the admittance changes its sign, when we adhere to the convention of taking admittances looking to the right. This inconsistency is removed by assigning *negative* signs to all distances to the apex of the *negative* cone. By this measure eq.(23.6) and other future expressions become valid for both positive and negative cones. The two types of cones are sketched in Fig. 23.1 together with the relevant geometrical quantities and their symbols. It is to be noted that the quantity designating the tube length, $l_1 = r_1 - r_0$, is positive in both tubes.

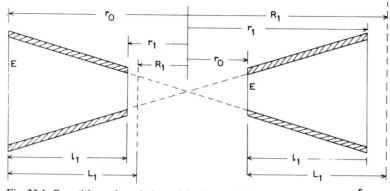

Fig. 23.1. Quantities and symbols used for "negative" cone, where r-quantities are negative (left) and for "positive" cone, where r-quantities are positive (right). Excitation at E.

At the open end $r = r_1$ the terminating impedance is given by eq.(22.14), with $\theta = 0$ here, since damping is neglected as a first approximation. Substitution in eq.(23.6) leads to the condition

$$\cot(w_1 + \psi) = -\frac{1}{\xi k a_1} + \frac{1}{k r_1}. \qquad (23.7)$$

Since always $r_1 > 30a_1$, the second term of the right hand member can be neglected with respect to the first term; an expansion of the tangent around zero can be effected: $w_1 + \psi = -\xi k a_1$, or

$$\psi = -w_1 - \xi k a_1. \qquad (23.8)$$

Introducing an end-corrected length R_1

$$R_1 = r_1 + \xi a_1, \qquad (23.9)$$

we may use the dimensionless variable $W_1 = kR_1$ which includes this open-end correction, so

$$\psi = -kR_1 = -W_1. \qquad (23.10)$$

Substituting this constant into eq.(23.6), we have the following expression for the admittance Y at the position w

$$Y = \frac{S}{j\rho c}\left[\frac{1}{w} - \cot(w - W_1)\right]. \qquad (23.11)$$

At the throat of the tube, taken at $w = w_0$, there are, as mentioned before, two possibilities, viz.

$$|Y_0| \gg S_0/\rho c, \text{ for flute-embouchure,} \qquad (23.12)$$

$$|Y_0| \ll S_0/\rho c, \text{ for reed-embouchure.} \qquad (23.13)$$

For the case of the *flute* it is found from eq.(23.11) that $|-\cot(w_0 - W_1)| \gg 1$ or approximately

$$W_1 - w_0 = kL_1 = m\pi, \ m \text{ integer}, \qquad (23.14)$$

where eq.(23.14) defines $L_1 = l_1 + \xi a_1$, the tube length including the end-correction. So the resonance frequency of a conical flute equals that of a cylindrical flute of the same length.

For the *reed*-embouchure we find $|1/w_0 - \cot(w_0 - W_1)| \ll 1$ or

$$W_1 = w_0 - \arctan w_0 + m\pi, \ m \text{ integer} \qquad (23.15)$$

Fig. 23.2. Two tubes with the same natural frequencies.

When w_0 is sufficiently small as compared to $\frac{1}{2}\pi$, this solution becomes $W_1 = m\pi$ with a good approximation. Apparently, the conical instruments with effectively closed top behave like a cylindrical flute of a length equal to the conical tube extended to the apex. In Fig. 23.2 two tubes are shown which resonate in the same frequency.

A discussion concerning the blowing mechanism is postponed to later sections; in this section only wall effects will be dealt with.

Since the thickness of the boundary layer, in which wall effects are perceptible, is very small with respect to the diameter, first order techniques are applicable, just as in the cylindrical tube. Unfortunately the mathematics is much more complicated here, since the extra terms in density and bulk modulus, due to the boundary layer, are dependent on the radius a, and this radius is linearly dependent on the distance r to the apex. So the ratio a/r is a constant, equal to ϑ_c, half of the angle of opening of the cone, also called the angle of conicity of the cone. For a negative cone, $\vartheta_c = a/r$ is negative. With this convention the derivations to follow are valid for both types of cones. Since the tube radius varies only gradually and slowly with r, and as the wavelength is always very large with respect to the tube diameter, it seems permissible to assume ρ and K to become complex in the same manner as in cylindrical tubes bearing in mind, however, that the boundary layer terms become dependent on the distance to the apex. The equations of motion, (23.1), and continuity, (23.2), are therefore used with the complex quantities ρ_w and K_w of eqs (22.1) and (22.2). In order to show explicitly that α_v' and α_t' are inversely proportional to r, new quantities $E_{v,t}$ are introduced as follows

$$(1-j)\alpha_{v,t}' = E_{v,t}/kr. \qquad (23.16)$$

The equations of motion and continuity then read

$$-\frac{\partial p}{\partial r} = j\omega\rho\left[1 + \frac{E_v}{kr}\right]u, \qquad (23.17)$$

$$-\frac{K}{r^2}\frac{\partial(ur^2)}{\partial r} = j\omega\left[1 + \frac{E_t}{kr}\right]p. \qquad (23.18)$$

From these equations* u can be eliminated. Neglecting higher order terms in E_v and E_t, and introducing $w = kr$, we get

$$\frac{d^2p}{dw^2} + \left[\frac{2}{w} + \frac{E_v}{w^2}\right]\frac{dp}{dw} + \left[1 + \frac{E_v + E_t}{w}\right]p = 0. \qquad (23.19)$$

The following quantities are introduced

$$\beta = \frac{1}{2}(E_v + E_t), \quad \epsilon_v = \frac{E_v}{E_v + E_t}, \qquad (23.20)$$

where we note that

$$\left.\begin{array}{l} \beta = (1-j)\,\beta' = \\[2mm] (1-j)k\dfrac{r}{2a}\left\{\sqrt{\dfrac{2\eta}{\omega\rho}} + (\gamma-1)\sqrt{\dfrac{2\lambda}{\omega\rho C_p}}\right\} \\[4mm] \epsilon_v = \dfrac{1}{1+(\gamma-1)(\lambda/\eta C_p)^{1/2}} \end{array}\right\} \qquad (23.21)$$

Introduction of the two new quantities into eq. (23.19) yields the wave equation

$$\frac{d^2p}{dw^2} + \left[\frac{2}{w} + \frac{2\epsilon_v\beta}{w^2}\right]\frac{dp}{dw} + \left[1 + \frac{2\beta}{w}\right]p = 0. \qquad (23.22)$$

The formulation of these basic equations and the method to find a first order solution I owe largely to D.W. van Wulfften Palthe.

Just as with cylindrical tubes, the boundary effects of conical tubes of real musical instruments are larger than theoretically predicted; we assume the same correction factor, viz. 1.6. With this and using the numerical values given in Section 22,

$$\left.\begin{array}{l} \beta' = 0.33 \times 10^{-3}\, k^{\frac{1}{2}}(r/a), \\ \epsilon_v = 0.685. \end{array}\right\} \qquad (23.23)$$

The solution to eq. (23.22) differs from the solution for the undamped case only slightly. Therefore we assume it to be of the form $[1+h(w)]\,(A/w)\sin(w+\psi)$, where $|h(w)| \ll 1$. The general solution then will be

$$p = \frac{A^+}{w}\,(1+h^+)\,\exp(+jw)\ +$$

$$+ \frac{A^-}{w}\,(1+h^-)\,\exp(-jw), \qquad (23.24)$$

with two constants A^+ and A^-. Substitution into eq. (23.22) and integrating twice gives to a first order accuracy [93]

$$h^{\pm} = \beta[\mp j\, \mathrm{Ei}(\pm 2jw)\exp(\mp 2jw) \pm j\ln w + \epsilon_v/w], \qquad (23.25)$$

where

$$\mathrm{Ei}(\pm jy) = -\int_y^\infty \frac{\exp(\pm jt)}{t}\,dt,$$

or

$$\mathrm{Ei}(\pm jy) = \mathrm{Ci}(y) \pm j\,\mathrm{si}(y) =$$

$$= -\int_y^\infty \left\{\frac{\cos t}{t} \pm j\,\frac{\sin t}{t}\right\}dt. \qquad (23.26)$$

After some rearrangement of terms it follows

$$h^{\pm} = \beta(\pm j\ln w \pm jg - f + \epsilon_v/w), \qquad (23.27)$$

where

$$\left.\begin{array}{l} f = f(2w) = -f(-2w) = \\ + \mathrm{Ci}(2w)\sin(2w) - \mathrm{si}(2w)\cos(2w), \\ \\ g = g(2w) = + g(-2w) = \\ - \mathrm{Ci}(2w)\cos(2w) - \mathrm{si}(2w)\sin(2w). \end{array}\right\} \qquad (23.28)$$

Functions Ci, si, f and g are tabulated or analytically known [1, 35, 62, 112].

Introducing $A^+ = A\exp j\psi$ and $A^- = -A\exp(-j\psi)$, the general solution, eq.(23.24), can be re-written as

$$p = \frac{A}{w}\left[(1+h^+)\exp j(w+\psi) - \right.$$

$$\left. - (1+h^-)\exp(-jw-j\psi)\right].$$

Since $|h^{\pm}| \ll 1$, we may write $1+h^{\pm} = \exp(h^{\pm})$. Introducing this into the previous equation and substituting for $h^{\pm}$ the expression of eq. (23.27) we can simplify the expression for p in the following way:

$$p = \frac{A'}{w}\exp(-\beta f + \beta\epsilon_v/w)\sin(w+\psi+\beta\ln w+\beta g). \qquad (23.29)$$

All terms with β are due to the fact that boundary layer effects are taken into account. Dropping these terms reduces the equation to the simple expression found in the beginning of this section where boundary layer effects were neglected. This applies equally to several equations to follow.

Using eqs. (23.17) and (23.20) for finding the velocity u and using, moreover, the relations $df/dw = -2g$ and $dg/dw = 2f - 1/w$, we can derive the admittance Y:

$$Y = \frac{S(r)}{j\rho c}\left[(1-2\beta wg - \frac{\beta\epsilon_v}{w})\frac{1}{w} - \right.$$
$$\left. - (1+2\beta f - 2\frac{\beta\epsilon_v}{w})\cot(w+\psi+\beta\ln w + \beta g)\right], \quad (23.30)$$

(compare eq. 23.6).

For brevity we introduce for the argument of the cotangent

$$B = w + \psi + \beta\ln w + \beta g. \quad (23.31)$$

The unknown quantity ψ in eq. (23.30) can be computed from the boundary condition at the open end, where we know the (radiation) admittance to be (see eq. 22.14)

$$Y_1 = \frac{S_1}{j\rho c}\frac{1}{\xi k a_1 - j\theta}. \quad (23.32)$$

When dealing with this boundary condition in the derivation without boundary layer-effects, it was argued that the cotangent in the expression for the admittance was the only term which could meet the large value of Y, the term with $1/w_1$ being of lower order of magnitude. This reasoning holds true, yielding

$$\tan(w_1 + \psi + \beta\ln w_1 + \beta g_1) = -(\xi k a_1 - j\theta), \quad (23.33)$$

or, since the argument of the tangent is very small, we find the following value for ψ:

$$\psi = -W_1 - j\theta - \beta(\ln w_1 + g_1), \quad (23.34)$$

where $W_1 = w_1 + \xi a_1$.

After substitution of this into eq.(23.31) we find for the argument of the cotangent:

$$B = w - W_1 + j\theta - \beta(\ln w_1 - \ln w + g_1 - g). (23.35)$$

The influence of the boundary layer on the wave number can be seen more clearly when the expression for the admittance, eq.(23.30), is

slightly modified. Taylor's expansion for the contangent. $\cot(x+dx) = \cot x - dx/\sin^2 x$, provided $(dx\cot x) \ll 1$, is used for bringing the expressions with β under the argument of the contangent. The result is

$$Y = \frac{S}{j\rho c}\left\{\frac{1}{w} - \cot\left[B - \beta\left(2g + \frac{\epsilon_v}{w^2} + 2(f-\frac{\epsilon_v}{w})\cot B\right)\sin^2 B\right]\right\}.$$
$$(23.36)$$

Substituting B from eq. (23.35) except in terms with β we find

$$Y = \frac{S}{j\rho c}\left[\frac{1}{w} + \cot(W_1 - w + \varphi - j\theta)\right], \quad (23.37)$$

where $\varphi = (1-j)\varphi'$ and (23.38)

$$\varphi' = \beta'\left[\ln(w_1/w) + g_1 - g\cos 2B + \right.$$
$$\left. + (f-\frac{\epsilon_v}{w})\sin 2B + \frac{\epsilon_v}{w^2}\sin^2 B\right]. \quad (23.39)$$

A first order approximation for B is

$$B = w - W_1, \quad (23.40)$$

which is substituted in eq.(23.39) to obtain a first order approximation for φ'.

The corrections on the wave number due to the boundary layer are contained in φ. In Sections 24 and 27 applications are given for flutes and conical reed instruments.

24. Flutes

A musical instrument is considered to be a flute when it is excited by means of a jet of air blown with relatively high speed (order 30 m/s, so 0.1 of the velocity of sound) against the edge of a lateral hole in the instrument. This jet of air can originate from human lips, as in various types of flutes commonly used in the orchestra, or from fixed lips as is the case with the flue organ pipe and the recorder. The recorder is a very simple keyless instrument with limited compass, low sound level and restricted means of variation in the sound level. These properties are in striking contrast to those of the modern Boehm-flute with its powerful tone and key-mechanism superior to the mechanism of any other woodwind. Beside the ordinary ('concert') flute other sizes are in use. The most common is the piccolo, sounding one octave higher.

The blowing mechanism of flutes has been studied extensively theoretically as well as experimentally and good qualitative descriptions are available [23, 31, 32, 33, 34, 37, 38, 41, 42, 77, 78, 95, 96, 97] sufficient for the present investigations. Though the various investigators have different views on the details of the blowing mechanism, they agree on the basic concepts. In Fig. 24.1 the situation at the embouchure-hole is sketched. From the left, air is blown in the direction of the opposing edge. Part of this air enters the instrument in such a way as to amplify the existing fluctuations. In order to understand this, we follow the air on its way from the moment it leaves the lips. The air flow resembles a ribbon of air moving in air at rest. The ribbon is subject to pressure fluctuations causing every particle of it to change its lateral velocity, which initially was zero. As the pressure in the tube fluctuates, and the ribbon moves to the right, it can take on the shape of a wave. Its motion may be compared

with a row of swimmers crossing the Channel swimming straight out from the coast, drifting sideways by tidal flows in the Channel. When the ribbon moves with the proper speed, its position at the sharp edge will be in phase with the air displacement in the tube and it will enter the tube and thus amplify this displacement. This stresses the importance of the ratio of the velocity of the ribbon, v, to its length, h. Apparently, this ratio, v/h, must take on a certain value for each frequency. Precise calculation of the behaviour of the air ribbon together with experimental evidence was presented by Cremer [41] and Coltman [37, 38]; they showed the matter to be slightly more intricate.

When v/h has the correct value the frequency is equal to the resonance frequency which is obtained when the flute is not blown but excited by a loudspeaker at a distance sufficient to ensure weak coupling. This was observed and measured by Coltman [36]. When v/h is lower, the frequency is lower, when v/h rises, the frequency rises too. v/h is different for every note. With increasing frequency, it must increase if we want to keep the blown frequency at the value of the weakly coupled one. Assuming the slit between the lips to be a constant, an increase in v with frequency means an increase in sound level, which is musically undesirable. Instead, h can be decreased (at least on a flute) by protruding the lips. This at the same time decreases the area of the embouchure-hole, causing an increase in its end-correction: the frequency decreases. Then, overblown notes would have a larger end-correction than fundamentals, which means that the upper register would be flat with respect to the lower register. To compensate for this, flutes have perturbations in the upper part of the bore: this part of the instrument shows a gradual contraction towards the embouchure-hole. Calculations are

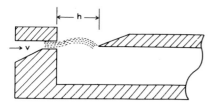

Fig. 24.1. The embouchure of the flute.

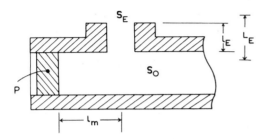

Fig. 24.2. Cylindrical flute with mouthpiece cavity.

postponed to Section 36.

One subject that strictly speaking belongs to the next chapter is considered here, viz. the so-called mouthpiece cavity. Such a cavity is found in flutes as well as in conical instruments blown with reeds. The action of the cavity is essential in conical reed instruments for the purity of the overblown notes and it is studied in the corresponding sections. Though being less essential for the flute, the action of this cavity is considered here too, for the sake of consistency.

In flutes, the mouthpiece cavity is formed by a short closed tube-piece at the left of the embouchure-hole (Fig. 24.2). It can be adjusted in volume by adjusting the position of plug P at the left. It is known to influence the pitch of the highest notes; this can be shown easily from a calculation. The sum of the admittances of the three joined tubes seen outwards from their junction point must be zero (see comments at eq. 15.4). Denoting the length of the cavity by l_m (m from mouthpiece), the length of the right hand part of the tube by L_1, the effective length of the embouchure-hole by L_E and taking into consideration that l_m and L_E are short with respect to wavelength, we have approximately

$$S_E/kL_E + S_0/\tan kL_1 - S_0kl_m = 0. \qquad (24.1)$$

From this it follows

$$(1 - k^2 l_m \lambda_E) \tan kL_1 + k\lambda_E = 0, \qquad (24.2)$$

where $\lambda_E = L_E S_0/S_E \qquad (24.3)$

denotes the transformed length of the hole, i.e. the length which the embouchure-hole would have if its diameter were equal to the diameter of the main tube. Investigating eq.(24.2) we find that when $\lambda_E/l_m = 3$, the solution is with a good approximation equal to

$$k(L_1 + \lambda_E) = m\pi, \ m \text{ integer, for } k\lambda_E < 1.5. \qquad (24.4)$$

For larger values of $k\lambda_E$ serious deviations are found. When $\lambda_E/l_m \neq 3$, condition (24.4) is valid in a smaller frequency range, the smaller, the more λ_E/l_m deviates from 3. It can be concluded that the mouthpiece-cavity is necessary for keeping overtones in tune.

As appears from an inspection of flutes and as is stated in tutors for flutes, l_m is about 17 mm. λ_E attains its lowest value when no lips are hanging above the embouchure-hole. In that case, the value can be calculated from geometrical data. The geometrical length of the embouchure-hole is taken $l_E = 4.3$ mm, its diameter $d_E = 11.2$ mm (in fact, the hole is slightly oval; the number given here is a mean), the diameter of the main tube $d_0 = 17.4$ mm. Using a formula of the next chapter (eq. 38.9), we find

$$\lambda_E = (l_E + d_E)d_0^2/d_E^2 - 0.45 d_0 = 30 \text{ mm}.$$

l_m being 17 mm, the minimum value for $\lambda_E/l_m = 30/17 = 1.77$. Since the lips partly cover the embouchure-hole, λ_E/l_m can be expected to be larger than this minimum value and especially so for higher notes (see above). Therefore it is not unlikely that it takes on the value of 3 for high notes, which is the preferred value for pure tuning of overblown notes. Since the mouthpiece cavity influences frequencies of high notes, it is only important for these notes that λ_E/l_m has the preferred value; deviations from this value for low notes do not cause serious impurities. Since $k\lambda_E = 0.2$ at the lowest fundamental and the upper limit to which corrections can be obtained is at $k\lambda_E = 1.5$, we expect about three octaves to be in tune.

To my knowledge, l_m is adjusted to the same value in every flute. Also, nearly all cylindrical flutes have a contracting (sometimes called "parabolic") head. The exact shape and dimensions of this "parabolic" head, of the diameter of the main tube at the embouchure and of the embouchure-hole itself are different from flute to flute but the variations remain within certain limits. Apparently, slight variations in design give about equally satisfactory results. Whether one design is better than another is difficult to decide, since musicians' ratings of flutes depend on other undefinable features such as ease of blowing and tone-colour. Moreover, by shaping his lips, the player is able to correct notes which are slightly out of tune, thereby blurring tuning differences between flutes. Especially for very high notes this technique is frequently used since the highest notes are not among the purest in intonation.

We conclude that a painstakingly accurate investigation of the various corrections is quite unnecessary.

Conical flutes have a mouthpiece cavity too. Although the expressions differ slightly from those for cylindrical flutes, results are essentially the same. For the conical piccolo we have, for example, $l_m = 7$ mm, $d_0 = 10.85$ mm, $d_E = 9.45$ mm and $l_E = 5$ mm. The calculated minimum value for $\lambda_E = 14.3$ mm, and the minimum of $\lambda_E/l_m = 2$.

To find the influence of the boundary layer effects at the wall the corresponding terms have to be included in the resonance condition. Influences of deviations from the ideal cylindrical tube will be neglected. We assume the flute to be "ideally" blown, so the blown frequency is equal to the resonance frequency found by loudspeaker excitation. This means that in the resonance condition, eq.(22.23), $\delta_E = 0$. Then the length of the substitution tube, L_{eff}, for a cylindrical tube is

$$L_{eff} = l + \xi a + \alpha' l. \qquad (24.5)$$

In this formula, ξa is an end-correction of the open end, and $\alpha' l$ gives the influence of the boundary layer. This influence can be expressed as a frequency shift D_w, using eq.(22.9):

$$D_w = -\alpha' = -0.33 \times 10^{-3} k^{-\frac{1}{2}} a^{-1}. \qquad (24.6)$$

For a conical flute, the resonance condition is found from eq.(23.37) when we prescribe Y_0 to become infinite at $w = w_0$. This yields, neglecting losses:

$$\tan(W_1 - w_0 + \varphi') = 0. \qquad (24.7)$$

When using the approximate solution $kL_1 = m\pi$, m integer, all sine-terms in eq.(23.39) disappear and a good approximation for φ' is:

$$\varphi' = \beta'(\ln w_1 - \ln w_0 + g_1 - g_0). \qquad (24.8)$$

In conical flutes, $2w_1 > 7.6$ and $2w_0 > 14$. Inspection of the terms between brackets reveals that in this case with an accuracy better than 2 percent

$$\varphi' = \beta' \ln(w_1/w_0). \qquad (24.9)$$

Note that β', which is given by eq.(23.21), becomes negative for a negative cone.

The effective resonating length follows from

$$L_{eff} = l_1 + \xi a_1 + (\beta'/k)\ln(r_1/r_0). \qquad (24.10)$$

The third term at the right hand side denotes the

length correction due to wall effects; it is always positive since β' is negative when $r_1/r_0 < 1$ and positive when $r_1/r_0 > 1$. This term can be expressed in a frequency shift as follows

$$D_w = -(\beta'/kL_1)\ln(r_1/r_0). \qquad (24.11)$$

Note that $r_1 = r_0 + l_1$, where r_0 is a constant and l_1 is the geometrical tube-length. The latter value is close to the acoustical length $L_1 = l_1 + \xi a_1$, which satisfies the relation $kL_1 = m\pi$, m integer.

25. Properties of reed excitation

Excepting flutes, all woodwind instruments are excited by either a single or a double reed. Descriptions of the action of reeds were first given by Von Helmholtz [50], Rayleigh [98] and Rockstro [104], more recently by Das [43] and others [2, 3, 6, 9, 48, 75].

The function of the reed(s) is to modulate the stream of air, which enters the pipe in such a way as to excite and maintain the vibrations in the tube. Clarinet and saxophone are provided with a single reed. These instruments have a rigid mouthpiece, one side of which (called the lay) is nearly flat (Fig. 25.1). The other side is tapered so that the two sides meet at the top of the instrument at an angle of about 30°. In the

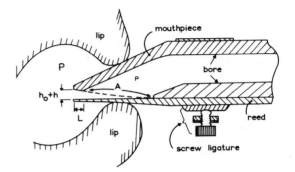

Fig. 25.2. Cross-section of single-reed embouchure.

flattened side of the mouthpiece is an oblong opening communicating with the bore (Fig. 25.2, A). The reed consists of a strip of cane thinned at one end. It is fastened with its thickest end to the right hand end of the mouthpiece with the screw ligature so as to cover the opening and reach to the upper end of the mouthpiece. The reed at this end is very thin and flexible and it stands at a small distance (around 1 mm) from the mouthpiece. The distance to the mouthpiece gradually decreases to zero as the reed nears the screw-ligature. In this way a passage from the mouth to the instrument is created which consists of a nearly rectangular portion (at the reed tip) flanked by two wedge-shaped passages. The length L (Fig. 25.1 and 25.2) of the passages is of the order of 1 mm. When in action, the reed moves to and from the mouthpiece, decreasing and increasing the height $(h_0 + h)$ of the passages, thus varying the stream of air, h_0 being the time-average.

The oboe, bassoon and other instruments of a similar nature are sounded by means of double reeds. A double reed consists of two blades of cane, the upper and thinner ends of which are slightly curved (Fig. 25.3). The lower ends are bound together and form a cylindrical tube through

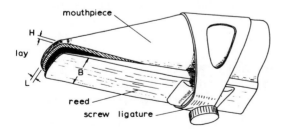

Fig. 25.1. Single-reed embouchure.

Fig. 25.3. Double reed (oboe).

which the air enters the instrument. The thin ends form an oval (lens-shaped) opening. When they vibrate the area of the opening changes, this has the same effect as that produced by the single reed.

The player takes the reed or reeds between his lips about halfway and by applying the proper lip force and air pressure in the mouth the excitation starts. The mouth-pressure is practically constant; the reed position, and hence the area of the opening to the tube, is determined by the (fluctuating) pressure difference between both sides of the reed. Because the resistance of the slit is strongly dependent on its area, the air stream increases as pressure in the instrument increases. When the right amount of air flows in the tube, (approximately) in phase with the pressure fluctuations, the oscillations in the instrument are maintained. A mathematical description of this action for a clarinet reed was given earlier by Backus [6]. Part of this theory is repeated here; it is extended to include reed motion and double reeds.

The following symbols are used.

C: displacement of the reed per unit pressure difference across the reed. C is dependent on the position along the reed; it may be called a position-dependent compliance of the reed. For double reeds C is the sum of the values for the single blades.

C_t: value of C at the reed-tip.

τ : relaxation time of the reed.

P: excess pressure in the mouth, assumed to be constant in time.

p: sound pressure, i.e. the acoustic excess pressure, in the top of the tube; the static excess pressure in the top of the tube is negligibly small with respect to P.

H: height of the slit (the distance between reed and mouthpiece at the top) in the absence of mouth pressure but with the lip force applied.

h_0: height of the slit when sounding the instrument, averaged over time.

h: oscillating component of the height of the slit.

M: acoustic mass of the air in the slit.

B: width of the slit, which is taken equal to the width of the reed at the tip (Fig. 25.1).

L: length of the slit (Fig. 25.2) at the reed tip (about 1 mm).

U_0: time-averaged mean value of the volume-velocity through the slit, positive in the direction down the tube.

U_{sl}: oscillative part of this volume-velocity through the slit.

U: oscillative part of the volume-velocity entering the pipe through a surface indicated by the dotted line A in Fig. 25.2.

S_r: effective area of the moving reed defined as ratio of volume displacement of the reed and displacement of the reed-tip.

E and q: empirical constants used for the description of the acoustic resistance of the slit.

The interaction of pressure, air flow and reed motion is described by three basic equations. They are first written down and then discussed.

The reed is considered to be an elastic plate with internal damping. Its mass is neglected since the natural frequency of the reed is at least ten times the playing frequency [6]. The balance of forces acting on the reed yields:

$$p - P = \frac{h_0 + h - H}{C_t} + \frac{\tau}{C_t}\frac{dh}{dt} \qquad (25.1)$$

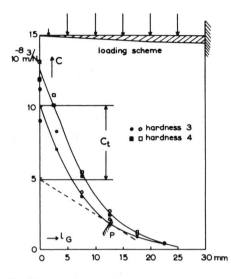

Fig. 25.4. Compliance C of four clarinet reeds, two of "hardness" 3 and two of "hardness" 4.

The equation of motion for the air in the slit is

$$P - p = E(U_0 + U_{sl})^q / B^2 (h_0 + h)^2 + M \, dU_{sl}/dt. \tag{25.2}$$

The oscillative flow U entering the instrument is composed of the oscillative flow U_{sl} through the slit and the oscillative flow due to the movement of the reed [18, 29]:

$$U = U_{sl} - S_r \, dh/dt. \tag{25.3}$$

The reed compliance C can be measured by observing the deformation of the reed when sucking at the instrument-side or by simulating the pressure drop by a static distributed load which can be applied by weighted (razor-type) blades resting on the flat side of the reed. Some illustrative results are shown in Figs. 25.4, 5, and 6. For double reeds the suction method was used. For single reeds, suction and distributed-load method were verified to yield identical results; the latter method, being the easiest one,

was preferred. The diagrams reveal that there is some spread between various commercial reeds, also between those sold under the same "hardness"-number. A reed in wet condition, which is the normal playing condition, has a compliance up to twice as large as a dry one. For the measurements shown here, the entire reed could move. In reality, however, the player presses the reed against the mouthpiece and partly immobilizes it. Then the pressure can act only on the free part of the reed. The reed more or less rolls on and off its lay. We assume it to be free from a point P on, as indicated by a hatched line in Fig. 25.4. To find the motion of the free part of the reed, we imagine that the complete reed is curved under influence of a pressure difference and fixed onto the mouthpiece at P. That part of the reed at the right of P is given such a shape that it touches the lay everywhere; it can be fixed on the lay in the usual way. This does not affect the shape of

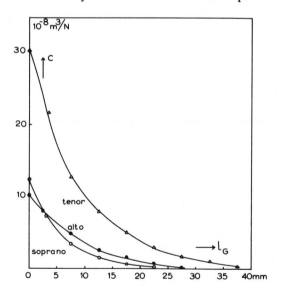

Fig. 25.5. Compliance C of saxophone reeds of "hardness" 3.

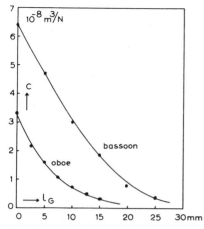

Fig. 25.6. Compliance C of an oboe-reed and a bassoon-reed.

the reed to the left of P. When the pressure difference across the reed is released the reed takes on a shape as indicated by the dashed line, i.e. according to the tangent to the curve at point P. The compliance of the reed-tip, C_t, is found from the vertical distance of the intersection points of the curve of C and the dashed line with the vertical axis. Since there is some spread among individual reeds and the position of point P can be varied, C_t is variable within certain limits. In Table 1 (page 103) values of C_t are listed valid for a reed of medium hardness which is completely free to move. In practice, C_t will be less, e.g. half as much.

The magnitude of the relaxation time τ of the reed, considered as a spring, is unknown; it may be frequency-dependent. In any case, it is small with respect to the period, as can be concluded from Backus' investigations [6].

The first term of the right hand member of eq.(25.2) describes the pressure drop due to frictional losses in the slit. Had the slit been a rectangle, this term would have been of the form [55, 56, 107] $\frac{1}{2}\rho(U_0 + U_{sl})^2/B^2(h_0 + h)^2$, for static

flow $\frac{1}{2}\rho U_0^2/B^2 h_0^2$. Note that the dynamic flow through the slit is assumed to be quasi-static, which assumption is not far from the truth [55]. Static measurements made by the present author on double reeds showed that the expression is essentially correct. Measurements on the clarinet reed, carried out by Backus, showed the pressure difference to be dependent on the 3/2 power of the flow. This apparently is due to the peculiar shape of the slit. No measurements are published or carried out on saxophone reeds; it is assumed that the results are similar to those for clarinet reeds. Results of my measurements and those of Backus are shown in Fig. 25.7. Lines were drawn

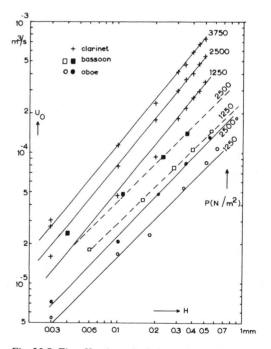

Fig. 25.7. Flow U_0 through clarinet, oboe and bassoon reeds as a function of stationary slit height H for various pressure drops P across the slit. Clarinet-reed measurements by Backus [6], oboe and bassoon-reeds measured by present author.

which gave the best fit with the measurements and it was found (in SI-units)

for single reed: $E = E_1 = 0.0056,\ q = q_1 = 3/2,$

for double reed: $E = E_2 = 2.6\quad,\ q = q_2 = 2.$

$$(25.4)$$

The E, found for double reed, can be compared with the theoretical expectation of $E = \frac{1}{2}\rho = 0.6$. By assuming that the effective width B is half the maximum value (reasonable because of the oval shape of the slit), E will be larger by a factor of 4, which is exactly the experimental finding.

The mean value of the acoustic mass M for a single-reed slit (the reed being at rest) was measured by Backus [6] and was found some three times higher than the mass of a rectangular slit, presumably due to the shape of the mouthpiece. According to these measurements the value for the acoustic mass M in the range $0.1 < h_0 < 1$ mm is

$$3000 > M > 1000 \text{ kg/m}^4 . \qquad (25.5)$$

As the influence of this mass on the natural frequency appears to be small, knowledge of its exact value is not very important.

An estimate of the magnitude of the area of the moving part of the reed, S_r, can be obtained. The maximally moving length of the reed is about 3 times its width. For a single reed, this length can be reduced considerable. These considerations yield $0.2\,B^2 < S_r < 2\,B^2$.

In order to be able to solve the set of three equations (25.1), (25.2) and (25.3) with four variables $(h_0 + h)$, $(U_0 + U_{sl})$, U and p, a fourth equation is necessary. It is provided by the throat impedance p/U of the tube of the wind instrument, the magnitude of which was derived in the preceding sections. For the moment, we will not consider this fourth equation, but solve the first three equations for the impedance p/U; in a later stage this impedance can be equated to the throat impedance of the tube.

An exact solution of the set of equations is difficult because of the many non-linear terms. Assuming small reed vibrations, i.e. small h, U, and p, a solution for the fundamental frequency can be obtained. For soft playing, this assumption was confirmed experimentally [3]. For loud playing, however, it is no longer true; the reed appears, then, to oscillate more or less with a square-wave form in which it alternates between two positions, an open one and one completely closing the aperture. Since, as is well-known, resonance frequencies for both soft and loud playing are about the same [5], we conclude that a calculation for infinitesimal fluctuations is meaningful. Apparently the fundamental in the square-wave type of motion is still of paramount influence.

In the derivations, M is assumed to be constant and the first term of the right hand member of eq.(25.2) is approximated to first order for relatively small U_{sl} and h. This gives

$$P - p = \frac{E}{B^2 h_0^2}\left[U_0^q\left(1 - \frac{2h}{h_0}\right) + q\,U_0^{q-1}\,U_{sl} \right] +$$
$$+ M\,\frac{dU_{sl}}{dt} \qquad (25.6)$$

The static parts of eqs.(25.1) and (25.6) yield

$$C_t\,P = H - h_0 , \qquad (25.7)$$

$$P h_0^2\,B^2 = E\,U_0^q . \qquad (25.8)$$

Assuming a harmonic oscillation, introducing complex notation, using eqs.(25.7) and (25.8) and eliminating U_{sl} with eq.(25.3), eqs.(25.1) and (25.6) give the following conditions

$$p = (1+j\omega\tau)h/C_t, \tag{25.9}$$

$$p = 2Ph/h_0 - (qP/U_0 + j\,\omega M)\,(U + j\,\omega S_r h). \tag{25.10}$$

After elimination of h between these equations the following expression is obtained for the acoustic admittance

$$Y_E = \frac{U}{p} = \frac{2PC_t/h_0 - 1 - j\,\omega\tau}{(1+j\,\omega\tau)(qP/U_0 + j\,\omega M)} - \frac{j\,\omega S_r C_t}{1 + j\,\omega\tau}. \tag{25.11}$$

The ratio of the magnitudes of imaginary and real terms can be estimated; for a clarinet, in SI-units, $\omega = 1000$, $M = 2000$, $U_0 = 10^{-4}$, $q = 3/2$,

$P = 2000$ N/m^2, $S_r = 0.5 \times 10^{-4}$, $C_t = 4 \times 10^{-8}$,

$Y_E' = 18 \times 10^{-9}$ (eq. 22.27), we find

$\omega M < 0.1\, qP/U_0$, $\omega S_r C_t < 0.2\, Y_E'$.

From Backus' experiments it may be found that presumably $\omega\tau < 0.3$ (see Section 26). So in the expression for the admittance $Y_E = Y_E'(1 - j\delta)$, the term δ is smaller than unity. We first consider the resistive part of the admittance. This is approximately equal to

$$Y_E' = (2\,PC_t/h_0 - 1)\,U_0/qP. \tag{25.12}$$

Using eqs.(25.7) and (25.8) to eliminate U_0 and P, eq.(25.12) can be written as follows

$$Y_E' = \frac{2}{q}\,B^{2/q}C_t^{1-1/q}E^{-1/q}h_0 H^{3/q-1}w, \tag{25.13}$$

where

$$w = \left(1 - \frac{3h_0}{2H}\right)\left(\frac{h_0}{H}\right)^{2/q-1}\left(1 - \frac{h_0}{H}\right)^{1/q-1}. \tag{25.14}$$

Using eq.(25.7) w can alternatively be written as

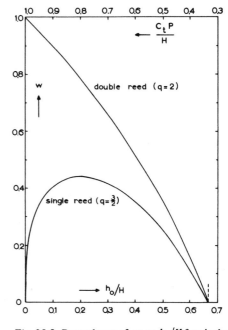

Fig. 25.8. Dependence of w on h_0/H for single and double reed.

$$w = \frac{1}{2}\left(\frac{3C_tP}{H} - 1\right)\left(1 - \frac{C_tP}{H}\right)^{2/q-1}\left(\frac{C_tP}{H}\right)^{1/q-1} \tag{25.14a}$$

Y_E' can be adjusted by the player through adjusting H and P; this at the same time fixes values for C_t and $w = w(C_tP/H)$. The quantity w can take on values between 0 and 1 for a double reed and between 0 and 0.45 for a single reed, as is illustrated in Fig. 25.8. As h_0 and Y_E' are both positive, we find limits for P and h_0 from eqs (25.14a) and (25.14) respectively

$$H/3C_t = P_{min} < P < P_{max} = H/C_t, \tag{25.15}$$

$$0 < h_0 < 2H/3 \tag{25.16}$$

When $P < P_{min}$, excitation is impossible. When $P > 3P_{min}$, the reed closes the aperture at all times, so excitation is impossible too. It appears that the variation in mouth pressure is a factor of one in three. From experiments [6] the minimum in the blowing pressure did appear to exist and its numerical value was as predicted by theory.

The highest possible value for the admittance Y'_E is attained for the largest possible values of H and w as appears from eq.(25.13). For a clarinet, in SI-units, $H_{max} = 0.001$, $w_{max} = 0.45$, $C_t = 4 \cdot 10^{-4}$; $E = 0.0056$, $q = 3/2$, $B = 0.0125$, it is found that $Y'_E < 10^{-6}$. This is about as large as the admittance for freely travelling waves, $\pi a^2 / \rho c = 3 \cdot 10^{-7}$ SI, so we conclude that the reed excitation is only able to sustain oscillations for which the tube admittance is low. As was shown before, $\delta < 1$, so $|Y_E| < S/\rho c$ and consequently there must be a velocity node near the reed. The admittance at the throat of the tube (see eq. 22.27) is some 50 times smaller than this maximum value, therefore w and/or H will be smaller. Smaller values of w mean that h_0/H is close to 2/3, or, for single reeds only, close to 0. This last possibility is not a very likely one as the reed amplitudes then become very small. Moreover, observations by Backus [3] showed that h_0/H is around 0.5.

There are two limits for H. The upper limit, H_{max}, follows from the position of the reed when no forces are acting upon it. This value is in between 1 and 2.5 mm, depending on the type of instrument. The lower limit, H_{min}, follows from eq.(25.13), when we solve it for H and insert the proper Y'_E of the bore, all slit constants and the highest possible value for w. It appears (see Sections 26 and 27) that H_{min} may vary between 0.02 and 0.2 mm.

As a matter of fact, the player adjusts a complex admittance and not a real one; but the real part of the tube admittance is not very dependent on a phase angle at the top, and the primary task of the musician therefore is to generate the proper real part of the admittance. Next to this, the imaginary part of the admittance can be changed by adjusting lip position and blowing pressure, providing means for a fine-adjustment of the frequency.

The imaginary terms in the denominator of eq.(25.11) are small and can be carried over to the numerator. We get

$$Y_E = Y'_E (1 - j\delta) = Y'_E (1 - j\delta_r - j\delta_T - j\delta_M),$$

where
$$\text{(25.17)}$$

$$\left. \begin{array}{l} \delta_r = \omega C_t S_r / Y'_E, \\ \delta_T = \omega \tau (H - h_0) / (H - 3h_0/2), \\ \delta_M = \omega M U_0 / qP. \end{array} \right\} \quad \text{(25.18)}$$

All three imaginary terms are negative, and according to eq.(22.28) they virtually increase the length of the tube, in other words, the note flattens. Their action can be compared with the action of a mouthpiece-cavity located close to the reed-tip. The influence of such a mouthpiece-cavity, say of volume V'_m can be calculated. The flow U entering the instrument is composed of the flow U_{sl} through the reed slit and the (negative) flow due to the compliance V'_m/K of the cavity ($K =$ bulk modulus):

$$U = U_{sl} - j\omega p V'_m / K, \quad \text{(25.19)}$$

which, after division of every term by p, can be written as follows

$$Y_E = Y'_E (1 - j\omega V'_m / KY'_E), \quad \text{(25.20)}$$

where we introduced $U/p = Y_E$, $U_{sl}/p = Y'_E$. Comparing this with eq.(25.17) we find

$$\delta = \omega V'_m / KY'_E. \quad \text{(25.21)}$$

This means that we have found a way of interpreting the term δ as a mouthpiece cavity. The length correction $\Delta l'_m$ due to this cavity onto a tube of cross-sectional area S is found from eqs.(22.26) ... (22.28). Eq.(25.21) implies a change in Y_E in eq.(22.26), which leads to a change in kl in eq.(22.28) amounting to kV'_m/S i.e. **to a correction in** l equal to

$$\Delta l'_m = V'_m /S. \tag{25.22}$$

Thus the terms δ in eq.(25.18) yield the following length corrections

$$\left.\begin{array}{l} \Delta l_r = V_r/S = KC_tS_r/S, \\[4pt] \Delta l_T = V_T/S = \tau\,(H - h_0)K\,Y'_E/S(H - 3h_0/2), \\[4pt] \Delta l_M = V_M/S = KMY'_E\,U_0/qPS. \end{array}\right\}$$

$$\tag{25.23}$$

The reason for this way of interpretation of the imaginary terms in eq.(25.17) was to show that the length corrections do not contain explicitly frequency or mode number any more, although many of the factors in these expressions are still frequency-dependent.

The correction due to reed motion, Δl_r, is dependent on the factor C_tS_r; this factor depends on how the player adjusts Y'_E When the player decreases H by a tighter clamping of the reed, C_t and S_r both decrease, showing that Δl_r increases with H.

The correction due to reed damping, Δl_T, is mainly dependent on H/h_0 and Y'_E, since τ can be assumed to vary slowly with frequency. In fact, as will be shown in Sections 26 and 27, Δl_T also increases with H.

The slit-mass correction is small, as can be shown when numerical values are inserted:
$M = 2000$ kg/m^4, $U_0 = 10^{-4}$ m^3/s,
$P = 2000$ N/m^2, $q = 3/2$, $Y'_E = 18 \times 10^{-9}$ SI,

$K = 1.4 \times 10^5$ N/m^2, $S = 0.00018$ m^2.
We find $\Delta l_M \approx 1$ mm, which is negligible for practical purposes.

26. The clarinet

A clarinet is a cylindrical instrument with a single-reed embouchure. It is a member of a family of 17 similar instruments which, essentially, are only different in size. The chief representative of this family is the common B-flat clarinet (Fig. 11.1)*. Some other sizes have gained some popularity such as the E-flat clarinet (a fourth higher), the A-clarinet (a semitone lower), the Basset-horn or alto-clarinet (a fourth lower) and the bass-clarinet (one octave lower).

The lower end of the tube is provided with a rapidly flaring horn, the top of the tube is tapered towards the reed embouchure. These perturbed parts of the tube are short with respect to the wavelength, at least for the lower notes, and therefore they can be replaced by fictitious pieces of cylindrical tube as a first approximation.

In the previous section the reed embouchure was proved to impose a velocity-node, hence the admittance at the reed is best described with eq.(22.26). For its real part Y'_E, neglecting θ with respect to $\alpha'kl$, we find (see eq. 22.27):

$$Y'_E = \alpha'kl\,S_0/\rho c, \tag{26.1}$$

where $kl \approx kL_{eff} = m\pi$, $m = \frac{1}{2}, 1\frac{1}{2}, 2\frac{1}{2}, 3\frac{1}{2}$, etc. and where L_{eff} denotes the acoustical length of the tube. α' is introduced from eq.(22.9). From eq.(26.1) it follows that the admittance is proportional to the mode number m and inversely

* *'Clarinet in B-flat' means 'clarinet sounding a tone lower than the written part'. So a written C sounds a B-flat, hence the name.*

proportional to the square root of the frequency. Its numerical value at the lowest note is given in Table 1 (see page 103).

The height of the slit between reed and instrument is found from eq. (25.13), where $q = 3/2$:

$$\left. \begin{array}{l} H = \dfrac{3\,Y_E'}{4w}\ \sqrt[3]{\dfrac{E^2}{B^4 C_t}}\,, \\[2ex] w = \left(1 - \dfrac{3h_0}{2H}\right)\left(\dfrac{H}{h_0} - 1\right)^{-1/3} \end{array} \right\} \qquad (26.2)$$

The lowest possible value for H, H_{min}, is reached for $w = w_{max} = 0.45$. C_t was assumed to be proportional to H: $C_t = 10^{-4}\,H$ (Fig. 25.4). For the lowest note, using values from Table 1, we find $H_{min} = 0.14$ mm. How H_{min} is dependent on the frequency is shown in Fig. 26.1, where it is plotted for fundamental and first overtone. It can be seen to vary between 0.05 and 0.16 mm over the whole tonal compass of the instrument. The lowest value is found at the upper end of the low register. Since, geometrically, H_{max} is about 1 mm, the variation in H is at least a factor of 10. This indicates that the player has a wide choice of lip positions. So the mere excitation of the instrument is not very critical. A certain choice in lip position also means that the frequency can be influenced within a certain range: in the previous section it was shown that the length-corrections at the embouchure-end are dependent on H. Further reference to this will follow in this section.

The natural frequency is directly connected to the effective length L_{eff} as it is found from eq.(22.28), neglecting θ:

$$L_{eff} = l + \xi a + \alpha' l + \delta \alpha' l \approx L(1 + \alpha + \delta \alpha').$$
$$(26.3)$$

L is the tube length including the open end correction ξa. The boundary layer yields a length correction of $\alpha' l$, corresponding to a relative fre-

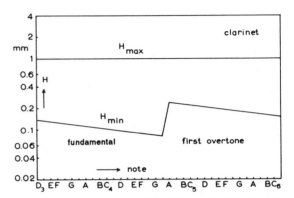

Fig. 26.1. Upper and lower limits of the rest height H of the reed slit for first and second register of a clarinet.

quency shift of $D_w = -\alpha'$; this is equal to the expression obtained for the flute, eq.(24.6).

The imaginary part of the impedance at the throat of the tube gives a length correction of $\Delta l = \delta \alpha' l$. It can be separated in corrections due to reed motion (Δl_r), reed damping (Δl_τ) and slit mass (Δl_M). These were calculated earlier, see eqs.(25.23). Slit mass influences were shown to be negligibly small. We may think in terms of fictitious mouthpiece cavities rather than length corrections. The former may be considered as related more closely to the reed action since they are calculated exclusively from the reed properties and do not contain constants related to the instrument, such as the cross-sectional area of the tube.

The magnitude of the fictitious cavity V_r, induced by the reed motion, was shown to depend strongly on the position of the reed on its lay. V_r is greatest when the reed is completely free to move. The magnitude of this greatest value is found by integrating the curve for C in the corresponding diagram, Fig. 25.4:

$$V_r = K \int B\,C\,dx. \qquad (26.4)$$

For a reed "hardness" of 4, V_r is found to be 1.1 cm^3 and $\Delta l_r = 6$ mm. For a reed of hardness 3 we obtain $\Delta l_r = 9$ mm. When the reed motion is decreased by tighter clamping, V_r decreases correspondingly. On the other hand, the reed softens in the wet playing condition and as it wears out, so V_r tends to increase by these effects.

The influence of reed damping, when expressed as a fictitious mouthpiece cavity V_T, is found from eq.(25.23) in which we substitute Y_E' solved from eq.(26.2):

$$V_T = \frac{4}{3}\frac{K}{} \sqrt[3]{\frac{C_t B^4}{E^2}} \left\{ \frac{h_0}{H} \left(\frac{H}{h_0} - 1 \right)^{2/3} \right\} H\tau .$$

$$(26.5)$$

The function between square brackets is equal to $\frac{1}{2}$ with a good approximation in the region $0.1 < h_0/H < 0.7$. Then the only remaining variable factors are H and τ and, to a lesser degree, C_t. Inserting numerical values obtained from Table 1 and eq.(25.4), we get

$$\Delta l_T = V_T/S_0 = 0.5 \times 10^5\, H\tau. \qquad (26.6)$$

Assuming a rather high value for τ given by $\omega\tau = 1$ at $\omega = 1000$ s^{-1} and taking $H = 0.2$ mm, it follows that $\Delta l_T = 10$ mm, corresponding to $D_T = -33$ cents for the lowest note in the register. From Backus' experiments [6] it is concluded that the absolute value of D_T at $H = 0.2$ mm is presumably less than 15 cents, so $\Delta l_T < 5$ mm. Using artificial damping, Backus was able to confirm experimentally the predictions of eq.(26.6) such as the numerical value of Δl_T as well as its linear dependence on H.

For both Δl_r and Δl_T only approximate values are known. In Section 44, where we will discuss the blowing tests combined with hole calculations, we will explain the choice which was finally made; it will appear to fall within the limits estimated here.

27. Saxophone, oboe and bassoon

This section is devoted to conical instruments blown with single or double reed. A single-reed embouchure is found on saxophones, which are built in various sizes, of which the most common ones are soprano, alto, tenor and baritone with lowest notes A_3-flat, D_3-flat, A_2-flat and E_2-flat respectively. Of these, the alto (Fig. 27.1) and the

Fig. 27.1. Alto saxophone. (Courtesy of Gérald Gorgerat, Encyclopédie de la Musique pour Instruments à Vent, 2nd ed. tome II, Rencontre, Lausanne 1955).

Fig. 27.2. Oboe.

Fig. 27.3. Bassoon.

tenor are by far the most common. A double-reed embouchure is found on the oboe (Fig. 27.2) and the bassoon (Fig. 27.3) as well as on related instruments, the cor anglais (one fifth below the oboe) and the contrabassoon (one octave below the bassoon).

Saxophones are usually made of brass, double-reed instruments of wood. Some rare instruments

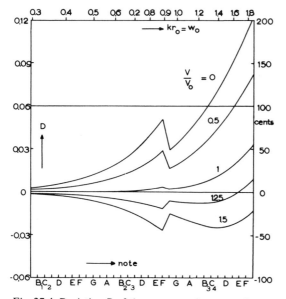

Fig. 27.4. Deviation D of the resonance frequency from the nominal value for various values of the ratio of mouthpiece-cavity volume V and volume of truncated part of the cone, V_0.

are an exception to this: the sarussophone (a metal instrument with double reed) and the tarogato, a saxophone-like wooden instrument, which is blown with double as well as single reed [14].

Like the clarinet, conical reed instruments are effectively closed at the top. The resonance frequency follows from eq.(23.15). When the truncation r_0 is sufficiently small to satisfy the relation $w_0 = \tan w_0$, where $w_0 = kr_0$ (Fig. 23.1), this condition simplifies to $W_1 = m\pi$, m integer, where $W_1 = kR_1$. This solution, the zero-order solution, is valid for low frequencies, since r_0 is about 0.1 of the tube length and at the lowest notes, then, $w_0 = 0.3$. To show the deviations which arise for higher notes in a bassoon we solved W_1 from eq.(23.15) for a number of w_0-values and plotted the deviation $D = W_1/m\pi - 1$ from the zero-order solution in Fig. 27.4 (uppermost curve).

An additional scale for the resultant notes is provided. In this diagram the high register can be seen to be completely out of tune with the lower one. As a matter of fact, no such deviations are experienced in reality. Therefore mechanisms must exist which provide compensations. Such effects may be expected from a mouthpiece cavity, from reed damping and from the air flow caused by the reed motion. It was shown in Section 25 that the last two effects can be described by a fictitious mouthpiece cavity. So all three mechanisms can be combined for a first approximation.

A cavity of volume V is imagined at the top of a loss-free conical tube, closed at its throat (Fig. 27.5). The cavity is supposed to be located exactly at the throat of the tube. Denoting the admittance of the conical tube by Y_0, then

$$Y_0 + j\,k\,V/\rho\,c = 0. \qquad (27.1)$$

Using eq.(23.11) this becomes

$$(1 - w_0^2\,V/3\,V_0)\tan(w_0 - W_1) = w_0, \qquad (27.2)$$

where $V_0 = \pi a_0^2\,r_0/3 \qquad (27.3)$

denotes the volume of the truncated part of the cone (Fig. 27.5). From eq.(27.2), W_1 can be solved numerically for various values of w_0 and V/V_0.

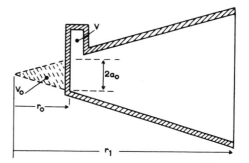

Fig. 27.5. Conical tube, closed at its throat and provided of a mouthpiece cavity at the throat.

Results $D = W_1/m\pi - 1$ for a bassoon are shown in Fig. 27.4 for various values of V/V_0. Apparently, for $V/V_0 \approx 1$ the zero-order solution $W_1 = m\pi$ is a good approximation within about two octaves, that is up to a frequency where the truncation is about as long as a quarter wavelength. Deviations from the preferred value of V strongly influence the high register and the upper part of the low register, whereas the lowest notes are altered less.

A mouthpiece cavity, either real or fictitious, of the right magnitude seems to be a conditio sine qua non. Before investigating its size in the various instruments, we proceed with refining the calculations, including damping and non-zero admittance at the reed. This reed admittance is written as (see eq. 25.17):

$$Y_E = Y_E' \, (1 - j\delta),$$

where Y_E' denotes its real part. The equation of continuity of admittances at the throat of the tube reads

$$Y_E' \, (1 - j\delta) = Y_0 + j k \, V_m/\rho c, \qquad (27.4)$$

where V_m, here, denotes the real mouthpiece-cavity volume only. Using eqs (23.37) and (23.38) this condition becomes

$$Y_E'(j + \delta)\frac{\rho c}{S_0} = \frac{1}{w_0} - \frac{w_0 \, V_m}{3 \, V_0} +$$

$$+ \cot \, (W_1 - w_0 + \varphi' - j\varphi' - j\,\theta). \qquad (27.5)$$

Since $\varphi' \ll W_1$, the expression for φ' as given by eq.(23.39) can be simplified by substitution of the approximate value $W_1 = m\pi$. This yields

$$\varphi' = \beta' \, [\, \ln (w_1/w_0) + \text{Ci}(2w_0) - \text{Ci}(2w_1) +$$

$$+ \frac{\xi v}{w_0^2} \, \sin^2 w_0 - \frac{\xi v}{w_0} \sin 2w_0 \,]. \qquad (27.6)$$

None of the terms between brackets can be neglected since they are all of the same magnitude.

A separation of imaginary and real parts of eq.(27.5) yields

$$Y_E' = \frac{S_0}{\rho c} \left[\frac{\varphi' + \theta}{\sin^2 \, (W_1 - w_0 + \varphi')} \right], \qquad (27.7)$$

$$\cot \, (W_1 - w_0 + \varphi') + \frac{1}{w_0} - \frac{w_0 \, V_m}{3 \, V_0} - \delta \frac{\rho c}{S_0} \, Y_E' = 0. \qquad (27.8)$$

A condition for δ is given by eq.(25.21) which can be rewritten as follows

$$\delta \, Y_E' \, \rho c/S_0 = V_m' \, w_0/3 \, V_0 = (V_r + V_T + V_M) w_0/3 \, V_0. \qquad (27.9)$$

V_m' denotes a fictitious mouthpiece-cavity volume due to combined influences of reed motion (V_r), reed damping (V_T) and slit-mass (V_M). The contributions to this volume were derived earlier and found from eqs.(25.23). Again, V_M is negligibly small. For single-reed instruments, V_T has the same value as for clarinets and is given by eq.(26.6). For double-reed instruments, a slightly different expression is found. To find this latter expression we need the admittance, given by eqs.(25.13) and (25.14), which $q = 2$:

$$\left. \begin{aligned} Y_E' &= B w \, \sqrt{\frac{C_t H}{E}} \, , \\ w &= (1 - 3h_0/2H)(1 - h_0/H)^{-\frac{1}{2}}. \end{aligned} \right\} \qquad (27.10)$$

Introducing this into the second equation (25.23):

$$V_T = \tau K B \, \sqrt{\frac{C_t}{E}} \, (H - h_0) , \qquad (27.11)$$

From this equation, V_T can be seen to increase with H, which is an analoguous effect as in single-reed instruments.

From eqs.(27.8) and (27.9) a condition is derived for the resonance frequency

$$[1 - w_0^2 \ (V_m + V_r + V_T + V_M)/3 V_0] \ \tan (W_1 - \ - w_0 + \varphi') + w_0 = 0. \quad (27.12)$$

The only difference with eq.(27.2) is the presence of a boundary layer term φ'; the cavity effects appear in exactly the same way.

The frequency being known, it can be substituted into eq.(27.7), so Y_E' can be calculated. Then δ is found from eq.(27.9).

The above results clearly show the important effects on the tuning of the volume of a mouthpiece cavity and of the shape and mechanical properties of the reed. They indicate the utmost care the reed requires in order that it shall act in the desired way on a woodwind.

A fair estimate of the magnitude of the mouthpiece-cavities of conical instruments, of which detailed data can be found in Chapter 4, is obtained by determining the excess volume of the mouthpiece over the main tube extrapolated to the reed tip and by assuming this volume to be concentrated at the reed tip. Results are given in Table 1. Saxophones were found to have a (real) cavity volume somewhere in the proper range, $V_m/V_0 \approx 1$. Double reed instruments do not show a cavity of significant volume; this volume appears to be very small. This leads to the supposition that in these instruments the reed motion is fully responsible for purity of tuning, contrary to saxophones where it has only an additional influence. This view is supported by measurements of Backus [10] on a bassoon: he found playing frequencies to be up to a semitone lower than resonance frequencies of the tube with immobilized reed.

The size of the fictitious cavity due to reed motion is estimated by using eq.(26.4) for single reeds and eq.(27.13) for double reeds:

$$V_r = \frac{2}{3} K \int B C \, dx. \quad (27.13)$$

The factor $2/3$ is introduced in order to account for the fact that the deformation of double reeds is maximal in the centre and decreases towards the sides of the reeds (Fig. 25.3): it very closely resembles a part of the circumference of a circle (Fig. 27.6); $2/3$ is the ratio of the area of a circle and its circumscribed rectangle, for slender segments. The results of the calculations can be found in Table 1; they suggest an appreciable influence of reed compliance on the tuning. The values given for the single reeds are maximum values (where the whole reed moves), while those for double reeds are probably closer to mean values. The numbers presented in the Table only intend to give an indication of the magnitude of the effect.

Hitherto the reed motion was translated into a fictitious cavity at the tip of the reed. Alternatively, we can transform the reed motion into a corresponding widening of the bore over the length which is bounded by the reed. It is easy to do this. Note that the pressures over the whole length of the reed are practically constant because there is a node here. Therefore the reed may be assumed to move entirely in the same phase. Then a position-dependent volume increase of the cross-sectional area, $d V_m'$, can be calculated from the curve for the compliance C as

Fig. 27.6. Curved blade of double reed and its circumscribed rectangle.

follows

$$d\,V_{\mathrm{m}}' = B_{\mathrm{eff}}\,C\,K\,dx,\qquad (27.14)$$

where x is the position along the reed. This volume-increase can be converted into a diameter change, if necessary. For single reeds, $B_{\mathrm{eff}} = B$, for double reeds, $B_{\mathrm{eff}} = 2B/3$. This procedure will be used in Chapter 4, Section 44, where various assumptions for the reed compliance will be studied.

The influence of the boundary layer effects on the tuning is accounted for in a frequency shift D_{w}, found from eq.(27.12):

$$D_{\mathrm{w}} = \frac{-\varphi'}{W_1} = -\left\{0.33\ 10^{-3}\frac{r\sqrt{k}}{a}\right\}\frac{1}{W_1}\,(\ln\frac{w_1}{w_0} + \\ + \ldots),\qquad (27.15)$$

where $\ln(w_1/w_0) + \ldots$ is an abbreviation of the term between brackets in eq.(27.6). The result can be rewritten so as to bring all frequency-independent factors together in a new constant T:

$$D_{\mathrm{w}} = -T\frac{\sqrt{w_0}}{W_1}\left[\ln\frac{w_1}{w_0} + \ldots\right],\qquad (27.16)$$

where

$$T = 0.33 \times 10^{-3}\frac{r}{a\sqrt{r_0}} = 0.33 \times 10^{-3}\sqrt{r_0}/a_0.$$
$$(27.17)$$

T is an instrumental constant and it is listed in Table 1. The remainder of the expression for D_{w} is frequency-dependent. It is plotted in Fig. 27.7 as a function of w_0/W_1 for two modes, $m = 1$ and $m = 2$. Additional scales are added to read D_{w} directly for every note of the various instruments. In the same figure, broken lines indicate a D_{w} for a cylindrical flute (of arbitrary dimensions) to show the essential difference in behaviour between conical and

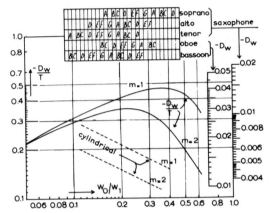

Fig. 27.7. Frequency deviation due to boundary layer effects, D_{w}, for various conical instruments, for first and second mode. Dashed line denotes D_{w} for an arbitrary cylindrical instrument

cylindrical instruments. For cylindrical instruments, D_{w} decreases monotonically with the square root of the frequency, independent of the vibrational mode. The shift in conical instruments follows a less regular pattern. For notes in the lower part of both registers, the shift increases with the square root of the fre-

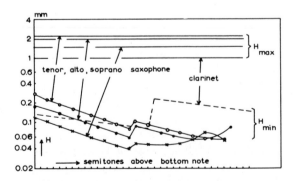

Fig. 27.8. Upper and lower limits of the rest height H of the reed slit, for first and second registers of clarinet and saxophones.

quency. For decreasing acoustical length this increase diminishes, the shift passes through a maximum and eventually falls at the highest notes of both registers. For these highest notes, the frequency shift of both modes differs markedly.

We may compare the results with those of Benade [16], who used an obvious and simple way of obtaining the influence of the boundary layer by integrating eq.(22.9) with respect to r from r_0 to r_1. He obtained

$$D_w = -\left\{ 0.46 \times 10^{-3} \frac{r k^{1/2}}{a} \right\} \frac{\ln (w_1 / w_0)}{W_1 - w_0} .$$

$$(27.18)$$

This is different from our expression, eq.(27.15), in two respects. Benade takes a slightly higher constant, 0.46 instead of 0.33, and his dependence on shape and frequency is different.

Deriving the magnitude of the damping by calculating the energy dissipated at the wall, when assuming a standing-wave pattern in the tube equal to that of the loss-free case, also leads to erroneous results, as Kuckes and Ingard have shown [68].

The minimum height of the slit at the reed-tip for which excitation of oscillations is possible can be calculated in the same way as was done for the clarinet. This is done for saxophones, by using eq.(26.2) into which eq.(27.7) is substituted. Results are plotted in Fig. 27.8 for the tenor, alto and soprano. For comparison, clarinet results, from Fig. 26.1, are inserted too. In the first register, clarinets and saxophones show similar values for H_{min}, but in the second register the clarinet-values are appreciably higher than those for saxophones. The consequences of this will become clearer in the last chapter.

28. Recapitulation

In this chapter the excitation mechanism of woodwind instruments was studied and explained. As a result, the specific influence of a number of effects was found and most attention was paid to those yielding a perceptible change in the tuning.

Flutes and similar instruments are excited by blowing a jet of air against the edge of a lateral embouchure-hole. For an even excitation over the whole compass, the hole is progressively covered by the lips as the frequency rises. However, with increasing coverage the end-correction of the hole increases and the frequency is reduced. The contraction of the bore towards the flute's embouchure-hole compensates for this effect.

The reed action and its coupling to the air column in the tube can be described mathematically by a set of differential equations. After certain assumptions, these can be solved numerically and yield relations between pressure and velocity and reed position. Experiments confirm predictions of the theory concerning the dimensions of the slit at the top of the instrument and the blowing pressure in the mouth.

The motion of the reed itself is damped and displaces air in the instrument; these effects are essential to ensure a pure tuning in all reed instruments. It was shown that conical instruments can be designed to overblow in the octave up to a frequency where the truncation of the cone equals a quarter of a wavelength. All reed effects are strongly dependent on the size and the stiffness of the reed. It can be explained why the frequency rises when the reed is clamped more firmly between the lips.

The short closed tube-piece in the flute, left of the embouchure-hole, was shown to have a function in the tuning of very high notes.

The vibrating air exchanges energy with its enclosing walls by friction and heat conduction. This slightly lowers the frequency and causes the vibrations to damp out when left to themselves. Both effects were investigated theoretically. The magnitude of the frequency shift was calculated, being as much as a semitone for instruments with a very narrow bore.

The sound energy radiated by the instrument proved to be small compared with that dissipated inside it.

chapter 3
holes and bore perturbations

31. Introduction

In Chapter 1, the principles of calculating the position and dimensions of holes so as to obtain a sequence of desired tones were briefly introduced. In Chapter 2, descriptions were given of the excitation mechanism of the various woodwind instruments and of the energy balance of vibrations. From these descriptions, formulae were obtained for frequency shifts due to excitation and boundary layers.

Effects of closed and open holes and of bore perturbations were not included in the discussions of Chapter 2, that is to say, the real instrument was replaced by a shorter one, ideally cylindrical or conical, without holes, resonating in the same frequency (substitution-tube). The problem of how to find the substitution-tube of a real tube with holes and perturbations is dealt with in the present chapter. Detailed methods of calculation are given for nearly all practical situations. All these calculations are performed on loss-free tubes with purely imaginary end-impedances; corrections for boundary-layer effects, perturbations et cetera are introduced afterwards where it is assumed that all frequency corrections derived in Chapter 2 for the idealized (substitution) tubes may be used unaltered for a real musical instrument. Because of the many unknown factors, a more accurate but much more intricate attack is obviously superfluous. So all corrections to the natural frequency, i.e. those due to embouchure, boundary layers, complex end-impedances and bore perturbations, are assumed to be additive and therefore they are calculated independently of one another.

32. Calculations for a tube with a single side-hole

a. The resonance condition

When a hole is opened, the tube is acoustically shortened. In the first chapter (Section 15) the resonance condition for a loss-free open-open cylinder with one open hole was derived. In this section it will be shown that this expression is of general validity for all woodwind instruments. In Fig. 32.1 the four types of instrument concerned are shown, each of them provided with a single

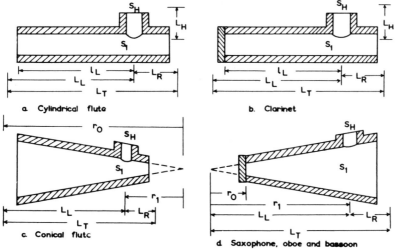

Fig. 32.1. The four types of instruments from acoustical point of view.

side hole. All quantities and symbols are explained in this figure.

The length of the side-hole is l_H without, and L_H with end-corrections. The length of the tube-part at the right of the hole is l_R excluding and L_R including the open-end correction.* The length of the tube to the left of the hole is l_L, measured from the centre of the hole to the centre of the embouchure-hole or to the top of the reed(s). When an embouchure correction is included, this length becomes L_L. For flutes, this correction is the usual passive open-end correction for a hole of the same size as the embouchure-hole. For clarinets, there is a correction for mouthpiece-cavity and complex throat-impedance. For conical reed instruments (Fig. 32.1 d) these corrections, as will appear below, include the length of the truncated part of the cone as well.

The total acoustical length of the tube with closed hole is denoted by

$$L_T = L_L + L_R . \qquad (32.1)$$

The length of the substitution-tube – still to be calculated – is L_S. All quantities L are always positive. The cross-sectional areas of hole and main tube at the hole are S_H and S_1 respectively.

The resonance condition for the pipe with open side-hole is found from eqs.(15.2) and (15.3) and gives a condition (Fig. 32.2) between admittances Y_L, Y_H and Y_R:

$$Y_L = Y_H + Y_R . \qquad (32.2)$$

The general expression for the admittance in a cylindrical tube at a position x, neglecting boundary-layer effects, is found from eq.(13.14)

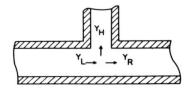

Fig. 32.2. Symbols used for the admittances at the tube junction.

$$Y = -(S/j\rho c) \cot (kx + \psi). \qquad (32.3)$$

At the extrapolated open end, where Y is infinite, we choose $x = 0$. This yields $\psi = 0$. Eq.(32.3) can be applied to the "cylindrical" open side-hole, S being equal, in this case, to S_H. The admittance at the throat of the hole, where $x = -L_H$, then is

$$Y_H = (S_H/j\rho c) \cot kL_H . \qquad (32.4)$$

In the same way the admittance of the right hand tube-piece, if cylindrical, is found to be

$$Y_R = (S_1/j\rho c) \cot kL_R , \quad \text{(cylinder)}. \qquad (32.5)$$

When the right hand tube-piece is conical, its admittance is found from eqs. (23.3) and (23.6). In deriving eq. (23.6), r_0 was chosen at the top of the cone. We adhere to this convention. The condition of zero impedance at $r = r_1 + L_R$ (see Fig. 32.1) yields $\psi = -k(r_1 + L_R)$, therefore at $r = r_1$:

$$Y_R = \frac{S_1}{j\rho c} \left[\frac{1}{kr_1} + \cot kL_R \right] , \quad \text{(cone)}, \qquad (32.6)$$

where S_1 is the cross-sectional area of the main tube at the hole.

The magnitude of Y_L must be calculated separately for each of the four situations shown in Fig. 32.1.

For a *cylindrical flute*, $Y = \infty$ at the corrected position of the embouchure, which is taken

---

* *In general we followed the rule of taking small print for geometrical lengths, and using capital print for corrected lengths.*

at $x = 0$. Substitution of this into eq.(32.3) yields $\psi = -m\pi$, m integer. The length of the substitution tube, L_S, for a flute is recalled to be determined by the condition $kL_S = m\pi$, m integer, so we may set $\psi = -kL_S$. With this, at $x = L_L$:

$$Y_L = -(S_1/j\rho c)\cot(kL_L - kL_S),$$
$$\text{(cylinder).} \quad (32.7)$$

For a (*cylindrical*) *clarinet*, $Y = 0$ at the embouchure, where again $x = 0$ is chosen, giving $\psi = -m\pi$, $m = \frac{1}{2}, 1\frac{1}{2}, 2\frac{1}{2}, 3\frac{1}{2}$ et cetera. Since the substitution tube is determined by $kL_S = m\pi$, with the same values of m, we here too may set $\psi = -kL_S$, so that we arrive, at $x = L_L$, at the same eq.(32.7) for the clarinet.

For a *conical flute*, the admittance is given by eq.(23.6). It becomes infinite at the throat $r = r_0$, which yields $\psi = -kr_0 - m\pi$, m integer. Introducing $L_L = r_1 - r_0$ and, in the same way as before, $kL_S = m\pi$, the admittance at $r = r_1$ becomes

$$Y_L = \frac{S_1}{j\rho c}\left[\frac{1}{kr_1} - \cot(kL_L - kL_S)\right],$$
$$\text{(cone).} \quad (32.8)$$

For a *conical reed instrument*, $Y = 0$ at $r = r_0$, which gives the condition

$$1 - kr_0 \cot(kr_0 + \psi) = 0. \quad (32.9)$$

Provided kr_0 is sufficiently small, $\psi = -m\pi = -kL_S$, m integer. L_S is the acoustical length to the apex of the cone. Usually, kr_0 is not negligibly small. In that case compensation is provided by the mouthpiece-cavity, see Section 27. When we set $r_1 = L_L$, eq.(32.8) is obtained.

When for each of the four situations the various admittances are substituted into eq.(32.2), for every instrument one and the same formula is found:

$$F(k) = S_1\cot(kL_L - kL_S) + S_1\cot kL_R +$$
$$+ S_H\cot kL_H = 0, \quad (32.10)$$

in which

$$kL_S = m\pi\begin{cases} m = n - \frac{1}{2} \text{ (clarinet)} \\ m = n \quad \text{(others)} \end{cases} n = \text{integer.} \quad (32.11)$$

In a somewhat different notation, this formula was first published by Richardson [101, 102], extended by Irons [58, 59] and Fouché [45], and for cylindrical instruments, still earlier by Bouasse [29].

b. First-order approximation

Since the hole is assumed to be located close to the open end of the tube, the trigonometric functions can be expanded in power series and all terms of a power higher than the first can be dropped. Writing $L_R = L_T - L_L$:

$$1/(L_L - L_S) + 1/(L_T - L_L) + 1/\lambda_H = 0, \quad (32.12)$$

where

$$\lambda_H = S_1 L_H/S_H. \quad (32.13)$$

λ_H is a transformed hole length; it is the length of a fictitious side-tube with the same diameter as the main tube and with the same throat impedance as the real side-tube.

Eq.(32.12) can be solved for either L_L, λ_H or L_S as desired. Solving the equation for L_S and for λ_H gives

$$L_S = L_L + \lambda_H(L_T - L_L)/(L_T - L_L + \lambda_H), \quad (32.14)$$

$$\lambda_H = (L_S - L_L)(L_T - L_L)/(L_T - L_S). \quad (32.15)$$

Since eq.(32.12) is quadratic in L_L, two solutions are obtained for L_L. The one giving $L_L > L_S$ has no physical meaning and is dropped. The other solution is

$$L_L = L_S(1 - z), \tag{32.16}$$

where

$$z = \tfrac{1}{2}g(1 + 4\lambda_H/gL_S)^{1/2} - \tfrac{1}{2}g, \tag{32.17}$$

$$g = L_T/L_S - 1. \tag{32.18}$$

From its definition in eq.(32.18) it is apparent that g is the relative frequency shift when the hole is opened. z is something like a relative end correction to a tube cut off at the hole (Fig. 32.3). The relation between g and the frequency shift, expressed in the number of semitones, ν, is

$$g = 2^{\nu/12} - 1. \tag{32.19}$$

The relation is valid for any value of ν but since most holes are intended for shifts of an integer number of semitones, these integer values appear frequently. A table for g for integer values of ν is given in Table 6 (see page 108). When $\nu = 1$, $g = 0.059463\ldots$ or approximately 6%.

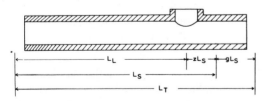

Fig. 32.3. Diagram showing the physical significance of

$$z = \frac{L_S - L_L}{L_S} \quad \text{and} \quad g = \frac{L_T - L_S}{L_S} \quad .$$

c. Exact solution of eq. (32.10)

There are situations in which the first order approximations are insufficiently accurate. Then eq.(32.10) may be solved exactly. Doing this for S_H or L_H we find

$$S_H = S_1 [\cot(kL_S - kL_L) - \cot kL_R] \tan kL_H. \tag{32.20}$$

For an exact calculation of the hole position we insert $L_R = gL_S - (L_L - L_S)$ into eq.(32.10) and solve the resulting equation for $\tan(kL_L - kL_S)$. The only meaningful solution is

$$\tan(kL_S - kL_L) = [a^2 + 2a(S_1/S_H)\tan kl_H]^{1/2} - a, \tag{32.21}$$

where

$$a = (\tfrac{1}{2}S_H \tan gkL_S)/(S_H - S_1 \tan kL_H \tan gkL_S).$$

From this, L_L can be solved directly, since $kL_S = m\pi$.

A calculation of the frequency or the wave number k from eq.(32.10) is more difficult since k is found as a factor in every argument. A quick iteration method (Newton-Raphson) is as follows. The starting point is an estimate for k, k', which can usually be obtained from eq.(32.12), using $k' = m\pi/L_S$. A second order approximation for k, k'', then follows from

$$k'' = k' - \left[\frac{F(k)}{dF/dk}\right]_{k = k'}. \tag{32.22}$$

The following result is found

$$k'' = k' + \frac{S_1 \cot(k'L_L - m\pi) + S_1 \cot k'L_R + S_H \cot k'L_H}{S_1 L_L/\sin^2(k'L_L - m\pi) + S_1 L_R/\sin^2 k'L_R + S_H L_H/\sin^2 k'L_H}. \tag{32.23}$$

This process can be repeated until a prescribed accuracy is obtained. When eq.(32.12) cannot be used for a first estimate, e.g. when one of the tubes is too long, mostly the knowledge of the properties of the instrument allows for a fruitful estimate for k, and the process converges rapidly. If not, a first approximation can be obtained by plotting $F(k)$ as a function of k.

d. Accuracy of first-order approximation

By an expansion in power series of the goniometric terms in the exact expressions for the various quantities, higher-order approximations can be derived. As long as the difference of first and second-order solution is small, this difference may be expected to give a good indication of the difference of first-order and exact solution. We therefore study the second-order approximation for the wave number. This second-order approximation is obtained by expansion of the terms of eq.(32.23) up to two terms. Using g and z, we find

$$k'' = k'(1 + D'') = k'\left[1 - \tfrac{1}{3}m^2\pi^2 z^2 g\left(1 + \right.\right.$$
$$\left.\left. + \frac{z(z+g)}{g^2}\frac{S_H^2}{S_1^2}\right)\right], \qquad (32.24)$$

where we used a symbol D'' for the relative frequency deviation between first and second order approximations. As a rule, $S_H/S_1 < 1$, and eq.(32.24) reduces to

$$k'' = k'(1 - \tfrac{1}{3}m^2\pi^2 z^2 g). \qquad (32.24a)$$

Expressions for S_H'' and L_L'' can be found in the same way from eqs.(32.20) and (32.21), but they can also be obtained easily by substitution of equation (32.24) into future eqs.(32.25) and (32.26), using $dk/k = -dL_S/L_S$.

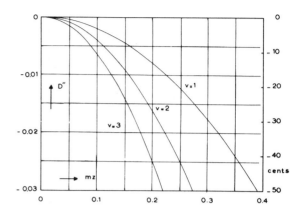

Fig. 32.4. Difference between first and second-order calculation of the resonance frequency as a function of the product mz, for various frequency shifts, plotted for three different shifts when opening the hole, expressed in number of semitones v.

As long as $|D''| \ll g$, D'' may be expected to be a good indication for the difference between first order and exact solution, and we therefore study its behaviour. In Fig 32.4, D'' is plotted versus mz for three values of g, for which $v = 1, 2$ and 3 semitones. At the right, a scale is given where the frequency shift can be read in a customary unit, the cent*, i.e. one-hundredth of a semitone, or $D'' = 0.0006$. It can be seen immediately that D'' increases with the mode-number and with the

---

* *Small frequency shifts may be expressed in other units [50]. We mention the skhisma (the difference between a tempered and a pure fifth) equal to about 2 cents, and the comma of Didymus, about 22 cents. Such a comma is the difference between a large major second, 9/8, and a small major second, 10/9. It differs slightly from the Pythagorean comma, i.e. the tuning error arising when a piano is tuned according to pure fifths, $(3/2)^{12}/2^7$*

frequency shift for which the hole is meant. Also, D'' increases with z; large values of z can be shown to pertain to long and shallow holes.

Since, normally, the same hole is used on two or more registers, D'' must be small on all these registers. On some instruments (especially flutes), musicians are able to detect deviations of less than 5 cents, on other instruments (notably bassoons) the perceptible threshold can be around 20 cents [39, 118]. When D'' is larger than the threshold, this may be annoying. Imagine one isolated hole having z and g values differing from those of adjacent holes. Its D'', which may be imperceptibly small in the low register, may be perceptable in a high register and, more important, be different from the adjacent holes. This causes unevennesses in the tuning which cannot be corrected for by bore perturbations since these act on a whole group of notes. These unevennesses can be avoided when all holes have the same z and g. This ideal is closely realized on a modern Boehm-flute and on a proposed clarinet with a new key mechanism based on the exclusive use of semitone-holes [91].

e. Variation of parameters

In order to get an impression of how sensitive the tuning is for small changes in dimensions (e.g. due to fluctuations in manufacture) and, at the same time, to find how to correct small impurities, we investigate the changes in the substitution-tube when small changes are introduced in position or size of the holes. Eq.(32.14) is differentiated with respect to L_L and S_H (or L_H) respectively, yielding

$$\frac{\partial L_S}{\partial L_L} = 1 - \left(\frac{z}{z+g}\right)^2, \qquad (32.25)$$

$$\frac{\partial L_S/L_S}{\partial S_H/S_H} = \frac{-\partial L_S/L_S}{\partial L_H/L_H} = -\left(\frac{z}{z+g}\right)g. \qquad (32.26)$$

We assume 10 cents (0.006) to be the threshold of perceptibility and both z and g to be about 0.06 (representative mean values). From the two equations we then find that this corresponds with a 1% change in distance to the (acoustical) top of the instrument, a 10% hole-diameter change or a 20% hole-length change. These theoretical results correspond with experiments by Meyer [81, 85] on small changes in the position and size of clarinet holes.

When the frequency of the tube with closed hole changes due to a change in L_T, but position and size of the hole remain the same, the resulting change of the frequency of the tube with open hole is found by differentiating eq. (32.14) with respect to L_T:

$$\partial L_S/\partial L_T = z^2/(z+g)^2. \qquad (32.27)$$

Obviously, a change in L_T is passed over to L_S in a reduced amount. When again $z \approx g$, this reduction is a factor of 4. When changes in L_T are due to changes in a row of open holes (for example, closing a hole for a semitone, while leaving open three holes below the row of closed holes), the influence of the closing of this hole on the frequency can be estimated to be $4 \times 4 \times 4 = 64$ times as small as a semitone, which can be neglected.

33. Tubes with more than one hole

To explain how to apply the equations to a real woodwind instrument in which many holes are drilled we have sketched in Fig. 33.1 a simplified cylindrical flute with six holes. This flute produces an incomplete scale. The key mechanism is constructed in such a way that hole 5 is closed

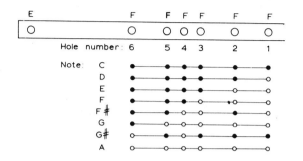

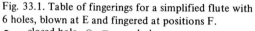

Fig. 33.1. Table of fingerings for a simplified flute with
6 holes, blown at E and fingered at positions F.
● = closed hole, ○ = open hole.

automatically when hole 2 or 4 is closed. By this
finger-saving arrangement 6 different notes can
be produced with only 4 fingers. Since the task of
the 10 fingers is already difficult enough on a
normal flute with its 17 holes at least, such
constructions are very useful.

We assume that our task is to calculate the
positions of the holes producing a scale when
using fingerings as indicated in Fig. 33.1. The
hole size is a degree of freedom which we delib-
erately ignore for the moment, so the hole-
diameters are specified.

To calculate the positions of holes 1, 2 and 3
(which are for the notes D, E and F respectively),
the simple procedure presented in Section 32 can
be used (e.g. eqs 32.16, 17 and 18). Its application
to hole 1 is self-evident. L_T is the acoustical
length of the fully-closed tube sounding note C and
L_S is the acoustical length for D. For hole 2,
L_T is the acoustical length with only hole 1 open
and this length is equal to L_S of hole 1. In the
same way, we deal with hole 3.

This procedure must be modified for the note F#;
it is true that in the usual way the next hole, 4,
is opened, but at the same time 2 is closed. To
calculate the position of hole 4, we must start

anew from the fingering for D (all holes but the
first closed) and perform a two-step calculation.
In a first step, L_S (or the frequency) is
calculated for holes 1 and 3 open (eq. 32.14). In
the second step, the position of hole 4 is determined in the usual way where L_T is equal to
L_S obtained from the first step. Since hole 2
is remote from hole 4, a quicker, though only
approximative way of calculating the position of
hole 4 is to ignore the fact that hole 2 is closed
and to use the simple procedure starting with 1, 2
and 3 open.

To play note G after F# the finger on hole 2
is lifted and, because of the coupling in the key
mechanism, hole 5 opens too. Calculations proceed
in the same way as before, viz. starting from
F, calculating firstly the frequency when hole 4
is opened, and secondly the position of hole 5.

The position of hole 6 for the note A is again
calculated in the usual way. The locations of all
holes on the main tube are now fixed. On many
instruments, however, we frequently encounter
cross-fingerings of the type as shown in Fig. 33.1
for G#. No hole is available to tune this note
independently. So there is nothing for it but to
verify whether this cross-fingering does indeed
produce the right frequency. Since at least one of
the tube-pieces is of a length comparable to the
wavelength, we have to apply the exact
equation, (32.10), twice, once for every hole.
When the frequency turns out to be wrong, and we
want to adhere to this fingering, we can try to
improve matters by using a degree of freedom which
was previously ignored, i.e. the hole diameter. We
can change the diameters of holes 4 and/or 6 and
repeat the calculations for the positions of these
holes, and finally for the frequency of the cross-
fingered G#. It may be that the cross-fingering
cannot yield the right frequency for any choice of
hole diameters, but if there is one solution there

can be expected to be a whole set of them since there is still one degree of freedom left. This degree of freedom can be used when the flute is also to be tuned in the second register: the upper register containing the first overblown notes. Then, from the set of hole positions obtained when tuning the first or lower register, the frequencies of all overblown notes on the second register can be calculated. Most of the notes turn out to be — with sufficient accuracy — one octave higher since most tube-pieces involved are short. Notes employing cross-fingerings, viz. F# and G#, constitute an exception. These might deviate from the octave-jump as the tube-pieces are now longer. The deviations found for F# usually appear to be negligible, but those for G# can be pronounced. Thus, to tune this note on the second register, we can use the extra degree of freedom mentioned above. Even so, in some cases, correct tuning will prove to be impossible.

On the third or high register, fingerings are usually even more complex, sometimes involving three or more isolated open holes followed by rows of closed holes. In principle, the methods are applicable in the same way, though it is rather cumbersome here since several of the tube-pieces are long.

In the two-step problems as encountered above, one hole of the two was fixed in position beforehand since it has a separate function. When, however, two holes are opened together by a single movement of a finger, and each hole separately has no other function, it is useful to combine the two steps of calculation into a single, more complicated one. As an example, we consider the transition from D to F# produced by opening holes 3 and 4 simultaneously (Fig. 33.1). Eq.(32.10) is applied twice. We introduce $L_R = L_T - L_L$. The quantities of hole 3 are provided of a dash to distinguish them from

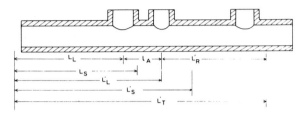

Fig. 33.2. Explanation of symbols used for a tube with three open holes.

those of hole 4 (Fig. 33.2). This yields the following two equations

$$S_1' \cot (kL_L' - kL_S') + S_1' \cot (kL_T' - kL_L') +$$
$$+ S_H' \cot kL_H' = 0, \text{ (hole 3)},$$
$$(33.1)$$

$$S_1 \cot (kL_L - kL_S) + S_1 \cot (kL_T - kL_L) +$$
$$+ S_H \cot kL_H = 0, \text{ (hole 4)}.$$
$$(33.2)$$

Note that in the present example of a cylindrical tube $S_1' = S_1$, but that the equations are equally valid for conical tubes where S_1' and S_1 are unequal. Two more equations are needed for "joining" the holes

$$L_S' = L_T, \qquad (33.3)$$
$$L_L' = L_L + l_A, \qquad (33.4)$$

where l_A is the mutual distance between the holes. Since the holes together are supposed to effectuate a frequency shift g, we have further the condition

$$L_T' = (1 + g)L_S. \qquad (33.5)$$

To calculate the positions of the two holes, we will take their mutual distance l_A a constant and calculate the position L_L of the upper hole. Hole sizes, L_T' and L_S are specified. Eqs.(33.3, 4, 5) are substituted into eqs.(33.1) and (33.2) and

L_T is eliminated between them.

When tube-pieces are short with respect to the wavelength the following quadratic expression in $y = L_S - L_L$ is obtained

$$(\lambda_H + \lambda'_H + l_A)y^2 + [gL_S(\lambda_H + \lambda'_H + l_A) - 2\lambda_H l_A - l_A^2]y -$$
$$- gL_S\lambda_H(\lambda'_H + l_A) + l_A^2 \lambda_H = 0, \quad \text{or:}$$
$$ay^2 + by - c = 0. \qquad (33.6)$$

There are two solutions of which only one is applicable:

$$y = \frac{b}{2a}\left\{\sqrt{1 + 4ac/b^2} - 1\right\}. \qquad (33.7)$$

The position of the upper hole is then found from $L_L = L_S - y$.

It is possible to use eq. (33.1) (and also 33.2) in the opposite way, that is as an expression valid for closing a hole instead of opening it. When, in this case, we want to call L'_T the acoustical length before and L'_S after closing the hole this means interchanging of L'_T and L'_S in eq.(33.1). Since these quantities appear in analogous expressions with a different sign, the sign of S'_H changes to negative in the original eq.(33.1). This stratagem can be used when applying eq.(33.6) to a two-hole problem, like this

● ● ● ● ○

● ● ● ○ ●

where two keys move in opposite direction. In that case, λ'_H is simply given a negative sign.

34. Register hole

On some instruments we find register holes, alternatively called overblowing-holes or speakers. These are small holes opened to facilitate over-blowing. Sometimes overblown notes do not sound without such a hole. The hole is positioned close to the pressure-*node* of the overtone which is mostly at the same time close to a pressure-*antinode* of the fundamental. A common view of the action of this hole is that it provides a way-out for the air and thus prevents the build-up of pressure-fluctuations and favours the formation of a pressure-node. Benade [24] presents an interesting explanation based on the strong coupling between the partials of the excitation mechanism and those of the tube. Since for every note the pressure-node is situated at a different place, each note would need a separate register hole. This would cause too much intricacies in mechanism or in fingering and therefore the maximum number of register holes in practice is three; often there is only one.

The register hole can cause a frequency shift if it is not too small. To calculate this frequency shift, we use eq.(32.10) in which we substitute

$$L_R = L_T - L_L = (L_T - L_S) - (L_L - L_S), \qquad (34.1)$$

yielding

$$\frac{1}{k\lambda_H} + \frac{1 + \tan(kL_T - kL_S)\tan(kL_L - kL_S)}{\tan(kL_T - kL_S) - \tan(kL_L - kL_S)} +$$
$$+ \cot(kL_L - kL_S) = 0.$$

Or:

$$[k\lambda_H + \sin(kL_L - kL_S)\cos(kL_L - kL_S)] \times$$
$$\times \tan(kL_T - kL_S) - \sin^2(kL_L - kL_S) = 0. \quad (34.2)$$

When the hole is very small, $\lambda_H \to \infty$, the solution of this equation is $L_T = L_S$ which is equal to the usual solution with closed hole. The correction due to the register-hole is expressed in a fractional frequency shift as a first approximation

$$D_{reg} = \frac{\sin^2 k(L_L - L_S)}{m\pi [k\lambda_H + \sin k(L_L - L_S) \cos k(L_L - L_S)]}.$$
(34.3)

Since $kL_S = (n-\frac{1}{2})\pi$ for clarinet and $kL_S = n\pi$ for other instruments (n integer), we have

$$D_{reg} = \cos^2 kL_L/m\pi(k\lambda_H - \cos kL_L \sin kL_L),$$
$$\text{for clarinet,} \qquad (34.4)$$

$$D_{reg} = \sin^2 kL_L/m\pi(k\lambda_H + \sin kL_L \cos kL_L),$$
$$\text{for others.} \qquad (34.5)$$

When the diameter of the hole is not too large, $k\lambda_H$ is larger than unity and $D_{reg} > 0$. When the hole is exactly located in the velocity antinode, $\sin kL_R = 0$ and $D_{reg} = 0$.

35. Closed side-holes

Closed side-holes in a resonating air column nearly always lower the frequency. This is due to the fact that a closed side-hole behaves mainly as a compliance, and only for a restricted part (in the order of 0.1 of its volume) as an extra negative mass.

First, the influence of a single closed hole is calculated as a function of its size, shape and position in a given sound field. A row of closed side-holes is accounted for by summation. In most cases the mean side-hole volume per unit length is constant in the perforated part of the instrument and we may replace the row of holes by a much larger number of much smaller side-holes of the same shape and of the same total volume. When the number of holes approaches infinite, the summation approaches an integration. This reduces the amount of calculation work to be done. When volume per unit length or shape are not constant, these properties are mostly constant in at least some regions so that the integration can be carried out in parts.

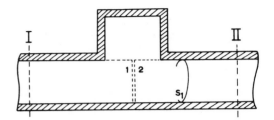

Fig. 35.1. Tube with a closed side-tube

The method for calculating the influence of a single hole was described in an earlier paper by Nederveen and Van Wulfften Palthe [90]; we therefore restrict ourselves to a short explanation. In Fig. 35.1 a tube with a closed side-tube is sketched. The side-tube dimensions are assumed to be very small with respect to the wavelength. The disturbing influence of the side-hole on the flow lines diminishes rapidly at some distance away from the hole; we assume that there are cross-sectional planes I and II (indicated in Fig. 35.1) at a mutual distance much less than the wavelength, but sufficiently far from the hole for the velocity to be constant over the cross-section. The influence of the side-hole can be described as an infinitely thin fourpole inserted into an unperturbed main tube. This fictitious substitution-fourpole replaces the side-hole and is bounded by the dashed lines 1 and 2 in Fig. 35.1. The compliance of this fourpole is assumed to be equal to compliance C_H of the entire hole, as follows

$$C_H = V_H/K, \qquad (35.1)$$

where K = bulk modulus of air and V_H = hole volume. The acoustic mass is assumed to be determined by only a part of the volume of the hole, since the flow only partly enters the hole:

$$M_H = \epsilon \rho V_H/S_1^2. \qquad (35.2)$$

The penetration factor ϵ which denotes the relative penetration of the flow in the hole was

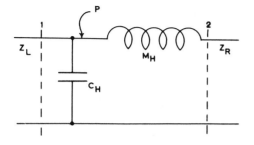

Fig. 35.2. Circuit for the substitution fourpole describing the behaviour of the side-hole between dotted lines 1 and 2 (Fig. 35.1.).

determined on (two-dimensionally) conducting paper and it appeared to be possible to describe it as a function of the ratio of width d_H to depth l_H of the side-hole:

$$\epsilon = (2/\pi)\arctan(2d_H/13l_H). \qquad (35.3)$$

Since in musical instruments mostly $d_H/l_H < 2$, a good approximation is

$$\epsilon = 0.1\,(d_H/l_H). \qquad (35.4)$$

So the flow effectively enters the side-hole to about 10% of its width. This number was found by measurements on a two-dimensional situation. In real woodwind instruments, the hole is cylindrical and fits onto a cylinder of a large diameter. The penetration factor can be expected to be different from the value for the two-dimensional example, but it is not known to what extent. Since ϵ is in any case small, and the effects of a variation in ϵ on the magnitude of the correction are likewise small, we assumed for the sake of simplicity that eq.(35.4) is also valid for a cylindrical side-hole with a diameter d_H.

The fictitious fourpole is described by a sub-stitution circuit given in Fig. 35.2, where mass and compliance are thought to act separately and in the way described here, which is an approximation to the real situation. An equally good approximation is the one where C_H is placed at the right of M_H; but results are alike since first order techniques are applied.

The condition of equality of admittances at point P, Fig. 35.2, yields

$$-\frac{1}{Z_L} + j\omega C_H = -\frac{1}{Z_R + j\omega M_H}. \qquad (35.5)$$

Substituting eqs(35.1) and (35.2), switching to admittances and neglecting terms with V_H^2 gives

$$\frac{j\rho c}{S_1}(Y_L - Y_R) + \left[1 - \epsilon\left(\frac{j\rho c}{S_1}Y_R\right)\left(\frac{j\rho c}{S_1}Y_L\right)\right]\frac{kV_H}{S_1} = 0 \qquad (35.6)$$

For cylindrical instruments, we introduce eqs.(32.5) and (32.7) for the tube admittances. Equating Y_L and Y_R in terms with V_H, we find the following resonance condition

$$\tan k(L_L + L_R - L_S) + k\,\Delta l = 0, \qquad (35.7)$$

where

$$\Delta l = (\sin^2 kL_R - \epsilon\cos^2 kL_R)\,V_H/S_1 \qquad (35.8)$$

is the length correction due to the closed side-hole.

For conical instruments, eqs (32.6) and (32.8) are inserted into eq.(35.6) and the same eq.(35.7) is obtained, only with a different Δl:

$$\Delta l = \left[\sin^2 kL_R - \epsilon\left(\cos kL_R + \frac{\sin kL_R}{kr_1}\right)^2\right]\frac{V_H}{S_1}. \qquad (35.9)$$

In both cases, Δl is the length correction to the acoustical tube length. L_R is measured from an open end.

The influence of the magnitude of ϵ is illustrated

for a cylindrical tube. In the extreme case of a very smooth perturbation of the diameter, $\epsilon = 1$ and the length correction becomes

$$\Delta l = -(V_H/S_1)\cos 2kL_R, \quad \epsilon = 1. \qquad (35.10)$$

This formula was originally derived by Rayleigh [98]. According to this equation the frequency increases when a widening is located in a velocity antinode and decreases when it is located in a velocity node. When the side-hole is very deep and thin, $\epsilon \approx 0$ and then

$$\Delta l = (V_H/S_1)\sin^2 kL_R, \qquad \epsilon = 0. \qquad (35.11)$$

In this case the frequency is always lowered and mostly so in a pressure-antinode. Since on musical instruments ϵ is small, closed side-holes tend to lower the frequency.

When the tube is provided with many closed holes in a row (Fig. 35.3) homogeneously spread out over a certain length L_P (P = perturbation)

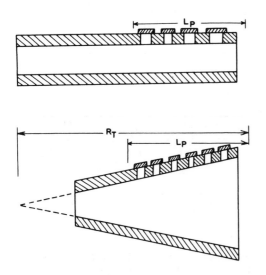

Fig. 35.3. Examples of tubes perturbed by closed side-holes over a length L_P.

such that V_H/S_1 is a constant, the length correction is found by summation from $L_R = 0$ to $L_R = L_P$. For practical purposes, the summation may be replaced by an integration. Thus for a cylindrical tube

$$\Delta l_v = \left[1 - \epsilon - (1+\epsilon)\frac{\sin 2kL_P}{2kL_P} \right] \sum \frac{V_H}{2S_1} , \quad (35.12)$$

where ΣV_H stands for the total volume of the closed holes. For a conical tube [93] we find

$$\Delta l_v = \left[1 - \epsilon - (1+\epsilon)\frac{\sin 2kL_P}{2kL_P} - \right.$$
$$\left. - \epsilon \frac{1-\cos 2kL_P}{kL_P(kR_T - kL_P)} \right] \sum \frac{V_H}{2S_1}. \quad (35.13)$$

R_T is the acoustical tube length including truncation regardless of the type of embouchure. Since the type of embouchure is not included in the derivations, all formulae are valid for flutes as well as for reed-blown instruments.

36. Flaring tube-ends and smooth diameter-perturbations

The bore deviates from the ideal cone or cylinder in many places and by widely varying amounts. Many of these perturbations have an historic origin and may be fortuitous; they may partly have been introduced intentionally, rightly or wrongly.

A striking deviation from the ideal bore is the rapidly expanding horn at the end of the tube, which is found on nearly all instruments. This horn starts below or just above the lowest hole and therefore only influences the tuning of the lowest notes in the register. Horns are said to improve the quality (tone-colour) of the instrument [14, 61, 100]. Morse [87] states that the horn improves the radiation of the lowest notes since it enlarges the resistive part of the radiation impedance. From this property the horn may have found its origination.

Conical horns will be dealt with later in this section; we will now consider a very specially shaped horn separately, viz. the catenoidal horn, which is used on the clarinet. The cross-section of this horn is defined as $S = S_0 \cosh^2(x/h)$, where x is the distance to the throat of the horn, S_0 the area at the throat and h a constant [87]. This horn fits onto the cylindrical tube without discontinuities, contrary to an exponential or conical horn. This property is said to diminish reflections at the junction. When the radius at the mouth of the horn is sufficiently small, the usual length correction for the open end can be applied. The geometrical length of the horn is l_h, its effective length including end-correction, L_h. Neglecting radiation losses, the input impedance of the horn, according to Morse but written in a slightly different way, is given by

$$Z_h = (j\rho ckh'/S_0) \ \tanh(L_h/h'), \tag{36.1}$$

where

$$h' = h/(1 - k^2 h^2)^{\frac{1}{2}}. \tag{36.2}$$

The condition of resonance of this horn, fitted onto a cylindrical clarinet-tube of length l_1 is found by equating impedances at the junction (cf. eq. 32.7)

$$(j\rho c/S_0)\cot kl_1 = Z_h, \tag{36.3}$$

from which the length-correction to l_1 is found:

$$\Delta l = (1/k) \arctan(Z_h S_0/j\rho c). \tag{36.4}$$

Referring the end-correction to the geometrical length of the cylinder including horn, and inserting eq.(36.1), we find

$$\Delta l_{\text{horn}} = - l_h + (1/k) \arctan [kh' \tanh(L_h/h')]. \tag{36.5}$$

In the two clarinets investigated, $L_h = 0.188$ m, $h = 0.085$ m and $k = 2.67$ for $m = \frac{1}{2}$ and $k = 8$ for $m = 1\frac{1}{2}$. Then it can be found numerically that a good approximation for the correction is

$$\Delta l_{\text{horn}} = - l_h + h. \tag{36.6}$$

Practically all other perturbations found on wood winds are such that the bore can be described by a succession of cylindrical and conical tube pieces, presumably because bore shapes other than cylindrical and conical are difficult to manufacture. Frequently found are perturbations which tend to reduce the diameter towards both tube ends; the bore more or less has the profile of a sword [14]. This type of perturbation mostly causes a lowering of the lowest notes of the instrument. Other types of perturbations are discontinuities in the diameter, mostly found near the embouchure of reed instruments. Whenever they occur at tube junctions, they seem to be a result of manufacture. If they tend to damage the tuning they are accompanied by other perturbations and discontinuities to compensate for this damage.

If the length of a perturbation is small with respect to the diameter, formulas derived for closed holes can be used, e.g. eqs (35.7) and (35.12). An apparently attractive feature of this method is that the penetration factor ϵ can be introduced in order to take into account the decreased influence of the negative mass at discontinuities. However, it is difficult to decide on the proper value of ϵ, and the deviations of the bore, especially near the ends, can be so substantial that it seems better to describe the tube as a succession of conical tube-pieces. The computational approach then is too cumbersome for a desk calculation, but can be handled easily by a computer.

We will start with the general derivation of the resonance condition of such a row of joined cones and then apply it to some special cases. Consider two cones of different diameters at their junction point. In Fig. 36.1 the symbols are explained, those of the second tube are provided with a dash. We recall the sign convention, mentioned before: quantities r_0 and r_1 are negative when the cone contracts to the right. The admittance of a conical tube is given by eq. (23.6). The condition of equality of admittances at the junction gives

$$S_1 [1/w_1 - \cot(w_1 + \psi)] =$$
$$= S_0' [1/w_0' - \cot(w_0' + \psi')] , \quad (36.7)$$

with two unknown constants ψ and ψ'. A similar expression is valid for the junction of second and third tube. When we use the same symbols for the third cone, only now provided with a double dash, the following condition is found for the continuity of admittances at the junction of second and third cone

$$S_1' [1/w_1' - \cot(w_1' + \psi')] =$$
$$= S_0'' [1/w_0'' - \cot(w_0'' + \psi'')]. \quad (36.8)$$

For $n + 1$ cones we find n equations. Two boundary conditions have to be met. At the open end at the right hand side, Y is infinite. This yields

$$\psi^{(n)} = - W_1^{(n)}. \quad (36.9)$$

At the throat, $r = r_0$, a reed embouchure gives the condition

$$\tan(w_0 + \psi) = w_0, \text{ or } \psi \approx 0. \quad (36.10a)$$

For a flute-embouchure, we have

$$\tan(w_0 + \psi) = 0, \text{ or } \psi = - w_0. \quad (36.10b)$$

In this way, $n+2$ equations are obtained for the $n+2$ unknowns: $k, \psi, \psi', \psi'' \ldots \psi^{(n)}$.

In principle, k can be solved, though this may be a cumbersome procedure. The best way is to

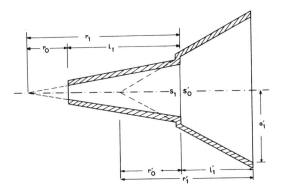

Fig. 36.1. Symbols used in the derivation of the resonance condition of two joined cones.

insert an estimate of k into all equations and to solve them in this sequence: $\psi, \psi', \psi'', \ldots \psi^{(n)}$. Then it appears that the last condition, eq.(36.9) is not fulfilled. The deficit can be interpreted as a length correction to the last cone:

$$\Delta l = \frac{1}{k}(-\psi^{(n)} + W_1^{(n)}), \quad (36.11)$$

or as a correction to k of

$$\Delta k/k = (\psi^{(n)} - W_1^{(n)})/m\pi. \quad (36.12)$$

Now k is corrected according to this equation and introduced in the equations. The calculation is repeated and again we find a correction to k, presumably smaller than in the first trial. This process can be repeated until a sufficient accuracy is obtained. The method is especially useful when the last cone is a long one and the effect of the perturbations on frequency is small. In that case a good estimate for k is derived from the length of the extrapolated last cone, the correction obtained is small and a single step suffices to find k with sufficient accuracy.

We now consider in more detail some aspects of the important case of two cones, where the second shows only minor deviations from the extrapolated first. An estimate for the acoustical length of the entire instrument is then

$$L_{est} = r_1 + L_1' + \psi/k, \qquad (36.13)$$

where ψ is given by eq.(36.10a) or eq.(36.10b) depending on the type of embouchure. Substitution of eq.(36.13) and of $\psi' = - W_1'$ (eq.36.9) into eq.(36.7) yields

$$S_1 \left[\frac{1}{w_1} - \cot(kL_{est} - kL_1') \right] =$$
$$= S_0' \left[\frac{1}{w_0'} + \cot kL_1' \right]. \quad (36.14)$$

The equation is solved for $\tan kL_{est}$. Introducing

$$A = \left(\frac{S_0'}{S_1 w_0'} - \frac{1}{w_1} \right) \sin kL_1' +$$
$$+ \left(\frac{S_0'}{S_1} - 1 \right) \cos kL_1' , (36.15)$$

we find

$$(1 + A \cos kL_1') \tan kL_{est} = A \sin kL_1'. \quad (36.16)$$

When A is zero this is the usual resonance condition for a single cone. The terms containing A are due to the perturbation. Note that L_{est} is equal to the total effective acoustical length of the two tube-pieces including the open-end correction of the second tube.

In the usual way eq.(36.16) yields an end-correction

$$\Delta l = -(1/k) \left[A \sin kL_1'/(1 + A \cos kL_1') \right]. \qquad (36.17)$$

Some special cases are considered now.

When the "dashed" horn is very short with respect to the wavelength we find

$$\Delta l = -AL_1'/(1+A), \qquad (36.18)$$

where $A = (S_0'/S_1 - r_0'/r_1)L_1'/r_0' + (S_0'/S_1 - 1)$.

When $S_0' = S_1$, and the corrections are small, it is found that

$$\Delta l = \frac{-(1 - r_0'/r_1) \sin^2 kL_1'}{k^2 r_0' + k(1 - r_0'/r_1) \sin kL_1' \cos kL_1'} . (36.19)$$

When, besides this, the conicities differ very little, so that $r_0' \approx r_1$, this becomes in first order approximation

$$\Delta l = -(1/k^2 r_0' - 1/k^2 r_1) \sin^2 kL_1'. \qquad (36.20)$$

When the second tube is cylindrical, r_0' becomes infinite, and when r_1 is very large eq.(36.19) is once more simplified:

$$\Delta l = \sin^2 kL_1'/k^2 r_1 . \qquad (36.21)$$

One property of the last two equations is mentioned, viz. that the correction rapidly decreases for high notes because of the k^2 in the denominators. In other words: perturbations of this type change the tuning of the low register but affect that of the high register much less.

These and many other types of compound pipes have been theoretically treated earlier, for which we refer to the literature [14a,28,45,57,58,59,63,64,102,110,113].

Finally we show how to calculate corrections due to a diameter change in part of a cylindrical tube (Fig. 36.2).

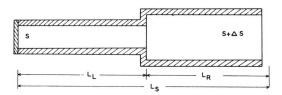

Fig. 36.2 Cylindrical tube with a small increase in diameter over part of its length.

Suppose that the cross-sectional area of the right hand part of the instrument is a small amount ΔS larger than the area of the left hand part, S. The resonance condition for this pipe-combination is found by equating admittances at the junction, applying eqs (32.5) and (32.7) with slightly modified values for the cross-sectional areas:

$$-\frac{S}{j\rho c}\cot(kL_L - kL_S) = \frac{S+\Delta S}{j\rho c}\cot kL_R. \quad (36.23)$$

This can be written as

$$\tan k(L_L - L_S + L_R) + \frac{\Delta S}{S}\sin(kL_L - kL_S)\sin kL_R = 0. \quad (36.24)$$

We set $L_L - L_S = -L_R$ in the second term and so obtain a correction to the frequency of a tube of an acoustical length $L_L + L_R$:

$$D_P = +\frac{\Delta S}{2Sm\pi}\sin 2kL_R. \quad (36.25)$$

The correction may be expressed as a function of L_L, by substitution of $L_R = L_S - L_L$. For a clarinet, $2kL_S = \pi, 3\pi.5\pi$ *et cetera* and we find

$$D_P = \frac{\Delta S}{2Sm\pi}\sin 2kL_L, \text{ (clarinet).} \quad (36.26)$$

The correction decreases with the mode-number, due to the presence of m in the denominator. When L_L is not small with respect to the tube length the correction can be positive on one and negative on another register.

37. Curved bore

To keep them within reasonable overall dimensions, low-pitched instruments are folded, i.e. the tube incorporates bends. In most instruments, bends follow approximately the shape of a cylindrical ring or tore (Fig. 37.1). Discontinuities of

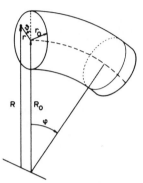

Fig. 37.1. Co-ordinates in a tore or cylindrical ring.

this kind affect the tuning: for sharp bends, the length of the bend taken along the centre line of the tube and its cross-sectional area do not correspond to the acoustical length and area.

A tore is generated by rotating a circle about a line in the plane of that circle. The distance from the centre of the circle to this line is called the radius of curvature R_0 of the ring.

The pattern of the waves in a cross-section of the tore is different from that in cylindrical tubes. If, as is usually the case, all dimensions of the tore are small with respect to the wavelength, its acoustical compliance and its inertia may be treated as separate, independent quantities. The compliance presents no difficulties, as it is determined by the volume of the bend (irrespective of its shape) and the bulk modulus of air. The inertia as represented by the acoustical mass presents more problems in that it is affected by the flow-profile in the bend.

Since in most musical instruments relatively short toroidal parts are found in between cylindrical (or conical) tube pieces, transition corrections can be expected. The magnitude of these corrections is not known; we neglect them.

On considering the effects of inertia, the

medium may be considered incompressible under the present restrictions; in that case it is justifiable to assume that the pressure in normal cross-sections of the bend is constant.

The longitudinal velocity of a particle at a distance R of the centre of the tore is given by (Fig. 37.1)

$$u = - \frac{1}{j\omega\rho} \frac{\partial p}{R\partial\varphi} . \qquad (37.1)$$

As p is independent of R, the mean velocity $\overline{u}$ over the cross-section S of the tube is found from

$$\overline{u} = \frac{1}{\pi r_0^2} \int u \, dS. \qquad (37.2)$$

Introducing

$$R = R_0 + r \cos\vartheta , \quad z = r \sin\vartheta , \qquad (37.3)$$

this becomes

$$\overline{u} = \frac{-2 \, \partial p/\partial\varphi}{j\omega\rho\pi r_0^2} \int_0^{r_0} \int_0^\pi \frac{r \, dr \, d\vartheta}{R_0 + r\cos\vartheta} =$$

$$= \frac{-2}{j\omega\rho r_0^2} \left[R_0 - \sqrt{R_0^2 - r_0^2} \right] \frac{\partial p}{\partial\varphi} . \qquad (37.4)$$

We now correct for the deviation of the acoustic mass of the bend from that of a straight tube having a length equal to that of the centre line of the bend by introducing an apparent density of the medium, ρ_B. When measuring along the centre line and introducing $x = R_0\varphi$, leaving out the bar above u, eq.(37.4) is replaced by

$$u = \frac{-1}{j\omega\rho_B} \frac{\partial p}{\partial x} , \qquad (37.5)$$

where

$$\rho_B = \rho \, \frac{\frac{1}{2} r_0^2}{R_0^2 - R_0 \sqrt{R_0^2 - r_0^2}} < \rho . \qquad (37.6)$$

In view of the previous considerations, no modification of the equation of continuity is required.

The expression for the acoustical impedance of a tore is similar to that of a cylinder, eq.(13.14), but we now introduce $k = \omega/c$, $c = (K/\rho)^{1/2}$ and replace ρ by ρ_B :

$$Z = \frac{-j\sqrt{K\rho_B}}{S} \tan\left(\omega x \sqrt{\rho_B/K} + \psi\right) . \qquad (37.7)$$

This impedance is equal to that of a cylindrical tube with apparent area S_B and position coordinate x_B:

$$Z = \frac{-j\sqrt{K\rho}}{S_B} \tan\left(\omega x_B \sqrt{\rho/K} + \psi\right) , \qquad (37.8)$$

where $\quad S_B = S \sqrt{\rho/\rho_B} \geqslant S ,$

$$x_B = x\sqrt{\rho_B/\rho} \leqslant x . \qquad (37.9)$$

For slightly curved bends, the tore may, with a good approximation, be replaced by a cylinder with the same cross-section and length as the tore. For sharp bends, however, corrections must be applied. When, for example, $r_0/R_0 = 0.55$, we find that $S_B = 1.04 \, S$ and $x_B = 0.96 \, x$. These are corrections of 4% as compared with the cylindrical tube. The effect of this is illustrated by an example in Fig. 37.2. With a solid line we indicate the diameter measured along the axis of a conical instrument with a bend. In this way of plotting, diameters and conicity join perfectly. Such a type of bore is very common, and at first sight it seems to be

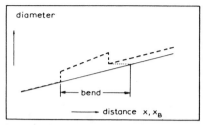

Fig. 37.2. Example of a conical bore before and after correction for a sharp bend ⌒ = measured along centre line, − − − = apparent diameter, as a function of apparent distance x_B

the best choice. When we apply the corrections, using eqs (37.9) we find the apparent bore (dashed line),as a function of the apparent position-coordinate x_B, to be widened and shortened. This will cause unevennesses in the tuning when the bend is part of the oscillating air column in more than one register. It would therefore be better to reduce a little both diameter and conicity in bends.

38. End-corrections for tubes and side-holes

In the preceding sections all calculations were performed on tube pieces with effective lengths equal to the sum of a geometrical length and an end-correction. In this section we consider the magnitude of this end-correction.

Some general remarks can be made on the subject of end-corrections, of which knowledge is restricted. As long as the cross-dimensions of the tube are sufficiently small with respect to the wave-length, the end-correction is a constant, that is not dependent on frequency, and which is determined by the geometry of the surroundings of the hole. The influence of the holes nearby affects the radiation impedance of the hole, but this effect can be shown to be small (Van Wulfften Palthe, personal communication). This means that the end-correction is a purely geometrical matter. Finding

its magnitude can be considered to be a practical problem which eventually can be solved by measurements. This appears to be the best method anyway, since, to my knowledge, only a few and relatively simple end-geometries have been investigated theoretically, viz. only open ends with no or with an infinitely extended flange [65,66,71,98]. Even these relatively simple end situations appear to imply cumbersome calculations. Other geometries such as that of a key hanging above a hole and that of a finite flange may be expected to be inaccessible for calculations, at least at the present state of the art.

For a number of configurations, end-corrections have been measured [21,28,49,51,73,88].Results of these measurements will be reviewed here and compared.

The end-corrections are expressed in a length correction Δl which is proportional to tube radius a

$$\Delta l = E \times a , \qquad (38.1)$$

where E is a geometrical factor depending on the end-geometry of the tube.

The correction is applied to a hole with a geometrical length l_H and a radius a, or cross-sectional area S_H. How are these quantities defined? The shape of the holes, especially the finishing of the end varies considerably; this can be seen from Fig. 38.1, where various types of holes are shown. The hole length l_H will be defined as the wall thickness in case A (Fig. 38.1) or as the shortest length in the other cases. The radius for oval holes (which are very rare) is defined as that value which gives the same area as for a cylindrical hole. When the hole is partly or completely conical, we can for this effect correct either the length or the radius. In most cases the conicity (sometimes called undercutting, also chamfering) is ignored and the hole is replaced by a cylindrical one with a radius equal to the smallest radius of the conical hole.

For a hole or tube of radius a, provided with a flange of outer radius $a+w$, the end-geometry factor was measured by Benade [21], and he found that the results could be described by

$$E_f = 0.821 - 0.13 (0.42 + w/a)^{-0.54} \qquad (38.2)$$

Results are shown graphically in Fig. 38.2. The magnitude of E_f varies between the well-known limits $0.613 \leqslant E_f \leqslant 0.821$ for a tube with no and one with an infinitely large flange.

The factor for the transition of tube to hole at the inner side of a hole of radius a_H in a tube with radius a_1 is [21]

$$E_i = 1.3 - 0.9 (a_H/a_1). \qquad (38.3)$$

In his publication Benade states that he measured this up to $a_H/a_1 = 0.72$, but in a later personal communication he has noted that it may be used up to $a_H/a_1 = 1$.

For the outside of the hole of radius a_H in a tube with outer radius R (Fig. 38.1) Benade found

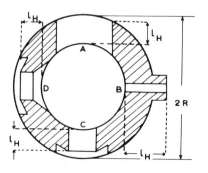

Fig. 38.1. Various hole shapes

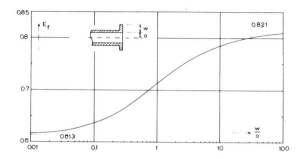

Fig. 38.2. Magnitude of flange correction-factor E_f according to eq.(38.2)

$$E_o = 0.64 + 0.205 \ln(0.3 \, R/a_H) , \quad 1.5 \leqslant R/a_H \leqslant 7. \qquad (38.4)$$

This correction varies between $0.48 \leqslant E_o \leqslant 0.821$. The very low value for the relatively wide holes (lower than the value for an unflanged tube, 0.613) is explained by the fact that the sides of these holes retract considerably (see Fig. 38.1, A). Since, however, nearly all holes in musical instruments are flat on the outside (for a better fit of pads or fingers) E_o can not be lower than 0.613. But even for a relatively large hole, the outer wall of the main tube acts as a flange for a considerable part of its circumference. Hence we assume that the lowest value for E_o will be the mean of the values for the flanged and the unflanged tube, viz. 0.70.

We now will proceed with referring the correction factor to the diameter, in which measure the dimensions of the hole mostly are given. The length correction then is given by $\Delta l = \frac{1}{2} E \cdot d_H$ The correction factor, in reference to the diameter, for the sum of inner and outer end of the hole is in between the limits

$$1 - 0.45 \, d_H/d_1 \leqslant \frac{1}{2} (E_i + E_o) \leqslant 1.06 - 0.45 \, d_H/d_1 . \qquad (38.5)$$

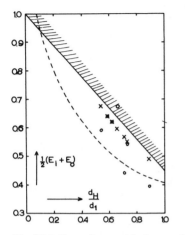

Fig. 38.3. Sum of geometrical correction factors, $\frac{1}{2}(E_i+E_o)$, referred to the hole/tube-diameter ratio d_H/d_1. Symbols are explained in the text; drawn line denotes present author's final choice.

This inequality is indicated by the shaded area in Fig. 38.3. In the same figure, measurements reported by Louden [73] are plotted (circles). Crosses indicate what the predictions according to Benade are for Louden's measurements (since the outside of the holes was not flattened, these points do not fall within our shaded area). Considering the scatter of the measurements, agreement with Benade's formula is very good. The dashed line is a formula according to Mühle [88]. Benade's measurements are to be preferred since these were much more extended, and on better defined tube combinations, than those of Mühle.

Since the outer end of the hole can take on various shapes (cf. B and C in Fig. 38.1), and because little is known about the exact value of E_o, we assume that for every hole $E_o = 0.70$. This corresponds to the lowest boundary (drawn) of the shaded area in Fig. 38.3. For wide holes, this will be approximately right. For narrow holes,

it can be expected to give an error of at most 10% in the end-correction factor. These holes are long in most cases, so that an error in the end-correction influences the effective length of the hole only slightly.

The effect of a key, hanging above a hole, was measured by Benade [21]. A disk with radius r is located perpendicularly to the axis of an unflanged tube with radius a_H at a distance h of the tube-end. The end-correction of the tube then increases with an amount

$$\Delta l_d = 0.613\, a_H \left[(r/a_H)^{0.18}\, (a_H/h)^{0.39} - 1 \right].$$
$$(38.6)$$

The range of validity is $1 \leqslant r/a_H \leqslant 4$ and $\Delta l_d > 0$. A reasonable mean value for r/a_H is 1.3. Assuming the expression to be valid also for a flanged tube, if we add $0.04\, a_H$ to the correction in order to obtain a convenient expression and changing to the variable $d_H = 2\, a_H$, we have

$$\Delta l_d = 0.325\, d_H \left[(d_H/2h)^{0.39} - 1 \right]. \quad (38.7)$$

This is plotted in Fig. 38.4. This equation appears also to describe quite well some similar measurements of Bouasse [28] and of Guittard [49].

Combining the results, the effective hole-length is given by the following expression

$$L_H = l_H + d_H - 0.45\, d_H^2/d_1 + \Delta l_d . \quad (38.8)$$

The transformed hole-length $\lambda_H = S_1 L_H/S_H$ is

$$\lambda_H = (l_H + d_H + \Delta l_d)\, (d_1/d_H)^2 - 0.45\, d_1 .$$
$$(38.9)$$

When the hole is very narrow, boundary-layer effects become important. The relative length increase is α', see eq.(24.6). Moreover, Benade has (in a personal communication) expressed the suspicion that end-corrections are different from the values given here for very narrow holes.

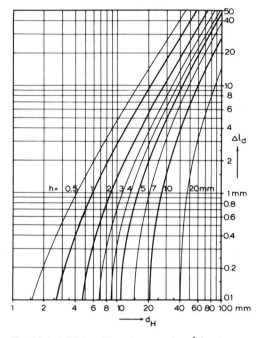

Fig. 38.4. Additional length correction Δl_d, due to a disk hanging h mm above a hole of diameter d_H, calculated with eq.(38.7).

39. Recapitulation

In the third chapter, a mathematical expression was derived that gave a relation between the frequencies with closed and with open hole, the size of the hole and its position. In its exact formulation, this condition is rather difficult to use. In most cases, a simplification is possible which reduces the exact formulation to an algebraic expression. Errors due to this simplification are normally small; they are always such that the frequency is calculated too high. These errors increase as frequency increases, so that notes on high registers are always relatively lower than the corresponding ones on the low register. The magnitude of the effect, as appears from formulae derived, is manifest especially for long and narrow holes which are meant for large frequency shifts (e.g. fork fingerings).

Variations of 10% in hole diameter, or of 1% in distance to the (acoustical) top of the instrument, could be shown to cause variations in the tuning of about 10 cents.

When, in a row of opened holes, one isolated hole is closed, and 3 or more open holes are found in between this closed hole and a row of closed holes, it can be shown that closing this isolated hole hardly influences the frequency.

Mathematical methods were presented for some cross-fingerings and for some special situations, where two or more holes are opened simultaneously and for cross-fingerings.

A register hole, which facilitates overblowing, may shift the frequency a little. The magnitude of this shift depends on the size and location of the hole.

Perturbations from the ideal cylindrical or conical bore change the frequency from that of an unperturbed tube. Perturbations consisting of a closed side-hole, or a row of closed side-holes in a resonating air column, are studied; a closed side-hole acts as an additional compliance mainly, and usually flattens the frequency.

Perturbations of a gradual character, which may be found anywhere in the instrument, change the frequencies for a whole group of notes. It is shown how to handle these perturbations generally, and a number of simple formulae for practical situations is derived. Sharply flaring horns at the ends of tubes influence almost only the lowest notes of the register.

Sharp bends in the bore have the effect of widening and shortening the bore, measured along its centre line.

End-corrections for holes and tubes in order

to obtain their acoustical lengths depend on the geometry of the surroundings of the hole, e.g. a key hanging above a hole. Formulae are given for most practical situations.

chapter 4
examples

41. Introduction

In the first three chapters, all the mathematics necessary for making calculations on woodwind holes was derived. In this chapter it will be shown how to use this mathematics. A procedure is given to calculate the position of a hole of specified dimensions, on an instrument with a specified bore, and yielding a specified frequency. This procedure is applied to the tuning of some existing woodwind instruments for which the predicted hole position was compared with the actual one. Observed differences were related to the tuning errors of instruments found by blowing them. Instruments of good quality as well as instruments with known defects were investigated in order to verify the validity of the theory. The investigations were restricted to the lower two registers of the woodwind instruments, except for the clarinet, where part of the third register was included. Although the methods can also be used for higher notes, the mathematical effort for these notes increases because the fingerings are more intricate and because there are more and bigger corrections; in this way correspondence between theory and experiment can be expected to diminish there.

At the end of the chapter, some consideration is given to the necessity of bore perturbations and to factors governing the timbre and ease of blowing of woodwind instruments.

42. Measurements

Specifications of the 24 instruments which were fully or partly investigated are given in Table 2 (see page 103).

For a detailed determination of the geometrical dimensions of a woodwind instrument, a vernier caliper and a measuring tape are the most important tools. For measuring flaring and conical bores, Russell developed a special device consisting of a very accurate continuously adjustable inside caliper [105]. We confined ourselves to simple cylindrical disks of non-scratching material (e.g. perspex) of various diameters. These are attached to a long rod which is shifted in the wide end of the bore until it sticks. This method cannot be used in bends or when the bore is oval. Since bends or oval bores are mostly found in metal tubes with well-defined wall thicknesses, the outer diameter can be measured and after subtracting twice the wall thickness the inner diameter is obtained.

Since wood is very sensitive to climatic conditions, all measurements on wooden parts should preferably take place within a short range of time.

A survey of all measurement data of bores and holes is given in Table 3.

All distances along the instrument are measured either from the centre of the embouchure hole or from the reed tip and along the centre line of the bore. These distances are introduced as position co-ordinate l_G (G for geometrical). The position co-ordinate of a hole is defined as located at the projection onto the instrument-axis of the intersection point of the hole-axis with the inner wall of the instrument.

For oval or elliptical holes, the values of the short and long elliptical axes are specified.

Holes with undercutting (conical widening towards the inside) were sometimes indicated merely with a +, sometimes largest and smallest diameters were given. On one of the oboes, holes are found which consist of a series of cylinders of different radii; also, some keys were perforated. The various dimensions are listed in the way explained in a little sketch next to the table.

When keys are coupled, we indicate the number

of the key which moves with (+) or against (−) the key in consideration. The listed interval is the one including the motion of the coupled key.

As was mentioned in Section 38, the geometrical hole-length l_H is defined as the shortest length; this is easily measured.

Near to the reeds, the bore is neither cylindrical nor conical. To incorporate such deviations, we measured the mouthpiece volume (as indicated in Table 3) and substituted the real cavity by a cylinder or cone with the same volume. The diameters obtained in this way were put between brackets in the table. In double-reed instruments, the mouthpiece volume was variable due to the variable lip-pressure on the blades. A reasonable mean was chosen. For single reeds the mouthpiece volume was defined as that obtained when the reed closed the aperture.

Where there are bends in the bore, their radius of curvature R_0 (Section 37) is given.

For most instruments investigated, frequencies of notes actually blown were measured. The sound was picked up by a microphone, amplified and fed into a one-third-octave filter to remove the higher harmonics. The period of the signal was measured with a digital counter. A mean of some three to five successive countings was taken as the reciprocal of the frequency of a single measurement. The relative frequency deviation from the nominal frequency based on $A_4 = 440$ Hz was then calculated and is denoted by D_{meas}, abbreviated as D. Since the player's intonation may vary somewhat and the temperature is not constant, the mean value, $\bar{D}$, of a number N of separate measurements was taken. Fluctuations in D are expressed in the standard deviation of a single measurement, s, defined as

$$s = \sqrt{\frac{\Sigma_i (D_i - \bar{D})^2}{N-1}} \qquad (42.1)$$

For a normal distribution, the probability of finding values for $|D_i - \bar{D}| > 1.96\, s$ is 5 percent. The standard deviation of the mean value is

$$s_{\bar{D}} = s/\sqrt{N}. \qquad (42.2)$$

The probability of the mean value $\bar{D}$ deviating more than $2.57\ s_{\bar{D}}$ from the mean value obtained after an infinite number of measurements is 5% for $N = 6$ [35, 46].

In the blowing tests, notes were blown in chromatic order upwards. The musicians were instructed to keep their lips as well as possible in the same position. As appeared from some additional experiments, this order of blowing yields slightly different results from alternative methods, e.g. where notes were played at random. Yet the chromatic order was preferred as the best way to investigate the intervals between adjacent notes, because temperature and lip position are more likely to be the same in the same run than in different runs. In this way the range of the intervals between adjacent notes is a minimum and the comparison with the predicted intervals by theory is most fruitful. A test of significance can be carried out by determining the mean values and standard deviations of the mean values of these intervals.

Register-hole influences were measured by blowing many times intermittently with the register-key open and closed. Since excitation of the overblown note without using the register key was sometimes difficult and required manipulations with the lips, the results may be expected to contain, and will indeed appear to show systematic errors.

43. Procedure

The theory can be verified by calculating the resonance frequencies of the instruments and comparing them with the frequencies obtained by actually blowing them.

The blowing test yields the resonance frequency f_{blow}, from which we obtain $D_{meas} = (f_{blow}/f_{nom}) - 1$, where f_{nom} is the nominal frequency in accordance with the equally tempered scale based on $A_4 = 440$ Hz.

The calculation of the resonance frequency can be done directly from the geometry of the instrument and after introducing the appropriate corrections and the parameters governing the excitation mechanism, e.g. the admittance. Although a theory predicting these latter quantities was presented, its results are insufficiently definite, and experimental determination (e.g. by blowing the instrument) is required. Since we want to have primarily a method which is useful for instrument design, where hole positions are sought with specified bore and hole dimensions, we prefer an indirect way. We calculate the fictitious position which should be given to each hole of the same dimensions as on the real instrument, were the instrument correctly tuned. In effect, we have designed a fictitious instrument (with the same bore and hole dimensions as the real instrument) which is correctly tuned, provided the theory is correct. The positions of all holes on the real instrument will probably differ from the corresponding ones on the fictitious instrument. This difference, ΔL_{calc}, is defined as the measured distance to the top on the real instrument minus the calculated distance to the top on the fictitious instrument. From ΔL_{calc} we find the relative frequency error expected for the real instrument as

$$D_{calc} = - a \, (\Delta L_{calc}/L_S), \qquad (43.1)$$

where L_S is the nominal acoustical length with open hole and a is a factor, almost unity, introduced to account for the effect of the adjacent holes. It will be discussed later in this Section. D_{calc} is the calculated deviation from the nominal tuning, and, provided the theory is correct, it equals D_{meas}. The discussion on the comparison of calculated and measured deviations is postponed to the next section.

The first step in determining D_{calc} is to decide on the internal admittance at the point of excitation, which determines the position of the acoustical top. This top lies at a distance Δl_G beyond the geometrical top; a negative value for Δl_G implies that the acoustical top is located somewhere in the instrument. Δl_G is one of the quantities hardest to estimate, due largely to our imperfect knowledge of excitation mechanisms. Various stratagems have been applied to circumvent the problems.

For flutes, Δl_G is determined from the geometry of the blowing hole (eq.38.9), but the effects of the player's lips nearby, the action of the excitation and the short closed tube-piece to the left of the embouchure hole are excluded (cf. D_E).

For cylindrical reed instruments (clarinets), additional compliances at the top of the instrument are taken into account, represented either by subscripted volumes V or length-corrections Δl. They are: V_r, Δl_r for the reed compliance, V_T, Δl_T for the reed damping and V_m, Δl_m for the mouthpiece excess volume, where V_m is the volume of the mouthpiece-cavity diminished by the extrapolated volume of the main tube, up to the reed tip. V_m may be negative. We refer to eqs. (26.4), (26.5) and (26.6); $\Delta l_G = (V_r + V_T + V_m)/S_1$.

For conical reed instruments (saxophones, oboes and bassoons) another approach is followed: Δl_G is introduced as the truncation, i.e. the distance between the top of the (extrapolated) cone and the geometrical top of the instrument.

In some cases a slightly different value was introduced for practical purposes. This nominal value is only a point of reference. Its error is corrected via D_{bore}.

The second step is to calculate the position of holes on the fictitious instrument with perfect tuning. In most cases this can be done with the first order approximation method yielding the hole position co-ordinate, referring to the acoustical top,

$$L_L = L_S - zL_S, \qquad (32.16)$$

where the nominal acoustical length L_S is calculated from the frequency f with $L_S = c/4f$ for the clarinet or $L_S = c/2f$ for other instruments; the velocity of sound $c = 346$ m/s (see eq. 22.13). L_S and f can be read from Table 4. z follows from

$$z = \tfrac{1}{2}g \sqrt{1 + 4\,\lambda_H/gL_S} \; - \tfrac{1}{2}g, \qquad (32.17)$$

where $g = 2^{v/12} - 1$ is the relative frequency shift when opening the hole, expressed in the (integer) number of semitones, v. In Table 5, g is given for a number of integer values of v. The transformed hole length λ_H can be calculated from

$$\lambda_H = (l_H + d_H + \Delta l_d)(d_1/d_H)^2 - 0.45\,d_1, \ (38.9)$$

where l_H is the hole length, d_H the hole diameter, and d_1 the diameter of the bore at the hole. The correction due to a key above a hole, Δl_d, is given by eq.(38.7) or Fig. 38.4. For narrow holes, boundary layer corrections have to be applied to the hole length l_H with eq.(24.6). The calculation of L_L is conveniently executed with a slide rule or a desk computer. Separately calculated tables of z as a function of λ_H/L_S are useful. When a limited accuracy suffices, Fig. 43.1 can be used.

The first order method for the calculation of L_L fails for some special cases such as double holes, cross-fingerings, coupled keys etc. Then the methods described in Section 33 must be applied.

The third step is the application of a number of corrections due to second-order effects such as the departure from the ideal geometry and air assumed in the preliminary calculations. These corrections may be divided into two groups viz. continuous corrections (where whole groups of notes are affected) and local corrections (affecting one or two notes).

The *continuous corrections* are indicated by subscripted D's, corresponding to relative frequency shifts. A positive value for D implies an increase in frequency due to the effect under consideration. The corrections are:

D_w, for boundary-layer effects; it applies to all instruments. For cylindrical instruments (flutes, clarinets) see eq.(24.6), for conical flutes see eq.(24.11) and for conical reed instruments (saxophones, oboes, bassoons) see eq.(27.15) or Fig. 27.7;

D_{reg}, for the effect of the register hole when overblowing; applied for the flute, clarinet and the saxophone but not for the oboe and the bassoon (eq. 34.3);

D_V, for the effect of closed side-holes, applied for all instruments. $D_V = -\Delta l_V/L_S$, for Δl_V see eqs (35.12) and (35.13) for cylindrical and conical instruments, respectively;

D_{bore}, which is a cumulative correction for all bore perturbations, e.g. changes in conicity (eq. 36.7 and further), diameter jumps (eq. 36.23), sharp bends in the tube (eq. 37.9), flaring ends of the instruments (treated as changes in conicity). Special corrections due to short flaring ends and for holes in such ends are excluded (cf. D_{horn}). For the conical reed instruments, an additional term ΔD_{bore} is included, where, formally, $\Delta D_{bore} = -(V_r + V_T + V_m)/S_1 L_S$, thus incorporating the reed effects. In fact, ΔD_{bore} is adjusted empirically, one of the stratagems for correcting Δl_G, as is also

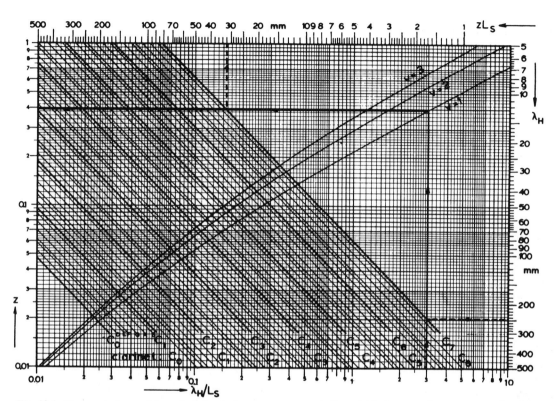

Fig. 43.1. Diagram to be used for calculating hole positions. Relative transformed hole length λ_H/L_S and relative hole position parameter z are interrelated by one of the curves for a frequency shift of ν semitones (in the example: plain line). Sloping lines are for notes desired with open hole; heavy lines are for C's as indicated (clarinet-type instruments are in reference to a separate scale). λ_H/L_S is obtained from the scale for λ_H and the note with open hole by drawing a horizontal line to the note-line (example: dotted line). zL_S is found by drawing a vertical line starting from the note-line (example: dotted line).

D_E, the embouchure correction for flutes, which takes the variation of the player's lip-position into account and is determined experimentally.

The following *local corrections* are applied:

D'', correction for finite acoustical length of tube pieces, applied to all instruments, usually being significant only for cross-fingerings (eq. 32.24);

D_{horn}, correction for the flaring ends and the positions of the holes there. For conical horns see the method yielding eq. (36.17) or one of its simplified versions ($D_{horn} = -\Delta l/L_S$), for catenoidal horns (clarinets), see eq. (36.5) with $D_{horn} = -\Delta l_{horn}/L_S$. Holes in the flare were given positional corrections according to $\Delta l_{horn} = -\Delta V/S_1$, where ΔV is the volume increase over the extrapolated main tube of the tube-piece lying above the hole under consideration.*

* *This choice of ΔV is rather arbitrary. It can be shown that, for a conical flare, it is more accurate to take the volume increase as that to the (fictitious) end point of the substitution tube.*

All continuous corrections are incorporated in:

$$D_{corr} = D_w + D_{reg} + D_V + D_{bore} + D_E, \quad (43.2)$$

which applies to all instruments, although a number of terms in the right hand side may disappear in some cases. The local corrections, D'' and D_{horn}, are added separately, when required. For flutes, D_E is retained as a separate correction, which facilitates its empirical adjustment. The other continuous corrections combine to the following:

$$D'_{corr} = D_w + D_{reg} + D_V + D_{bore}. \quad (43.3)$$

The calculated hole position co-ordinate (in reference to the acoustical top of the instrument) is given as $L_L + (D'' + D_{horn} + D_{corr}) L_S$.
The measured hole position on the real instrument, being l_G in reference to the geometrical top, is $l_G + \Delta l_G$ in reference to the acoustical top. Now eq. (43.4) gives the calculated positional error for the real hole:

$$\Delta L_{calc} = l_G + \Delta l_G - L_L - (D'' + D_{horn} + D_{corr}) L_S.$$
$$(43.4)$$

In this context it should be recalled that the calculated hole positions are based on perfect tuning. This also applies to the case of overblowing: the ideal hole positions are then calculated anew.

From eqs (43.4) and (43.1) we obtain the

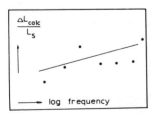

Fig. 43.2. Example of plot of relative positional errors obtained from comparison of actual and predicted hole position.

predicted relative frequency deviation for the real instrument D_{calc}. This transformation incorporates the factor a which accounts for the effect of the adjacent holes. The magnitude of this factor a is now discussed. When we plot $\Delta L_{calc}/L_S$ against the (logarithm of the) frequency we observe two phenomena (see Fig. 43.2), the mean line through the points does not coincide with the horizontal axis (this axis signifies that the tuning of real and fictitious instruments is identical) and the individual points scatter around this mean line. A shift $\Delta L'_{calc}/L_S$ of this mean line with respect to the zero-line can be understood as an average frequency shift with respect to the nominal tuning of the magnitude $-\Delta L'_{calc}/L_S$. i.e. $a = 1$. This may be an actual error in the mean tuning of the instrument, but it can also indicate that the assumptions on which the calculations are based are unsound. A coincidence does not necessarily prove the soundness of the assumptions! The fluctuations around the mean line are related to errors in the intervals between the individual notes. Errors in adjacent holes tend to reduce fluctuations: according to eq. (32.27) a deviation in a hole causes a deviation in an adjacent one, higher in the tube, of the same sign and about one-fourth as much. So we may expect the fluctuations to be somewhat less than they would appear from the diagram (Fig. 43.2), as $a < 1$. Although it is not impossible to correct for this effect, it is rather cumbersome to do so and we therefore assume $a = 1$.

44. Results

a. Comment on the diagrams and the calculation of closed side-hole influences

The results of the hole-position calculations (including all corrections) of the various instru-

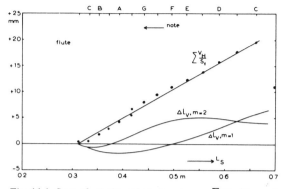

Fig. 44.1. Sum of relative side-hole volume, $\Sigma V_H/S_1$, and length correction Δl_V due to this volume, for two modes of a flute, as a function of the acoustical length L_S.

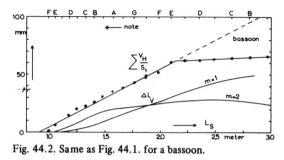

Fig. 44.2. Same as Fig. 44.1. for a bassoon.

ments are presented in diagrams in which are plotted $D_{calc} = -\Delta L_{calc}/L_S$. For those instruments for which a transposed notation is customary, the diagrams are provided with an additional scale for reading off this notation. On the vertical scale, relative frequency deviations and cents can be read off.

The deviations as obtained from the blowing measurements, D_{meas}, are plotted in the same diagrams as D_{calc}. Circles are used for D_{meas} and crosses for D_{calc} wherever possible. When D_{meas} is the result of several measurements, standard deviations of the mean value are indicated by vertical lines if this value exceeds the radius of the circle (0.01). Points concerning notes on one and the same register are connected by lines. In this way it is possible to see immediately to which register a note belongs. If notes can also be made by cross-fingering, they are connected to the keyed notes by a line and they are slightly shifted to the left of the keyed note.

For the length correction due to closed side-holes, Δl_V, details are given here since the methods are alike for all instruments. To determine this correction, $\Sigma V_H/S_1$ is calculated as

$\Sigma l_H d_H^2/d_1^2$ and plotted versus L_S. An example for a flute is given in Fig. 44.1 and for a bassoon in Fig. 44.2. We recall that eqs (35.12) and (35.13), which are used for the calculation of Δl_V, are only applicable when $\Sigma V_H/S_1$ is a linear function of L_S. This can be seen to be approximately so for a flute. It is true also for other instruments excepting the bassoon, where two separate regions are found in each of which $\Sigma V_H/S_1$ is a linear function of L_S, so that in each region the formula must be used separately. Table 6 lists, for the various instruments, the co-ordinates (L_a, y_a) and (L_b, y_b) of the terminal points of the best straight line through the points $y = \Sigma V_H/S_1$ as a function of the acoustical length L_S. In the same table, the penetration factor ϵ is given as obtained from eq. (35.4) where the mean value for all holes of the straight region is inserted for d_H/l_H. In Figs 44.1 and 44.2 the results of the calculated length correction Δl_V are plotted for two modes. From these, the deviations $D_V = -\Delta l_V/L_S$ are obtained. This deviation is plotted in future diagrams for the various instruments.

b. Flutes

Investigations were made of six contemporary Boehm flutes, one historical old-system conical flute, a modern Boehm piccolo and an old-system piccolo.

74

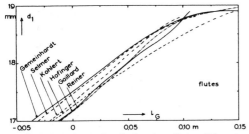

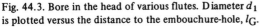

Fig. 44.3. Bore in the head of various flutes. Diameter d_1 is plotted versus the distance to the embouchure-hole, l_G.

For the historical conical flute, which had 8 keys, we used data on dimensions and resonance frequencies as gathered (on or before 1890) and published by Rockstro [104]. For all other instruments data were obtained by actual measurements. Two of the Boehm flutes (the Gemeinhardt and the Reiner) and both piccolos were blown, and frequencies were measured.

In Fig. 44.3 the "conical" bore in the head joints of the cylindrical flutes is shown. Lines were obtained by drawing a smooth line through the individual measured data as given in Table 3. The piccolo bores are plotted in Fig. 44.4.

The effect on the tuning of both the conical head on cylindrical and the cylindrical head on conical instruments is found by application of either eq. (36.21) or a slight modification of this equation. Mean results are plotted as D_{bore} in Figs. 44.5 and 44.6 for flute and piccolo respectively.

The corrections for the boundary-layer effect

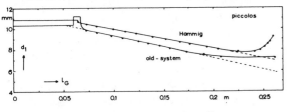

Fig. 44.4. Diameter d_1 as a function of the distance to the embouchure hole, l_G, for the two piccolos.

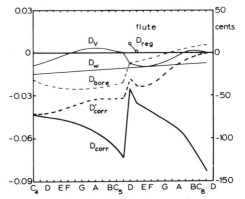

Fig. 44.5. Diagram showing various continuous corrections for the flute. For explanation of symbols see Section 43.

were calculated with eq. (24.6) for the cylindrical and with eq. (24.11) for the conical instruments. Results are plotted as D_w in Figs. 44.5 and 44.6 for flute and piccolo respectively.

The determination of the influence of closed side-holes is explained in subsection a; results are plotted as D_V.

For the two lowest notes on the second register, (D_5 and D_5 # on flutes) a register hole is opened. However, the same hole also serves as a note-hole for C_5-sharp on the low register, therefore it is

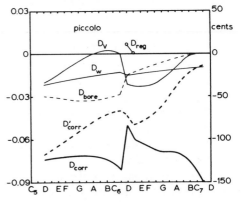

Fig. 44.6. Diagram of corrections for piccolo. For explanation of symbols see Section 43.

rather wide for its function as register-hole. Nevertheless, since it is approximately located in the velocity-antinode of the two notes under consideration, it causes only a small frequency-shift. In mathematical language this means that kL_L is close to π (which can easily be verified to be so from the geometry). Since $\sin kL_L$ goes through zero in the neighbourhood of π, slight changes in the embouchure have a large influence on the correction D_{reg}. Therefore it is difficult to calculate the correction accurately. From measurements the correction appeared to be about zero for D_5-sharp, so $kL_L = \pi$ for this note. For D-natural, $kL_L = \pi/1.06$, so $\sin kL_L \approx 0.18$ and $\cos kL_L \approx 1$. Using eq.(34.5), after inserting $k\lambda_H(\approx 0.60)$ we find $D_{reg}=0.007(12\,\text{cents})$. This corresponds very well with our measurements for D_{reg}: Gemeinhardt flute: 0.008, Reiner flute: 0.004, Hammig piccolo: 0.007, old piccolo: 0.017 and with those of Coltman [36] on a Powell flute: 0.007.

The sum of all corrections is

$$D'_{corr} = D_V + D_w + D_{bore} + D_{reg},$$

and is shown in Figs. 44.5 and 44.6 with a heavy dotted line.

To the conical horns of the piccolos, eq.(36.18) was applied. Holes in the horn were given positional corrections according to $\Delta l_{horn} = -\Delta V/S_1$, where ΔV is the volume increase of the tube-piece lying above the hole under consideration (cf. Section 43). The horn corrections were not included in D'_{corr}.

One continuous correction remains to be dealt with, viz. the frequency-dependent part of the embouchure correction, D_E. This correction is not accurately known and is not studied independently here. But in order to present the hole calculations in a convenient form and to make a comparison with blowing tests more fruitful, a reasonable estimate of D_E was introduced, after a study of the results from the hole calculations.

The minimum of the embouchure correction, from the purely geometrical point of view, can be calculated from the dimensions of the embouchure hole, using eq. (38.9). We find $\lambda_E = 30$ mm (flute), 14 mm (Hammig piccolo) and 12 mm (old piccolo). These values were added as geometrical corrections Δl_G to the hole positions (i.e. the distance between the hole centers) at an early stage of the calculations. Then results were compared with blowing tests.

We consider the deviations from the nominal frequencies for blown notes on the Gemeinhardt as shown in Fig. 44.7b. Open circles are mean values of 6 runs by a skilled professional player, closed circles mean values of 7 runs by an amateur player (the owner of the flute). Both players were asked to blow "straight" and not to correct any impurities that they heard or knew of. Apparently, the experienced player maintains a more constant relative frequency shift than does his amateur colleague. On the other hand, specific local "errors" are detected equally well by both players. This experiment shows that there is no standard embouchure correction: all depends strongly on the player. Taking the embouchure correction as a constant would be unrealistic, as is shown in Fig. 44.8 where we plotted the calculated deviations for a constant embouchure correction of 30 mm (+ signs). The higher notes are predicted progressively sharper than measured. This was to be expected, since the effect of progressive hole coverage by the player's lip for increasing frequency was not incorporated. In the same figure, and in Fig. 44.7b, crosses show the calculated deviations when the embouchure correction was assumed to be 25 mm for the lowest note and to increase with a fixed amount per semitone, where we took on the low register 1 mm per semitone starting from C_4 and on the high register 2 mm per semitone

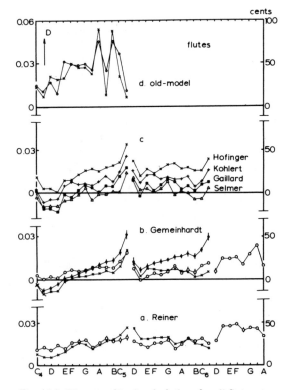

Fig. 44.7. Diagram of tuning deviations for all flutes investigated. The open and filled circles are measured frequency deviations, all other symbols concern calculated values. The Reiner was blown by E. Mesman, the Gemeinhardt by E. Mesman (open circles) and P.J. Napjus (filled-in circles).

starting from C_5. From Fig. 44.7b it can be seen that this assumption fits the blown notes quite well, especially those of the professional player. It is remarkable, that when we take the increase in embouchure correction as 0.75 and 1.5 mm, instead of 1 and 2 mm, the measured points of the amateur player's scale are covered almost throughout by calculated values within ± 0.002.

This deviation from the professional's results may well be due to the amateur's faulty blowing technique. We therefore adhere to the "1 and 2

mm increase" of the embouchure correction.

Additional evidence for the influence of the increasing hole coverage can be obtained from a paper of Coltman [36], who measured blown frequencies as well as externally excited resonances of the flute with a fixed (artificial) lip position. Coltman observed that for higher frequencies the embouchure correction increases, progressively lowering the higher notes.

Results of blowing tests and hole calculations on the Reiner, which was a high-quality professional flute, are shown in Fig. 44.7a. The instrument was blown 4 times. The same assumption for the embouchure correction was used as for the Gemeinhardt. The results are similar to those of the Gemeinhardt.

Having decided upon the magnitude of the embouchure correction, it is added to D'_{corr} and the sum is plotted as D_{corr} with a heavy line in Fig. 44.5.

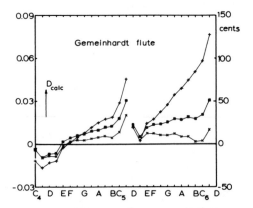

Fig. 44.8. Calculated deviations for the Gemeinhardt flute for three different degrees of embouchure-correction. + symbols are for a constant correction of 30 mm. Crosses and rectangles assume the correction to be 25 mm at the lowest note of each register and to increase a fixed amount per semitone, which is on first register 1 and 0.75 mm respectively, and on second register 2 and 1.5 mm respectively.

For the piccolo similar investigations were' made and similar results were obtained. The embouchure correction Δl_G for the (non-existent) note C_5 was taken as 14 mm for the Hammig and as 12 mm for the old-model piccolo, and their increase was taken as 0.5 mm per semitone on the low and 1 mm per semitone on the second register. The resulting D_{corr} is shown in Fig. 44.6.

Results of calculated and blown frequencies for both piccolos are shown in Fig. 44.9a and b. The Hammig was blown 6 times by a professional, the old-model 8 times by an amateur player. Theory and experiments coincide satisfactorily.

From the results on flutes and piccolos we conclude that, at least qualitatively, the embouchure corrections agree with the expectation formulated in Section 24. In order to overblow the instrument, i.e. to sound the second register, the player increases the velocity of the air stream directed at the embouchure hole [36]. As the critical quantity is the travel time of the air from the lip to the hole edge, this means that the player must withdraw his lips from the hole when shifting from the highest note of the first

register to the lowest note of the second, thus reducing the embouchure correction. So the embouchure corrections may very well be the same for the lowest notes of both registers.

Two cross-fingerings are used on the piccolo (and on old-model flutes too), viz.

● ● ○ ● ● ○   for B_6-flat,
○ ● ○ ● ● ○   for C_6 and C_7

(The first six symbols indicate the fingerholes, the last symbol is the E-flat key; the flute is blown from the left end). For these three notes it was necessary to use the methods given in Section 33. The results are plotted in Fig. 44.9, b. Points corresponding to notes obtained by cross-fingering are connected with a line to the keyed notes and are shifted slightly to the left to improve clarity. The cross-fingerings appear to fit in reasonably well between the other points, except C_7, for which no explanation can be given. In any case, this calculation is very sensitive to small changes in the dimensions of the tube-pieces; the explanation should be sought in this direction. Note also that, in the case of cross-fingerings, the intermediate step of first calculating the theoretical hole position, comparing that to the hole position on the real instrument and converting the result to an expected frequency deviation, was bypassed; expected frequency deviations were calculated directly from the hole positions, applying the appropriate corrections.

The remaining four Boehm flutes, for which the same corrections were used as for the Gemeinhardt, were investigated theoretically only. Calculated deviations are shown in Fig. 44.7c. The results are similar to those of the other flutes. No blowing tests were performed for these instruments. Whether the slight differences in mean relative frequency deviation are real is

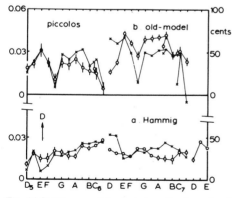

Fig. 44.9. Diagram of tuning errors for two piccolos. X = calculated, o = measured frequency deviations. The Hammig was blown by E. Mesman, the old-model by C.J. Nederveen.

difficult to decide, since the embouchure-holes and the bore there vary among the flutes. For simplicity we took the same embouchure correction for all flutes. The fluctuations seem to be larger than on the Gemeinhardt or Reiner, but this might be due to the fact that the accuracy of the geometrical measurements was less reliable.

Rockstro [104] gave fairly accurate data on the dimensions and blown resonance frequencies of the low register of an old-model flute. For the calculations we used D_{corr} from the cylindrical flute. Results are shown in Fig. 44.7d; D_{meas} and D_{calc} appear to coincide reasonably well. Calculated fluctuations are larger than measured ones, but it should be recalled that relative positional fluctuations are larger than real frequency fluctuations (see Section 43). Since Rockstro states this flute to be a good specimen, we conclude that the old 8-keyed flute was far inferior to a modern Boehm-flute regarding the tuning, cf. Fig. 44.7a. The same conclusion can be reached from a comparison of the diagrams of the Boehm and the old-system piccolo (Fig. 44.9).

Consideration of the tuning diagrams, Figs. 44.7 and 44.9, leads to a number of remarks.

First of all it can be concluded that the theory is capable of spotting notes which are out of tune. A further check on this was made for the Gemeinhardt, where the difference between adjacent notes was compared with theoretical expectations. Analyzing the amateur player's blowing results it appeared that in 9 out of 10 cases predictions from the theory were within the 95% confidence limits found from the measurements. This finding is in proper accordance with statistical laws.

The lift-height of the pads above the holes has a slight, but nevertheless perceptible influence, e.g. changing this height from 1.8 to 3.5 mm changes the calculated frequency about 10 cents. In this respect it is interesting to pay attention

to the slight relative flatness of both G#-s on the Reiner flute (Fig. 44.7a), which was measured as well as theoretically predicted. On inspecting the data of this flute, the G#-key appeared to lift to a height of 1.8 mm instead of 2.8 mm as did all other keys. Calculation shows a frequency rise of 0.004 for a 1 mm increase in key lift. This would just bring the note in line with its adjacent notes.

The sharpness of D_5, observed on most flutes, is due to the register hole. With the present set of holes, there is no simple way to reduce this deviation.

Most of the Boehm flutes investigated here as well as the Haynes flute reported by Young [116] show a tendency to be sharp at the fundamental (C_4) and at the last note of the low register (C_5#). With respect to the C_5# Rockstro [104] states that this note-hole has so many functions that its sharpness is due to a compromise. The absence of a pronounced sharpness of C_5# on the Reiner throws a dubious light on this statement. The same is true for the sharpness of the lowest fundamental, also absent on the Reiner (Fig. 44.7a), which according to Rockstro serves to facilitate excitation. This is supposed to

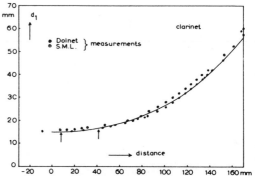

Fig. 44.10. Diameter d_1 as a function of the distance from the throat of the catenoidal horn at the open end of clarinets. The line denotes the function 15 cosh (x/85); arrows indicate positions of the holes.

be difficult for the large-diameter open end. Apparently, the same argument should hold for the note E-flat on the Boehm piccolo (Fig. 44.9a), which is vented via a hole with a diameter larger than the bore and which is also somewhat sharp.

c. Clarinet

Two Boehm clarinets, a Dolnet and an S.M.L., were investigated. Those parts of the bore which deviate from the cylindrical are plotted in Figs. 44.10 and 44.11, where the flare at the open end and the contraction towards the reed are plotted (curve I). The flare is almost a catenoidal horn as is shown by plotting (drawn line) a catenoidal horn with a horn constant $h = 85$ mm in the diagram.

The holes of the S.M.L. were cylindrical, those of the Dolnet showed undercutting (alternatively called chamfering) in a number of cases. In the hole calculations, a chamfered hole was treated as cylindrical with a diameter equal to its smallest diameter. Observe that this assumption tends to predict notes which are flat with regard to the result of an approach which would take this undercutting into account.

Corrections for the boundary layer were

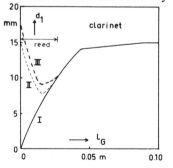

Fig. 44.11. Apparent diameter d_1 of a clarinet mouthpiece (curve I), corrected value for reed motion (curve II), and value corrected for reed motion and reed damping (curve III), as a function of distance to reed tip l_G.

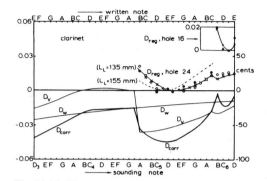

Fig. 44.12. Diagram showing corrections for clarinets. For explanation of symbols see Section 43.

calculated with eq.(24.6) and plotted as D_w in Fig. 44.12. In the same figure we plotted the deviation D_V due to closed side-holes, determined in the way explained in Subsection a.

As was shown in Section 25, reed motion and damping can be described as a fictitious mouthpiece-cavity. The volume of this cavity depends on the reed properties in combination with the lips of the player, notably reed stiffness and damping and the length over which the reed is immobilized on the lay of the mouthpiece. A decisive estimate of all these variables for "normal" playing is impossible (not least because "normal" is ill defined), but the limits can be indicated approximately.

From a measurement of volume and length of the (Selmer) mouthpiece, the mouthpiece cavity (= the volume of mouthpiece with reed clamped minus extrapolated volume of bore of the main tube to reed tip) was found to be $V_m = -5.3$ cm^3, which corresponds to a length correction of $\Delta l_m = V_m/S_1 = -30$ mm, where S_1 is the cross-sectional area of the main tube. The length correction due to reed motion, Δl_r, was estimated in Section 26 to be between 6 and 9 mm (provided the complete reed could move), that due to reed damping $\Delta l_r < 5$ mm. The total correction due to both reed effects therefore is

$$\Delta l_r + \Delta l_T = 10 \pm 4 \text{ mm}.$$

Adding to this the mouthpiece-cavity correction Δl_m, the total effective geometrical embouchure-correction (Δl_G) is found to be

$$\Delta l_G = -20 \pm 4 \text{ mm}.$$

The reasoning given above is rather speculative, but some experimental evidence is available to support it. Before presenting this we shall illustrate the reasoning in more detail.

In Fig. 44.11, curve I gives the equivalent diameter with the reed in rest position and clamped onto the mouthpiece. This curve was obtained via the volume measurements and replacing non-circular cross-sections by circular ones of the same area, e.g. the bore is far from cylindrical in the upper part of the mouthpiece. Curve II shows the effective bore after adding to curve I an amount corresponding to the compliance due to the reed motion of a reed of hardness 4, when not pressed against the lay by the lips. The amount to be added to curve I was obtained by calculating (see eq. 27.14) the cross-sectional increase $\Delta A = dV'_m/dx = CKB$, where C is found from Fig. 25.4, $K = 1.4 \times 10^6$ N/m^2 and $B = 0.0125$ m (Table 1). The additional increase in compliance due to reed-damping is estimated (from the ratio $\Delta l_T/\Delta l_r$) to yield an additional increase in area of $0.4 \, \Delta A$. On adding all corrections, curve III results. The volume in a tube given by curve III is equal to that of a cylindrical tube-piece with the same diameter as the main tube but 20 mm shorter than the mouthpiece; so: $\Delta l_G = -20$ mm.

It should be noted that, even should Δl_G be confirmed experimentally, this does not imply that the individual contributions of reed motion and reed damping are correct.

Independent support for the magnitude of the corrections due to reed effects is obtained from data in a paper by Backus [6]. Our Fig. 44.13 is partly copied from Backus' Figure 1. Open circles are resonance frequencies measured with weakly coupled external source, the reed being clamped tightly onto the mouthpiece. Vertical bars indicate the range of actually blown frequencies. When applying a correction of $\Delta l_r + \Delta l_T = 10$ mm to the externally excited frequencies we get the results indicated with filled-in circles. These can be seen to fall well within the range of the real frequencies. Also, the theoretically predicted spread of ± 4 mm more or less corresponds with the spread as measured by Backus.

Further support for the correctness of the mouthpiece-cavity correction is obtained from a study of the results from hole calculations and register-hole effects, as will be shown below.

The influence of register-hole 24 (also used as a note-hole) is calculated with eq. (34.4). The position of this hole can be found from Table 3 to be $l_G = 155$ mm. Assuming $\Delta l_G = -20$ mm, the value of L_L becomes 135 mm. Calculated results are plotted as a drawn line, D_{reg}, in Fig. 44.12. They correspond very well with our measurements on the S.M.L. clarinet (open circular symbols) and with those reported by Backus [6] (filled-in circles). For comparison, D_{reg} is plotted for $L_L = 155$ mm in the same figure with a dotted line. This curve shows poor agreement with the experimental results, which is an independent, though not very accurate, indication that the top correction is about -20 mm.

In the same way, the influences of note-hole 16, used as register hole in the third register, are calculated and measured. Results are plotted in Fig. 44.12 in the insert.

The sum of all corrections, $D_{corr} = D_V + D_w + D_{reg}$, ($D_{bore} = D_E = 0$) is plotted in

Fig. 44.12 with a heavy line.

The catenoidal horns at the open ends of the clarinets (see Fig. 44.10) yield length corrections. These are calculated with eq.(36.5) and they are −86 mm for the first-register note and −82 mm for the second-register note. When calculated with the first-order approximation, eq.(36.6), we find −85 mm for both modes, which proves that first-order approximation can can be applied.

The holes located in the slowly expanding part of the flare were assigned a positional correction (see Section 43).

Hole 24, used both as a note-hole and a register-hole, is a rather narrow hole. Corrections were applied for boundary-layer effects, using eq.(22.9), which gave a 6% length increase. Incorporation of the boundary-layer effects gives a correction of −12 cents for use as a note-hole.

The results of the calculated frequency deviations, D_{calc}, are plotted in Fig. 44.14 for both clarinets.

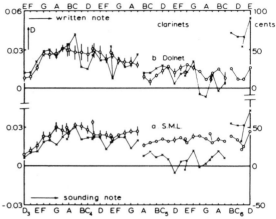

Fig. 44.14. Tuning diagram of clarinets.
o = measured, X = calculated frequency deviations.
Both instruments were blown by C.J. Nederveen.

Blowing tests in an ascending chromatic scale were carried out, where the S.M.L. was blown 6 times and the Dolnet 4 times. Results are plotted as D_{meas} with circles in Fig. 44.14. Standard deviations of the mean values are indicated with vertical lines. The standard deviation from the mean value of an interval between adjacent notes on repeated blowing was also calculated; this was carried out over various intervals. In general, these standard deviations were found to be a factor of two lower than the standard deviations as plotted in the diagram.

It appears that experiment and theory coincide satisfactorily although the instruments are more evenly tuned than the calculations suggest. In the case of the Dolnet this can be partly explained by the undercutting of the holes.

Both theory and experiment show the tendency of part of the low register to be sharp, except for the bottom notes which tend to be flat. This shortcoming of the clarinet is well-known and has been reported earlier [6, 119]. Fig. 44.12 reveals that this is due to the combined action of the

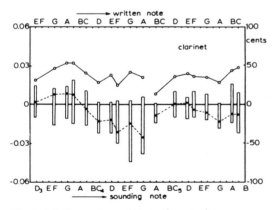

Fig. 44.13. Comparison of blown frequencies (vertical bars) with those measured with weakly coupled external source (open circles) and those after applying a correction of +10 mm to the "open circles" (filled-in circles). Measurements by Backus [6].

register hole and the closed side-holes in the second register. Improvements can be expected by reducing the diameter of the register hole when relieving it from its duplicate function as note-hole for B-flat, combined with a slight widening of the bore in the upper half of the clarinet. The first measure suppresses the bottom notes of the second register so that by rearranging the bottom holes the lower notes of the first register can be sharpened. The bore-widening causes a lowering (see eq. 36.26) of the lower half of the first register. A bore-widening of as little as 2% would yield the anticipated effect, i.e. a flattening of 20 cents.

It is interesting to study the second-order correction D'' by comparing mutual tuning errors between duplicate fingerings in various registers. For instance, the fingering for A_3-E_5-C_6# can be either a fork for a whole tone or a key for a semitone. The second-order correction for the fork is greater than that for the key, and the forked note should flatten with respect to the keyed note in the higher registers. Fig. 44.14 clearly shows this to be true for the S.M.L. The change in measured differences between key and fork on the three registers corresponds to those calculated.

d. Saxophones

Six saxophones were investigated, among which two tenors (a Schenkelaars and a Racso), one alto (a Schenkelaars) and three sopranos (a Selmer, a Schenkelaars and a Solotone). From cursory blowing tests, the Schenkelaars tenor and alto and the Sélmer soprano seemed to be tuned satisfactorily but the other instruments gave rise to difficulties in intonation for some parts of the registers.

In Figs. 44.15 and 44.16 the bore measurements are plotted.

Boundary-layer corrections D_w were read from Fig. 27.7, and closed side-hole corrections

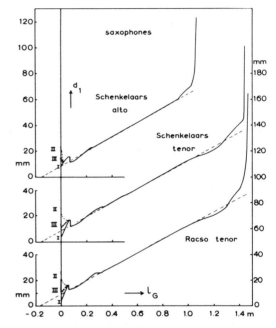

Fig. 44.15. Diameter d_1 as a function of distance to reed tip, l_G, of alto and tenor saxophones.

were calculated along the lines described in Subsection a. Results are plotted in Figs. 44.17, 19 and 20.

On saxophones, two register holes are in use, one being opened for written* D through G # and one for written A on upwards. Results of calculations (eq. 34.5) and measurements are plotted in Figs. 44.17 to 20 with crosses and circles respectively. (Note that L_L diminishes for the highest notes of alto and soprano because of the large truncation-correction.) The measured influences (see Section 42) of the register-hole seem to be somewhat smaller than the calculations suggest. This might be explained by the lip-manip-

*A written C sounds a B-flat on tenor and soprano, and a E-flat on alto saxophones.

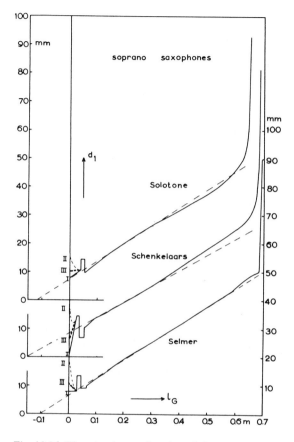

and the largest length as length. In fact, this simplification has the same effect as increasing the end correction. In the diagrams, we indicated with drawn lines the values of D_{reg} which were used in the calculations. For the three sopranos, the corrections are shown separately.

The mouthpiece cavity and the reed compliance are essential factors in the tuning. As was shown in Section 27, the sum of real and fictitious cavity volumes must approximately be equal to the volume of the cone-truncation, to ensure purity between first and second register. The application of this simple rule of thumb is obscured by the influences of diameter perturbations in the crooks and upper parts of the instruments.

Besides, the position of the mouthpiece on the saxophone can be shifted over a wide range, which is another variable factor. For the present investigations, the mouthpiece was adjusted for what the player (i.e. the author) considered the best compromise.

It is especially noticeable for saxophones that the theory of the reed-exitation mechanism does not yield very definite results. Thus, as in the case of the flute, experimental investi-

ulations necessary to force the notes in their overtones when deprived of the aid of the register-hole. Another possibility is that the impedance calculation of the rather narrow holes (corrected for boundary layer) is slightly in error; the end-corrections may be higher. Many register holes (cf. Table 3) appear to be conically widened at both ends. In the calculations, it was always assumed that the hole is cylindrical throughout, with the smallest diameter as diameter

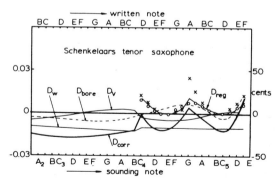
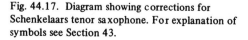

Fig. 44.17. Diagram showing corrections for Schenkelaars tenor saxophone. For explanation of symbols see Section 43.

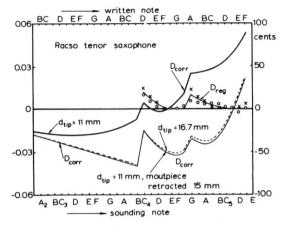

Fig. 44.18. Diagram showing corrections for Racso tenor saxophone. (D_V and D_W are the same as Fig. 44.17.). For explanation of symbols see Section 43.

gation is required to determine the excitation parameters. Here the following procedure was adopted. The combined effects of reed motion and damping were introduced as a variable and characterized by an equivalent diameter at the reed tip, d_{tip}. The active part of the reed may be adjusted theoretically. For various values of d_{tip}, D_{calc} was obtained (using D_{bore} as obtained from a computer) and a value for d_{tip} was selected which gave the best overall correspondence between D_{calc} and D_{meas} as obtained from the blowing tests. The effects of bends were neglected in calculating D_{bore}, the other perturbations were introduced in accordance with eqs.(36.7) to (36.10). The results for the best correspondences are plotted in Figs. 44.22, 44.23, 44.24. In Figs. 44.17, 19 and 21, D_{bore} is separately shown; the bore, which gave these results is indicated with heavy dots (curve III) in Figs. 44.15 and 16. D_{bore} for the soprano saxophones was, for convenience, referred to a truncation of 0.110 m for all three instruments though it is apparent from Fig. 44.16

that, geometrically, their truncations are different. The computer calculation was programmed in such a way that it corrected for the difference of the geometrical truncation and the formal reference truncation.

For the alto and the soprano saxophones, D_{corr} increases sharply for the highest notes of the second register. The corresponding holes are not intended for use in the low register and may thus be expected to be seriously out of tune when used as such. We can verify this effect by a simple experiment where we first blow such a high note and then, using the same fingering except the register-key, blow the instrument in its lowest mode and estimate the deviation of the interval from the octave. Since D_{corr} for the low register is small, we may estimate its value on the second register. It can amount to nearly a whole tone.

For at least two of the three soprano saxophones, theory predicts that correct tuning for both

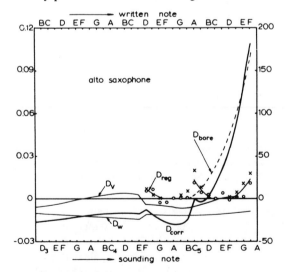

Fig. 44.19. Corrections for alto saxophone. For explanation of symbols see Section 43.

registers seems to be unattainable — and it is
indeed so. Many soprano saxophones are seriously
out of tune. Instrument makers, well aware of
this, tried to do away at least with some of the
sharpness of the upper register by a device for
improving one note, B_5: when the register key
is pressed, a separate key keeps a small hole
closed (which hole stays open for B_4). Thus
the sharpness of B_5 is indeed reduced, but unfortunately too much so, which makes the device
equally annoying. On the Selmer, very ingeniously,
the key is perforated so that the venting for B_5
is reduced less drastically. It can be seen from the
tuning diagrams that this measure is satisfactory.
The best cure for the soprano troubles, as it
evolves from the present investigations, would
be to make the bore purely conical, reduce the
truncation and leave out the above-mentioned
coupling for B_5. The Selmer comes very close
to this ideal: its bore is the straightest and
its truncation is the lowest; it was found to
be the best-tuned instrument of the three.

If the angle of conicity of the lower part
of the bore of a conical instrument exceeds that

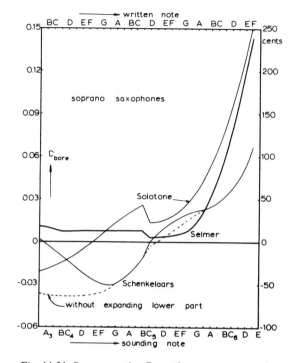

Fig. 44.21. Bore correction D_{bore} for soprano saxophones.

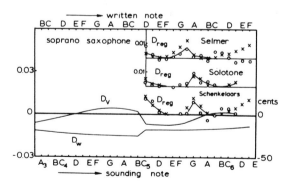

Fig. 44.20. Corrections D_V, D_w and D_{reg} for soprano
saxophones. D_{reg} is separately shown for the three
sopranos, using two inserts. For explanation of symbols see Section 43.

of the upper part, as does the Schenkelaars
saxophone, the mutual tuning between registers
is strongly influenced. This appears from
eq.(36.20), and from Fig. 44.21. In this figure,
the broken line indicates the effect on D_{bore}
when the lower part of the bore is assigned the
same conicity as the upper part (the broken line
in Fig. 44.16). Since D_V, D_w and D_{reg} are
practically frequency-independent, D_{bore} is a
good measure of D_{corr}. The lower part of
the first register becomes annoyingly flat, to the
disadvantage of the instrument which is already
a trifle flat in this range.

The reed compliance was assumed to be the
same for the whole frequency range, although this
is presumably incorrect. This simplification

hardly appears to affect the results.

Shifting the mouthpiece produces the same kind of effect as altering the reed properties, which can be represented as a change of d_{tip}. This is so because both effects may be interpreted as a change in volume at the reed tip, since the length of the reed is always smaller than one-tenth of the wavelength. The effects are illustrated in Fig. 44.18, where D_{corr} is plotted for the Racso saxophone for a retraction of the mouthpiece of 15 mm and for a change in diameter at the tip from 11 to 16.7 mm.

In Figs. 44.15 and 16, the bore of the mouthpiece without reed influences, (drawn line, curve I) is the circular bore having the same volume as the (non-circular) real bore. Using the reed compliance curves for static displacements of the whole reed, Fig. 25.5, dashed lines (II) were constructed. Curves III are supposed to incorporate both reed motion and damping for a reed partly pressed against the lay. In this respect the transformation from curves II to III differs here from that for the clarinet where the reed motion was assumed to be free in both cases. Whereas, for the clarinet, curve III shows an increase over curve II (Fig. 44.11), for the saxophone curve III shows a decrease. Translating the diameters back to reed compliances, this indicates that the reed compliance is lower for saxophones than it is for clarinets. A qualitative explanation for this fact is available. The lowest values of the reed slit, H_{min}, are plotted for the various saxophones and the clarinet in Fig. 27.8 together with H_{max}, the slit height in rest position of the reed. From this diagram we see that the ratio H_{max}/H_{min} has approximately the same value (about 8) for the lowest notes of saxophones and clarinets. However, the ratio can be up to 5 times larger on saxophones for the higher notes. Assuming that for normal playing H is proportional to H_{min}, reed-tip

compliance C_t is, in the mean, a much smaller fraction of the maximum value on saxophones than it is on clarinets. Moreover, the reed motion influence is determined by the area between the reed compliance curve and its tangent at the last point of contact on the lay; it will therefore be smaller by even more than a factor of 5, since this decrease of the reduction factor in the resultant reed compliance is more than linear in C_t and will thus exceed 5. This means that the saxophone reed is clamped on the lay over a relatively larger portion of its length and will thus have less influence on the tuning (as compared with the 'static' prediction) than in the case of a clarinet reed. The lowest notes constitute an exception, but, as can be seen from Fig. 44.18, the influence on the tuning of the reed motion is not very large in this range.

As the rapidly expanding flare at the end of the tube resembles a flange, it was treated as

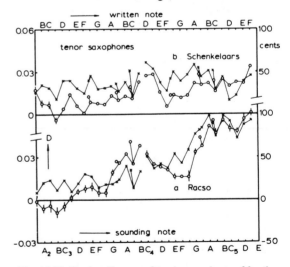

Fig. 44.22. Tuning diagram of tenor saxophones. Mouthpieces were shifted 45 and 36 mm on crook for Schenkelaars and Racso respectively. Both instruments were blown by C.J. Nederveen.

such with eq.(38.2). The flange is preceded by a short conical horn, to which eq.(36.18) was applied.

In two places, tenor and alto saxophones have bends in the bore. The crook in the upper part of the bore shows very low curvature and does not exercise any appreciable influence. The reverse is the case for the sharp bend in the lower part. This bend affects only the lowest notes and does not even come into play for the upper register. The length of the bend is about 12% of the acoustical length of the lowest fundamental. In Section 37 it was shown that such sharp bends correspond to a shortening and widening of the equivalent straight tube, where the differences may be of the order of 5% for the curved parts. This means that a perceptible increase of the resonance frequency is not unlikely. No correction was applied, however, since, as was argued in Section 37, no accurate numerical values are available yet.

Results of the blowing tests are plotted in the corresponding diagrams, Figs. 44.22, 23 and 24. The Solotone was blown five times, the Selmer seven times, the other instruments each six times, by the author.

Comparing the results for D_{calc} and D_{meas}

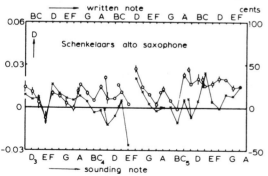

Fig. 44.23. Tuning diagram of Schenkelaars alto saxophone. Mouthpiece was shifted 30 mm on crook. Instrument was blown by C.J. Nederveen.

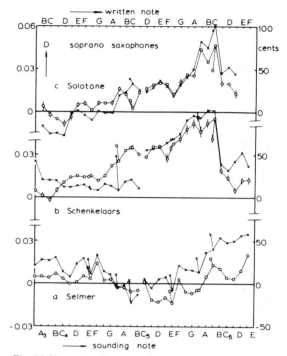

Fig. 44.24. Tuning diagrams of soprano saxophones. Mouthpieces were shifted 25, 25 and 12 mm on the instrument for Selmer, Schenkelaars and Solotone respectively. Instruments were blown by C.J. Nederveen.

we conclude that, in general, the fluctuations are predicted satisfactorily, whereas the mean relative frequency deviation shows discrepancies of the order of 0.02.

The Schenkelaars tenor and alto and the Selmer soprano saxophone are reasonably well tuned with the exception of some fluctuations which are amenable to improvement, usually a shifting of the holes.

The Racso seems to be designed for a standard-A somewhat below the present-day one: when the mouthpiece is pulled out some 1 or 2 cm, the evenness of the tuning is much better.

The Solotone and Schenkelaars soprano saxophones

88

show sharpnesses of the upper register. Both
instruments would be much better with a lower
standard-A, after retracting the mouthpiece.
Also, the Schenkelaars could be improved considerably by either enlarging its upper four and
lower three holes or shifting them upwards.

We conclude that three of the six instruments
seem to have been built to a slightly lower
standard-A, presumably 435 Hz. Part of their
lower register is disturbingly flat compared with
other instruments tuned to 440 Hz or, as seems

to be becoming common practice, 445 Hz. Such a
rise in pitch means that many excellent instruments of older make become useless, which is a
pity for those who have to rely on second-hand
instruments [115].

e. Oboe

Two oboes were investigated, a Buffet and a
Mönnig. Both were equipped with a modern Con-
servatoire-system key mechanism. As can be seen
from Table 3, some holes of the Buffet are of
intricate shape; they consist of a sequence of
two cylinders of different diameters. Some finger-
plates are perforated. For simplicity, we used
the smallest diameter as hole diameter and the
total length as hole length, neglecting the
perforations in the keys.

The bore as a function of the distance to the
reed tip, as obtained from the data of Table 3,
is plotted in Fig. 44.25.

Corrections for boundary layer, D_w, were
read from Fig. 27.7, closed side-hole corrections
D_V were calculated as described in Subsection a.
Both deviations are plotted in Fig. 44.26.

There are two register holes, one which is
opened at a time, to aid overblowing. The upper

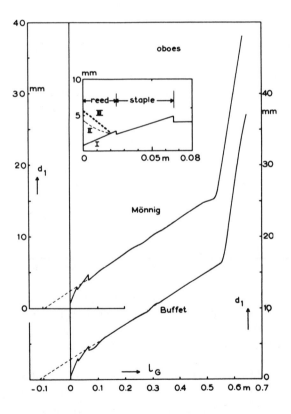

Fig. 44.25. Bore of the oboe. Diameter d_1 as a function
of distance to reed tip, l_G.

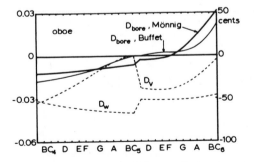

Fig. 44.26. Diagram of continuous corrections for
oboes. For explanation of symbols see Section 43.

holes are less than 0.5 mm in diameter and have a negligible influence on the frequency. The register-hole, for the lowest three notes of the upper register, is fairly large, but its key opens only slightly. It was difficult to calculate the effect of this hole, as was measuring its influence, so we neglected its effects entirely.

In the same way as for saxophones, the best-fitting reed-tip position was determined by trial and error using a computer simultaneously with hole position calculations. On both oboes the same staple and reed were used and the same d_{tip} was assumed. Those assumptions giving the best results are shown as curve III (cf. Subsection d) in the insert in Fig. 44.25. Fig. 44.26 gives the tuning corrections including D_{bore} as found from these investigations, for both instruments. The nominal acoustical top was placed at a distance of 95 mm beyond the geometrical

top for both instruments. This value corresponds to the truncation of the Mönnig, that of the Buffet being somewhat larger (116 mm). The nominal acoustical top merely serves as a reference point for the calculations, the computer programme yielding the correct values for D_{bore}. The results are not exactly the same for both instruments, but they are very similar. This correspondence between two essentially different instruments may be understood by taking into account that (a) the slight conicity reduction on the Mönnig flattens the lower notes, and (b) the larger truncation on the Buffet sharpens the higher ones. (See the remarks concerning the truncation of the soprano saxophone in the previous subsection.)

The final results of the calculations, D_{calc}, and those of the measurements are summarized in Fig. 44.27*. On the Buffet, seven chromatic runs were carried out, one with the staple in completely pushed-in position (triangular symbols) and six with the staple retracted 7 mm (circular symbols). For the Mönnig 6 runs were made, but with various reeds and various staple positions and on different dates. For this reason we only indicate the mean values of the measurements and omit the standard deviations.

There are several intricate mechanical linkages on oboes which necessitated the use of the double-hole procedure explained in Section 33.

On the Buffet, a small vent-key in the bell opens when the low B-flat-key is pressed; this key closes when B is fingered. To calculate the frequency of the bottom note, B-flat, we use eq.(32.14). The position of the hole for B is found with the one-step-double-hole equation (33.6) where λ'_H

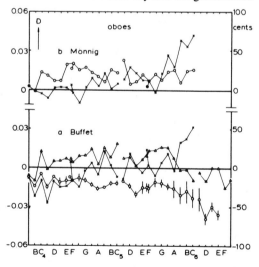

Fig. 44.27. Tuning diagram for oboes. o, Δ = measured, X = calculated frequency deviations. The Buffet was blown by E.J. Spelberg, Δ = with completely pushed-in reed, o = with staple retracted 7 mm. The Mönnig was blown by A. de Bruijn, with various reed positions.

The measurements on the Mönnig were carried out by A. de Bruijn in the National Research Council, Ottawa, Canada.

must be taken negative, since the keys move in opposite direction.

When comparing D_{meas} and D_{calc} in Fig. 44.27 we observe that the correspondence is not as good as for the instruments previously investigated. However, some predicted fluctuations can be seen to occur also in the measured results, such as those in the lowest notes of the Buffet. Despite prediction, the upper part of the second register is scarcely sharp, except that a notable increase in spread of the blown frequencies is found here. This part of the register is difficult to play in tune; most oboists are experienced in correcting these notes downwards. The great flexibility of the oboe allows for these large corrections, and it was having no reference to other instruments that apparently caused the large fluctuations during the test. The principal reason for the poor agreement referred to above is that since the excitation mechanism is very flexible, any assumption introduced into the calculations tends to become more or less fictitious.

We note that the oboe has the same fundamental note and about the same compass as the soprano saxophone, and that both instruments have the same tuning troubles at the end of the second register. Just as for the soprano saxophone, we can expect an improvement by reducing the truncation of the oboe.

f. Bassoon

Of the bassoons that we investigated, both the Riedl and the Heckel were modern instruments provided with modern German key mechanism. The other three instruments, the Kohlert, the Mahillon and the Thibouville were specimens from the historic collection of W. Jansen; they were provided with French key mechanisms in various stages of historic development and perfection.

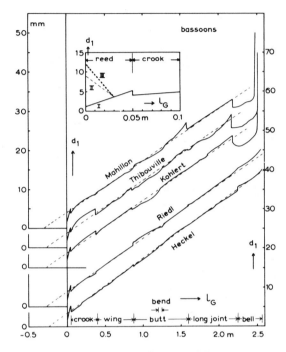

Fig. 44.28. Diameter d_1 as a function of distance to reed tip, l_G, for bassoons.

The tuning of the two oldest instruments, the Mahillon and the Thibouville, was very inferior. This emerged from cursory blowing tests as well as from hole calculations. The Kohlert was somewhat better, but of this last instrument no blown frequencies were measured.

For all five instruments, the bores are plotted in Fig. 44.28. Data in Table 3 are only given for the Heckel, the Riedl and the Kohlert.

D_w was read from Fig. 27.7, D_v was calculated as described in Subsection a, results are plotted in Fig. 44.29. Since bore and holes for all bassoons are approximately the same, these corrections apply to all instruments alike.

Even a modern bassoon is provided with an

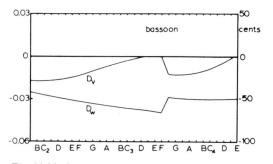

Fig. 44.29. Continuous corrections D_V and D_w for bassoons. For explanation of symbols see Section 43.

impractical key mechanism that is difficult to handle. Although the low register of the bassoon is extended to cover an octave plus a fifth, it overblows in the octave. For the low register, eight semitones have to be fingered with two thumbs, and the little finger of the left hand. The distribution of the holes over the tube is very irregular. This has its roots in the historical bassoon, which had only a few keys. A modern bassoon still retains five holes which are closed -directly by the fingers. These fingerholes are long and narrow, running obliquely through 3 cm of wood so as to bring them closer together within the range of the fingers. Keyholes, on the contrary, are shorter and wider and positioned at acoustically correct places, which, apparently, the fingerholes are not. This lay-out causes certain notes to be weak and out of tune, even on modern instruments where certain improvements have been achieved: (a) by altering positions and sizes of the holes, (b) by fitting an additional key coupled to a ring around the hole which is thus simultaneously moved down when the finger closes the hole. These idiosyncrasies seem to be essential for the characteristic sound of the bassoon, since every attempt until now to rationalize the instrument has failed because of serious damage to the tone-colour.

None of the bassoons had a perfectly conical bore. Deviations due to these fluctuations were computed in the way explained for the saxophones, varying the reed motion until a satisfactory agreement with the simultaneously performed hole-calculations was obtained. The results are shown in Fig. 44.30, where the apparent diameter at the reed tip was the same for all three instruments viz. 12 mm. The mutual tuning between the registers is not very good for the Kohlert, at least not with the particular reed used. If the instrument was designed for another size of reed and tuned to another frequency for standard-A, the fluctuations under the original circumstances might well be lower.

Only the Heckel and the Riedl were subjected to blowing tests and each was blown six times, by the same musician. Results of blown and calculated deviations are plotted in Fig. 44.31. Some of the predicted fluctuations are realized. The mean frequency deviation of the Riedl was predicted to be somewhat higher than that of the Heckel, which was confirmed by the blowing tests. It can be observed that the fluctuations on the Kohlert are larger than those of the other two instruments; this would confirm a generally

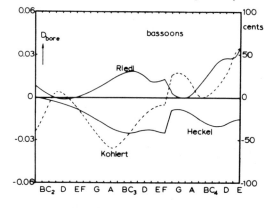

Fig. 44.30. Bore correction D_{bore} for bassoons.

accepted idea that old French bassoons are very unevenly tuned.

Agreement between prediction and measurement is not very impressive for the bassoons. No obvious arguments can be adduced, but the irregularity in hole sizes combined with the hazardous and flexible excitation may well be beyond the capacity of the present relatively simple theory.

The apparent reed-tip diameter of the bassoon indicated with III in Fig. 44.28 was larger than the value indicated with II. Since the moving part of the reed cannot be altered, as can be

done for single reeds, the difference of II and III can be attributed to reed damping. Considering the positions of II and III with respect to I, we are inclined to conclude that reed damping contributes to the apparent mouthpiece-cavity around one-half as much as reed motion. The same can be concluded from comparison of curves II and III for the oboes (Fig. 44.25). This corresponds with the assumption made in this respect for the clarinet. This conclusion, however, is subject to a restriction. By increased lip pressure, the player of double reeds can reduce the *real* mouthpiece cavity between the reeds, curves I and II shifting downwards by the same amount in the diagram. Then the ratio of influences of damping and motion increases since curve III keeps its place here because it already incorporates the effects of lip pressure variations.

45. On the necessity of bore perturbations

The number and magnitude of bore irregularities varies from instrument to instrument; this raises the question whether or not all these irregularities serve a definite purpose. Heckel bassoons are closer to the pure cone than are saxophones and oboes, the latters showing important deviations from the pure cone. Even so, even the high-quality representatives of these instruments require substantial corrections in the frequency calculation when a quarter of the wavelength becomes larger than the truncation length of the cone.

The question formulated above initiated a little additional investigation into this matter. In Fig. 45.1 we show the frequency correction for an oboe according to the bore shown in the insert, curve A. The bore was assumed to be perfectly conical below $l_G = 0.15$ m. On changing the bore according to the dotted line (curve B), i.e. making

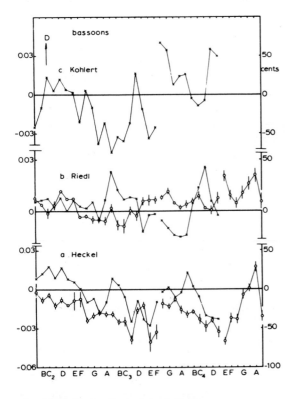

Fig. 44.31. Tuning diagrams for bassoons, o = measured, X = calculated frequency deviations. Instruments were blown by W. Jansen.

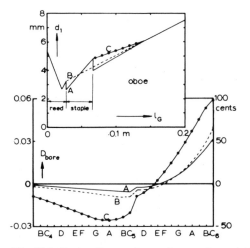

Fig. 45.1. Tuning diagram for an oboe, unchanged (A), and changed in two different ways (B and C) as shown in the diameter plot in the insert.

it perfectly conical, we see that the calculated frequency corrections practically coincide with the results for the real bore. We conclude that a straightening of the bore does not change the tuning. The only difficulty arising with this bore would be how to fix the reed onto a staple with enlarged diameter at the upper end. Using a reed of a larger diameter might be impossible in view of the close tolerances for the reed dimensions. So the reed specifications may very well have occasioned the top irregularities. A similar sort of argument may well apply to irregularities in saxophones: at the lower end of the crook we find a short cylindrical tube-piece which facilitates the joining of the crook to the tube (cf. Fig. 44.15).

The bore according to curve B appears to the eye to be a kind of mean value between the real bore and it is not unreasonable to experience that such a bore yields the same results. When, however, the bore is changed erratically, e.g. when the contraction is removed (curve C in the insert), the result is disastrous. Russell [105] and Young [117] report the story of an oboist who actually did this: he ruined his oboe. According to the calculation shown in curve C of Fig. 45.1, the low registers flattens, the high register sharpens and the octave stretches more than a quarter of a tone: disastrous indeed.

This short investigation clearly showed the tremendous influence of the bore on tuning. It shows that a truly conical bore can be acoustically equivalent to one with many perturbations, e.g. constrictions and abrupt changes in diameter. This leads to the conclusion that, in the absence of compelling reasons, the simplest possible bore is preferable to any other shape because of easier manufacture — and perhaps because of a decrease in sound energy losses.

Some instruments feature a "sword-profile" bore, by which is meant that the bore contracts towards the open end. From the above investigation we might conclude that this is not a desirable bore-shape, but Figs 27.4 and 44.21 suggest otherwise. A sword-profile bore can give good results provided the mouthpiece cavity is somewhat enlarged. A large cavity leads to sharpness for the lowest notes (see Fig. 27.4, lowest curve). This sharpness is compensated by the reduced conicity of the bore, as can be seen from comparing the continuous and dotted lines for the Schenkelaars saxophone in Fig. 44.21. The mean level of the tuning is somewhat lowered.

46. Tone-quality of woodwind instruments

The straightforward calculations presented in the foregoing might suggest that any mathematician can design any woodwind instrument at his desk. This section is intended to discourage such attempts, since sound-frequency is only part of the picture. Other aspects such as tone-quality (timbre or tone-colour) and ease of blowing are also important. These aspects were not studied here but we mention some of the results of studies reported elsewhere.

In recent years, the subjet of tone-quality has been investigated extensively [4, 8, 20, 22, 25, 47, 70, 74, 76, 79, 80, 81, 82, 83, 84, 85]. From experiments by panels, listening to distorted and artificially created waveforms [108, 109], it appeared that two factors largely determine the characteristics of an instrument for the listener. The composition of partials in the steady state (partials which need not necessarily be harmonics of the playing frequency) as well as the initiation of the sound (its initial transient) appear to be crucial in the correct identifications by the listening panel.

Ease of blowing, "resistance", "feel" or whatever name the musician attaches to his feelings of comfort in blowing his instrument are presumably related to the correct matching of the acoustical impedances of generator and tube. The strong partial content which is inherent in reed and hole excitation requires this condition to be fulfilled not only for the fundamental component of the playing frequency but also for the frequencies of its overtones [12, 24]. It means that the tube itself must have a harmonic set of overtones. The frequencies of these overtones are sensitive to minor changes in the bore, to hole lengths and to tube segments between holes in that part of the tube where all holes are open. The oboe and the bassoon especially are known for their particular sensitivity to changes in hole arrangements. There are notes which become unstable and difficult to blow steadily when (open) hole positions on the lower tube piece are modified.

A subject of repeated discussions is the influence of wall vibrations on the tone quality. Most musicians claim that the wall material is important [14, 100]; with a few exceptions, scientists deny this. Let us consider the facts.

First of all, it is quite certain that the walls vibrate. This can be felt with the fingertips and it has also been measured. But the contribution of wall vibrations to the harmonic composition of the total of radiated sound is very small: it has been measured as well as calculated [8, 13] that the sound power radiated by the walls is about 40 dB (10000 times) below that given out from the holes. Investigations on the steady-state partial composition of woodwind instruments made from various materials have revealed [8, 13, 27] that only in rare cases (e.g. thin-walled tubes of non-circular cross-section) are the wall materials found to influence the composition of partials. It seems that other opinions on this matter, as reported by some authors [72, 86, 89], are based on questionable or no evidence at all. These investigators apparently did not take all possible precautions by ruling out any slight differences in geometry when they compared instruments of different material. This leads us to some reflections on minor geometrical fluctuations.

A minor geometrical change can have a large influence on the composition of the partials of a blown tube and hence on the tone quality. This can be understood when we realize that the excitation mechanism oscillating in steady state produces a set of partials which constitute a harmonic series (*exact* integer multiples of the fundamental frequency). If, due to some small change in the bore, the resonance frequency of a partial changes in an amount comparable to the width of its resonance curve, we may expect a considerable change in the amplitude of this partial; a similar effect would appear had the partial been excited by some external source, first in resonance and then, after a slight frequency shift in the source, out of resonance. Slight changes in the bore may thus enhance some partials and suppress others, leading to changes in the timbre of the instrument.

Although many seemingly mysterious matters appear to have a simple scientific explanation, it must be admitted — also by scientific musicians — that there are phenomena which *seem* to be related to the material of the tube and for which no convincing explanation has been offered yet. These problems should be investigated since only when they are all solved will we be able to design a woodwind scientifically with specified properties and free of malfunctions. Now we must still rely for a large part on a craftmanship which, undisputably, has achieved impressive results but which, unfortunately, is disappearing in this technical age.

47. Discussion

All calculations on woodwind instruments presented here are based on elementary acoustical laws. Because of the intricate geometry of woodwind instruments the accurate application of these laws is sometimes too cumbersome or even impossible, so that we must rely on simplifications or experimentally obtained functions. This naturally restricts the accuracy of the results obtained.

The methods of calculation enable us to recognize an isolated mistuned note and to indicate how to correct it. The origin of tuning-differences between instruments bearing the same name can sometimes be revealed. Certain defects in the tuning can be identified as being due to register holes, closed side-holes, diameter perturbations or excessive truncations of the cone.

The tuning strongly depends on the properties of the excitation mechanism which have not been investigated in sufficient detail yet. The resonance frequency as affected by excitation can be varied within certain limits, giving the player means for compensating small fluctuations in tuning and temperature, e.g. in flutes the embouchure-hole coverage is varied, or in reed instruments the lip pressure is adjusted. Theoretical estimates of the embouchure effects can be made, but they must be corrected empirically after a comparison of calculated and blown frequencies.

The flexibility in pitch implies that instrumental geometries are not critical within certain limits. Hence mouthpieces, reeds, blowing methods, bores and holes may somewhat vary and yet yield equally satisfactory results. Deviations from the ideal bore need not yield an acoustically inferior instrument compared with an instrument with an ideal bore; these deviations may be preferable when they constitute conveniences for the manufacture of the instrument.

The diagrams in which the deviations from the nominal frequencies are plotted show a scatter around a mean line. This scatter is only significant in so far as it exceeds plus or minus 10 cents, since this is about the uncertainty of blown as well as calculated frequencies. Also, the player can easily correct the tone 10 cents by re-adjusting his lips; fluctuations of this magnitude are common in normal playing [39, 118].

Correlation between predicted and measured frequencies was best on flutes and worst on bassoons. This is not surprising since flute holes are shaped regularly whereas on bassoons the holes vary considerably in dimensions.

It is easy to detect notes which are out of tune either by calculations or by simple manifold blowing tests using a chromatic stroboscope (Stroboconn), or the like. When they concern an isolated note it is easy to correct the error (Section 32 e), but when they concern a whole group of notes which are out of tune with respect to another register, only a radical change of the bore can bring the solution. The theory presented here may help to indicate in which direction these bore changes should go.

general summary and conclusions

For cylindrical as well as for conical woodwind instruments, resonance frequencies were derived taking into account boundary-layer effects, radiation of sound, the excitation mechanism and bore irregularities. Formulae were presented for calculating hole positions in a prescribed tuning.

The methods were applied to a number of existing woodwind instruments: flutes, piccolos, clarinets, saxophones, oboes and bassoons. Of these instruments, dimensions were determined, and frequencies predicted by theory were compared with actual, blown frequencies. After some constants had been determined experimentally (notably those related to the excitation) a satisfactory correspondence between theory and practice was found. Some effects known from practice, such as notes or groups of notes being out of tune, could be confirmed; causes and means of correcting these shortcomings were discussed. It is suggested that the methods developed can be fruitfully used in the blueprint-stage of the design of a woodwind instrument.

A number of findings and conclusions is worth recapitulating:

1. The way in which the column of air is excited into vibration can be described qualitatively and partly quantitatively. From these descriptions the individual acoustical behaviour of the various woodwind instruments is found. A flute behaves as a two-sided open cylindrical tube, a clarinet as a tube with one end open and the other closed at the reed. Saxophones, oboes and bassoons, which consist of a truncated cone closed at the narrow end by one or two reeds, behave in the same way as a cylindrical flute of a length equal to the cone measured to its apex.

2. Simple algebraic expressions may be derived for the calculation of the hole position when its size is given, or vice versa. It is necessary to specify only the frequencies which sound when the hole is closed and when it is opened. These calculations are rather simple and accurate when the position of a hole between correctly placed adjacent holes must be determined. To predict the positions of a row of holes yielding a prescribed musical scale it is necessary to introduce corrections, such as those due to a row of closed side-holes, boundary layers, excitation effects and perturbations of the ideal cylindrical or conical bore. When this procedure is applied for predicting the hole positions on an existing instrument, the deviations from the predicted positions on the actual instrument could usually be correlated with tuning deviations on the instrument.

3. Corrections were derived for boundary-layer effects at the walls, due to the excitation mechanism and due to radiation from the holes and the open end. Solving the wave equation including boundary-layer effects up to first-order terms, in cylindrical and conical tubes, yields the boundary-layer corrections. The resonance frequency is diminished up to 2/3 of a semitone for a narrow bore. The energy dissipated in the boundary layer along the wall was found to be much larger than the energy dissipated by radiations at the openings of the tube. The purpose of the excitation is to sustain the oscillation. At the same time however, it affects the tuning and the player can shift the frequency slightly via variations in the way of excitation.

4. Corrections due to irregularities in the main tube (bore perturbations, closed side-holes) yield frequency-dependent corrections and hence influence the mutual tuning between registers. Perturbations of the bore, if carefully designed, can be intentionally used for this purpose. Closed side-holes mostly lower the frequency — up to half a semitone.

5. In flutes, the nature of the excitation mech-

anism requires an increasing lip coverage of the embouchure hole with rising frequency. As a result of this increasing coverage the note flattens, an effect compensated for by a bore contraction in the head of the flute towards the embouchure hole.

6. A mouthpiece-cavity, as in flutes is found left of the embouchure-hole and in conical reed instruments in the mouthpiece or between the reeds, is essential for keeping overblown notes close to the harmonic sequence.

7. In reed-blown instruments the reed properties, such as size, shape, compliance and damping, are essential for proper tuning. The reed compliance causes a lowering of the frequency. In conical instruments, the reed compliance has the same effect as a mouthpiece cavity and, therefore, it has an important function in keeping the upper register in tune with the lower one.

8. The player can correct errors in the tuning within certain limits since in flutes, the tone flattens as the embouchure-hole is increasingly covered and in reed instruments the tone sharpens as the lips are tightened.

9. When the theoretically predicted position of a hole (in reference to its neighbours) deviates from the actual position by an amount equivalent to a fractional frequency shift of 10 to 25 cents, the corresponding note is likely to be detected through blowing tests. Moreover, the musician will recognize deviations of this magnitude. The theory is useful in eliminating such impurities in the design stage.

10. Roughly speaking, a 10% change in hole diameter, or a 1% positional change relative to the (acoustical) top of the tube, causes a frequency shift of 10 cents.

11. There is strong evidence that wall vibrations do not contribute perceptibly to the total of radiated sound; the material of the wall therefore has no influence on the timbre. Frequency, initial transient, stability, ease of blowing and timbre of a note are solely determined by the inner geometry of the entire instrument (including the player's mouth).

references *

1. M. Abramowitz and I.A. Stegun, Handbook of Mathematical Functions, Dover, New York 1965.
2. V. Aschoff, Experimentelle Untersuchungen an einer Klarinette, Ak. Zeitschrift **1** (1936) 77–93.
3. J. Backus, Vibrations of the Reed and the Air Column in the Clarinet, JASA **33** (1961) 806–809.
4. J. Backus, Variation with the Loudness of the Harmonic Structure of Clarinet and Bassoon Tones, JASA **34** (1962) 717.
5. J. Backus, Frequency Shifts for Loud Tones of the Clarinet, JASA **35** (1963) 771.
6. J. Backus, Small Vibration Theory of the Clarinet, JASA **35** (1963) 305–313.
7. J. Backus, Effect of Steady Air Flow on the Resonance Frequencies and Q's of the Clarinet, JASA **36** (1964) 2014.
8. J. Backus, Effect of Wall Material on the Steady-State Tone Quality of Woodwind Instruments, JASA **36** (1964) 1881–1887.
9. J. Backus, Clarinet-Reed Parameters, JASA **39** (1966) 1220.
10. J. Backus, Resonances in the Bassoon, JASA **41** (1967) 1608–1609.
11. J. Backus, A Plea for Conformity, JASA **44** (1968) 285.
12. J. Backus, Resonance Frequencies of the Clarinet, JASA **43** (1968) 1272–1281.
13. J. Backus and T.C. Hundley, Wall Vibrations in Flue Organ Pipes and their Effect on Tone, JASA **39** (1966) 936–945.
14. A Baines, Woodwind Instruments and their History, Faber, London 1962.
14a. A.E. Bate, Resonance in Coupled Pipes, Phil. Mag. **16** (1933) 562–574.

15. P.A.T. Bate, The Oboe, Williams and Norgate, London 1956.
16. A.H. Benade, On Woodwind Instrument Bores, JASA **31** (1959) 137–146.
17. A.H. Benade, On the Mathematical Theory of Woodwind Finger Holes, JASA **32** (1960) 1591–1608.
18. A.H. Benade, Horns, Strings and Harmony, Anchor, Garden City N.Y. 1960.
19. A.H. Benade, Thermal Perturbations in Woodwind Bores, JASA **35** (1963) 1901.
20. A.H. Benade, Relation of Air-Column Resonances to Sound Spectra Produced by Wind Instruments, JASA **40** (1966) 247–249.
21. A.H. Benade and J.S. Murday, Measured End Corrections for Woodwind Toneholes, JASA **41** (1967) 1609.
22. A.H. Benade, Search-Tone Measurements in Blown Wind Instruments, JASA **42** (1967) 1217–1218.
23. A.H. Benade and J.W. French, Analysis of the Flute Head Joint, JASA **37** (1965) 679–691.
24. A.H. Benade and D.J. Gans, Sound Production in Wind Instruments, Proc. Conf. Sound Production in Man, Acad. Sci. New York 1966.
25. K.W. Berger, Some Factors in the Recognition of Timbre, JASA **36** (1964) 1888–1891.
26. T. Boehm, The Flute and Flute-Playing, 1871, Reprint by Dover, New York 1964.
27. C.P. Boner and R.B. Newman, The Effect of Wall Materials on the Steady-State Acoustic Spectrum of Flue Pipes, JASA **12** (1940) 83–89.
28. H. Bouasse, Tuyaux et Résonateurs, Delagrave, Paris 1929. (end corrections: p. 236).
29. H. Bouasse, Instruments à Vent, Delagrave, Paris 1930. Tome I & II. (hole calculation: Vol II, pp. 117–128; reed motion: Vol I, pp. 74–92).

* J. Acoust. Soc. Am. is abbreviated by JASA

30. A. Bouhuys, Sound-Power Production in Wind Instruments, JASA 37 (1965) 453–456.

31. G.B. Brown, On Vortex Motion in Gaseous Jets and the Origin of their Sensitivity to Sound, Proc. Phys. Soc. London 47 (1935) 703–732.

32. G.B. Brown, The Vortex Motion Causing Edge Tones, Proc. Phys. Soc. London 49 (1937) 493–507.

33. G.B. Brown, The Mechanism of Edge-Tone Production, Proc. Phys. Soc. London, 49 (1937) 508–521.

34. R.C. Chanaud and A. Powell, Some Experiments Concerning Hole and Ring Tone, JASA 37 (1965) 902–911.

35. Chemical Rubber Publishing Co., Handbook of Chemistry and Physics.

36. J.W. Coltman, Resonance and Sounding Frequencies of the Flute, JASA 40 (1966) 99–107.

37. J.W. Coltman, Acoustics of the Flute, Physics Today 21 (1968) 25–32.

38. J.W. Coltman, Sounding Mechanism of the Flute and Organ Pipe, JASA 44 (1968) 983–992.

39. J.F. Corso, Unison Tuning of Musical Instruments, JASA 26 (1954) 746–750.

40. I.B. Crandall, Theory of Vibrating Systems and Sound, Van Nostrand, New York 1927. (wall damping: appendix A).

41. L. Cremer and H. Ising, Die selbsterregten Schwingungen von Orgelpfeifen, Acustica 19 (1967) 143–153.

42. H. Dänzer, Ueber die stationären Schwingungen der Orgelpfeifen, Z. Physik 162 (1961) 516–541.

43. P. Das, Theory of the Clarinet, Indian J. Phys. 6 (1931) 225–232.

44. R.D. Fay, Attenuation of Sound in Tubes, JASA 12 (1940) 62–67.

45. M. Fouché, Acoustique des Instruments à Vent, Cent. of Assoc. Eng. Liége, Section Art de l'Ingénieur et Art de la Musique (1947) pp. 13–34.

46, R.A. Fisher, Statistical Methods for Research Workers, 6th ed., Oliver & Boyd, Edinburgh 1936.

47. M.D. Friedman, Analysis of Musical Instrument Tones, JASA 41 (1967) 793-806.

48. R.N. Gosh, Theory of the Clarinet, JASA 9 (1938) 255–264.

49. J. Guittard, Tuyaux Sonores, Variations de Fréquences Propres, Acustica 20 (1968) 264–270.

49a. H.C. Hardy, D. Telfair and W.H. Pielemeier, The Velocity of Sound in Air, JASA 13 (1942) 226–233.

50. H.L.F. von Helmholtz, On the Sensations of Tone, 1885, Reprint by Dover, New York 1954. (reed action: appendix VII).

51. S.A. Higgs and L.C. Tyte, Effect of Various Flanges on the Open-End-Correction of a Square Organ Pipe, Phil. Mag. 4 (1927) 1099–1125.

52. C.M. Hutchins, Comparison of the Acoustical and Constructional Parameters of the Conventional 16 to 17-inch Viola and the New 20 inch Vertical Viola, JASA 36 (1964) 1025.

53. C.M. Hutchins, Acoustic Parameters of Violin Design Applied to the Development of a Graduated Series of Violin-Type Instruments, JASA 35 (1963) 771–772.

54. C.M. Hutchins, Bass Violin and the Seven-Foot Contrabass Violin, JASA 37 (1965) 1203.

55. U. Ingard and H. Ising, Acoustic Nonlinearity of an Orifice, JASA 42 (1967) 6–17.

56. U. Ingard, On the Turbulence Limit for Sound Through Apertures, JASA 22 (1950) 680.

57. E.J. Irons, On the Effect of Constrictions in Kundt's Tube and Allied Problems, Phil.

Mag. **7** (1929) 873—886.

58. E.J. Irons, On the Free Periods of Resonators, Phil. Mag. **9** (1930) 346—360.

59. E.J. Irons, The Fingering of Wind Instruments, Phil. Mag. **10** (1930) 16—27.

60. A.R.P. Janse, Sound Absorption at the Soil Surface, Dissertation Delft 1969.

61. W. Jansen, Personal communication to F.G. Rendall, see ref. 100, p. 46.

62. E. Jahnke and F. Emde, Tables of Functions, 1938, Reprint Dover, New York 1945.

63. A.T. Jones, Resonance in Certain Non-Uniform Tubes, JASA **10** (1939) 167—172.

64. F.C. Karal, The Analoguous Acoustical Impedance for Discontinuities and Constrictions of Circular Cross Section, JASA **25** (1953) 327—334.

65. L.V. King, On the Electrical and Acoustic Conductivities of Cylindrical Tubes Bounded by Infinite Flanges, Phil. Mag. **21** (1936) 128—144.

66. L.E. Kinsler and A.R. Frey, Fundamentals of Acoustics, J. Wiley and Sons, New York 1950. (radiation impedance: p. 211; wall damping: p. 231).

67. G. Kirchhoff, Ueber die Einflusz der Wärmeleitung in einem Gase auf die Schallbewegung, Ann. Phys. Leipzig **134** (1868) 179—193.

68. A.F. Kuckes and U. Ingard, A Note on Acoustic Boundary Dissipation Due to Viscosity, JASA **25** (1953) 798—799.

69. H. Lamb, Hydrodynamics, Cambridge, University Press 1932, Reprint Dover, New York 1945. (Wave damping: p. 653).

70. P.R. Lehman, Harmonic Structure of the Tone of the Bassoon, JASA **36** (1964) 1649—1653.

71. H. Levine and J. Schwinger, On the Radiation of Sound from an Unflanged Circular Pipe, Physical Review **73** (1948) 383—406.

72. W. Lottermoser, Der Einflusz des Materials von Orgel-Metall-Pfeifen auf ihre Tongebung, Akust. Z. **2** (1937) 129—134.

73. M.M.E. Louden, Untersuchung von Reflexionsvorgängen in Rohren mit Hilfe akustischer Impulse, Dissertation Braunschweig 1964.

74. D. Luce and M. Clark, Physical Correlates of Brass-Instrument Tones, JASA **42** (1967) 1232—1243.

75. C.S. McGinnis and C. Gallagher, The Mode of Vibration of a Clarinet Reed, JASA **12** (1941) 529—531.

76. H. Meinel, Musikinstrumentenstimmungen und Tonsysteme, Acustica **7** (1957) 185—190.

77. D.M.A. Mercer, The Voicing of Organ Flue Pipes, JASA **23** (1951) 45—54.

78. D.M.A. Mercer, Organ Pipe Voicing Adjustments as a Guide to Theories of the Mechanism of the Pipe, 5e Congrès International d'Acoustique, Liège, paper M 52.

79. J. Meyer, Ueber die Resonanzeigenschaften offener Labialpfeifen, Acustica **11** (1961) 385—396.

80. J. Meyer, Ueber die Messung der Frequenzscalen von Holzblasinstrumenten, Das Musikinstrument **10** (1961) 614—616.

81. J. Meyer, Ueber die Stimmung von Klarinetten, Das Musikinstrument **11** (1962) 540—544.

82. J. Meyer, Die Klangspektren von Klarinetten, Das Musikinstrument **13** (1964) 685—694.

83. J. Meyer, Die Richtkarakteristieken von Klarinetten, Das Musikinstrument **14** (1965) 21—25.

84. J. Meyer, Die Richtkarakteristieken von Oboen und Fagotten, Das Musikinstrument **15** (1966) 598—604.

85. J. Meyer, Akustik der Holzblasinstrumente in Einzeldarstellungen, Das Musikinstrument, Frankfurt am Main 1966.

86. J. Meyer, Akustische Untersuchungen über den Klang alter und neuer Fagotte, Das

Musikinstrument **17** (1968) 1259–1266.

87. P.M. Morse, Vibration and Sound, McGraw-Hill, New York, 2nd ed. 1948. (radiation impedance: p. 333, horns: p. 281).

88. C. Mühle, Untersuchungen über die Resonanzeigenschaften der Blockflöte, Dissertation Braunschweig 1966.

89. D.C. Miller, The Influence of the Material of Wind Instruments on the Tone Quality, Science **29** (1909) 161–171.

90. C.J. Nederveen and D.W. van Wulfften Palthe, Resonance Frequency of a Gas in a Tube with a Short Closed Side-Tube, Acustica **13** (1963) 65–70.

91. C.J. Nederveen, New Key Mechanism for Clarinet, Acustica **14** (1964) 55–58.

92. C.J. Nederveen, Calculations on Location and Dimensions of Holes in a Clarinet, Acustica **14** (1964) 227–234.

93. C.J. Nederveen and A. de Bruijn, Hole Calculations for an Oboe, Acustica **18** (1967) 47–57.

94. W.H. Pielemeier, Velocity of Sound in Air, JASA **10** (1939) 313–317.

95. A. Powell, On Edge Tones and Associated Phenomena, Acustica **3** (1953) 233–243.

96. A. Powell, On the Edgetone, JASA **33** (1961) 395–409.

97. A. Powell, Aspects of Edgetone Experiment and Theory, JASA **37** (1965) 535–536.

98. J.W.S. Rayleigh, The Theory of Sound, Vols 1 and 2, 1894, Reprint Dover, New York 1945. (wind instruments: vol 2, p. 234; wall damping: vol. 2, p. 312; bore perturbations: vol. 2, p. 66).

99. J. Redfield, Certain Anomalies in the Theory of Air Column Behavior in Orchestral Wind Instruments, JASA **6** (1934) 34–36.

100. F.G. Rendall, The Clarinet, Williams and Norgate, London 1954.

101. E.G. Richardson, The Acoustics of Orchestral Instruments and of the Organ, Edwards, Arnold & Co., London 1929.

102. E.G. Richardson, Technical Aspects of Sound, Elsevier, Amsterdam 1953. (musical instruments: pp. 487–496).

103. E.G. Richardson, The Transient Tones of Wind Instruments, JASA **26** (1954) 960–962.

104. R.S. Rockstro, The Flute, Rudell, Carte & Co, 1890, Reprint 1928. (flute-data on p. 229–298).

105. M.E. Russell, The Oboe, Dissertation Iowa State Teachers College, Cedar Falls, Iowa 1953 (ruined oboe: p. 99).

106. F.D. Shields, K.P. Lee and W.J. Wiley, Numerical Solutions for Sound Velocity and Absorption in Cylindrical Tubes, JASA **37** (1965) 724–729.

107. L.J. Sivian, Acoustic Impedance of Small Orifices, JASA **7** (1935) 94–101.

108. W. Strong and M. Clark, Synthesis of Wind-Instrument Tones, JASA **41** (1967) 39–52.

109. W. Strong and M. Clark, Perturbations of Synthetic Orchestral Wind-Instrument Tones, JASA **41** (1967) 277–285.

110. J.D. Trimmer, Resonant Frequencies of Certain Pipe Combinations, JASA **11** (1939) 129–133.

111. D.E. Weston, The Theory of the Propagation of Plane Sound Waves in Tubes, Proc. Phys. Soc. London **B66** (1953) 695–709.

112. W.P.A. Tables; Table of Sine, Cosine and Exponential integrals, 2 Vols. New York 1940.

113. F.J. Young, The Natural Frequencies of Musical Horns, Acustica **10** (1960) 91–97.

114. R.W. Young, Terminology for Logarithmic Frequency Units, JASA **11** (1939) 134–139.

115. R.W. Young, Why an International Standard Tuning Frequency, JASA **27** (1955) 379–380.

116. R.W. Young, The Tuning of Musical Instruments, the Flute, Gravesaner Blätter **3** (1957) 87–91.

117. R.W. Young, The Tuning of Musical Instruments, the Oboe, Gravesaner Blätter **3** (1957) 111–119.

118. R.W. Young, A Decade of Musical Acoustics, 4th International Congress on Acoustics, Copenhagen 1962.

119. R.W. Young and J.C. Webster, The Tuning of Musical Instruments, the Clarinet, Gravesaner Blätter **3** (1957) 174–178.

120. C. Zwikker and C.W. Kosten, Sound Absorbing Materials, Elsevier Amsterdam 1949. (wall damping: p. 24).

tables

Table 1. Numerical data concerning woodwind instruments

	embouchure		hole		single reed				double reed		for
						Saxophone					
instrument:		flute	pic-colo	clar-inet	tenor	alto	so-prano	oboe	bas-soon		explanation see page

instrument:	flute	piccolo	clarinet	tenor	alto	soprano	oboe	bassoon	explanation see page
H_{max}, mm	–	–	1.0	2.2	2.0	1.5	1.0	1.2	34
B, mm	–	–	12.5	16	15	13.2	7	15	29
$C_{t max}$, 10^{-8} m^3/N	–	–	10	30	10	12	3	6.5	31
$V_{t max}$, cm^3	–	–	1.1	6.7	2.2	1.7	0.2	0.8	36, 41
1) throat radius a_0, mm	8.7	5.3	7.5	4.1	4.1	3.5	1.5	2.0	
$S_0 = \pi a_0^2$, mm^2	238	88	177	53	53	39	7.0	12.5	
1) r_0, mm	–	–635	–	150	155	110	95	260	21
V_m / V_0	–	–	–	0.4	0.7	0.7	0	–0.1	41
V_t / V_0	–	–	–	2.6	0.9	1.0	0.6	0.6	41
2) top angle $2\vartheta_c = 2a/r$	–	–0.019	–	0.053	0.057	0.071	0.025	0.014	22
T	–	–	–	0.032	0.030	0.028	0.085	0.092	42
Lowest fundamental frequency f, Hz	C_4 261.6	D_5 587.3	D_3 146.8	$A_2{}^b$ 103.8	$D_3{}^b$ 138.6	$A_3{}^b$ 207.7	$B_3{}^b$ 233.1	$B_1{}^b$ 58.27	
ac. length L_s, mm	661.3	294.6	589.1	1666	1248	833.1	742.2	2969	12
wave number k, m^{-1}	4.75	10.65	2.67	1.88	2.52	3.77	4.24	1.06	7
$w_0 = k r_0$	–	–6.8	–	0.28	0.39	0.49	0.40	0.30	20
rel. truncation r_0/L_S	–	–2.2	–	0.09	0.12	0.13	0.13	0.09	
1) open-end radius a_1, mm	9.5	3.5	7.5	44	34	25	9	19.5	
$\theta/\pi = k^2 a_1^2/2\pi$, 10^{-3}	0.32	0.22	0.064	1.1	1.2	1.4	0.23	0.07	18
$-D_w$, 10^{-3}	16	22	27	9	10	11	31	26	27, 36, 42
Y'_E, 10^{-9} m^{4}s/kg	11700	3000	18	48	28	15	11	29	19, 41
H_{min}, mm	–	–	0.14	0.24	0.18	0.12	–	–	36, 43
number of semitones in low register	14	12	19	14	14	14	14	19	

1) For reed instruments, obtained by extrapolation of the mean cylindrical or conical bore
2) Obtained graphically

Table 2. Specifications of instruments investigated.

FLUTES
1. **Gemeinhardt** (brass, Boehm system). K.G. Gemeinhardt, Elkhardt, Ind., no. M2S 221690.
2. **Reiner** (silver, Boehm). Hans Reiner, Schöneck SA, no. 953.
3. **Hofinger** (wood, brass head, Boehm). F. Hofinger, Bruxelles.
4. **Kohlert** (brass, Boehm). Kohlert & Co., Winnenden, no. 64655.
5. **Selmer** (brass, Boehm). Bundy, Selmer, Elkhardt, Ind., no. 107064.
6. **Gaillard** (brass, Boehm). Gaillard, Loiselet, Lyon-Paris.
7. **Old-model** (wood, 8 keys). Rudall and Rose (around 1827).

PICCOLOS
8. **Hammig** (wood, brass head, Boehm). Philipp Hammig, Markneukirchen, no. 2911.
9. **Old-model** (wood, 7 keys). Nameless.

CLARINETS
10. **Dolnet** (wood, Boehm). Dolnet & Lefèvre, Paris, no. 6070. Mouthpiece: Selmer HS**.
11. **S.M.L.** (wood, Boehm). Strasser/S.M.L., Paris, no. 5686. Mouthpiece: Strasser SML 7.

SAXOPHONES
12. **Schenkelaars tenor.** Schenkelaars, Eindhoven, no. 57085.
13. **Racso tenor.** Oscar Adler, Markneukirchen, no. 5981.
14. **Alto.** Schenkelaars, Eindhoven, no. 85321.
15. **Selmer soprano.** Henri Selmer, Paris, Mark VI, no. 138592. Mouthpiece: D.
16. **Schenkelaars soprano.** Schenkelaars, Eindhoven, no. 2640.
17. **Solotone soprano.** Imported by W. Hampe, Amsterdam, made in Italy, no. 9682.

OBOES
18. **Mönnig** (Conservatoire system). Mönnig, Markneukirchen, no. 1055.
19. **Buffet** (Conservatoire system). Buffet-Crampon, Paris, no. 3204.

BASSOONS
20. **Heckel** (German system). W. Heckel, Biebrich, no. 9919.
21. **Riedl** (German system). V. Kohlert, Graslitz, no. 296757.
22. **Kohlert** (French system). V. Kohlert, Graslitz, no. 276774.
23. **Thibouville** (French system).
24. **Mahillon** (French system).

Table 3. Survey of measurements on woodwinds

d_1 = inner diameter of main tube (mm).
l_G = distance to tip of reed or to centre of embouchure-hole (mm).
d_H = hole diameter or its smallest value (mm). For oval holes, smallest and largest values are given.
l_H = minimum hole length (mm).
h = mean distance of cup to hole end, in opened position (mm).

R_0 = radius of curvature of bended part of the bore.
+ = denotes undercutting of a hole.
= in the h-column, denotes that the hole is not covered by a key
- denotes no hole present.
( ) tube diameters between brackets are estimates obtained via volume-measurements.

A. FLUTES

Gemeinhardt		Reiner		Hofinger		Kohlert		Selmer		Gaillard		Hammig		Old piccolo		old flute	
d_1	l_G	d_1	l_G	d_1	l_G	d_1	l_G	d_1	l_G	d_1	l_G	d_1	l_G	d_1	l_G	d_1	l_G
17	-26	16.8	-20	16.6	-63	16.5	-61	16.9	40.8	16.9	-23	10.85	7.1	10.35	7	18.8	0
16.2	-16	17.0	-12	17.0	-28	16.9	-23.5	17.2	-25.8	17.0	-13	10.85	64.1	10.35	61	18.8	132
16.65	14	17.5	19.9	17.6	22	17.8	26.5	17.8	19	17.3	7	10.7	64.1	11.2	61	15.2	340
17.0	24	17.4	20	17.7	32	17.9	36.5	17.9	29	17.5	17	10.5	73.4	11.2	67	13.5	452
18.0	34	17.8	30	17.9	42	18.1	46.5	18.1	39	17.65	27	10.25	83.1	10.0	67	11.2	583
18.1	44	17.9	40	17.9	52	18.3	56.5	18.2	49	17.85	37	10.0	99.7	9.75	72.5		
18.3	54	18.0	49.4	18.1	62	18.4	66.5	18.3	59	17.95	47	9.75	111.4	9.5	83.1		
18.45	64	18.0	50	18.2	72	18.6	76.5	18.5	69	18.05	57	9.5	122.5	9.25	97.5		
18.55	74	18.25	60	18.3	82	18.8	86.5	18.6	79	18.25	67	9.25	139.0	9.0	109.1		
18.60	84	18.4	70	18.4	92	18.8	96.5	18.7	89	18.4	77	9.0	151.9	8.75	124.7		
18.65	94	18.5	78.2	18.5	102	19.0	106.5	18.9	99	18.5	87	8.75	166.6	8.5	134.8		
18.8	104	18.55	80	18.95	152	18.8	156.5	19.0	109	18.65	97	8.5	176.8	8.25	145.7		
18.85	114	18.68	90	19.05	465	18.9	156.5	18.9	159	18.95	107	8.25	193.6	8.0	155.8		
18.9	154	18.75	100	18.9	594.4	18.9	599.7	18.9	604	18.95	601	8.0	204.7	7.75	172.6		
18.9	603	18.8	110									7.75	224.6	7.5	189.7		
		19	160									7.75	240.9	7.25	207.1		
		19	596.4									8.0	247.4	7.3	262.5		
												8.25	251.3				
												8.5	254.3				
												8.75	256.6				
												9.0	258.6				
												9.2	259.6				

hole			Gemeinhardt				Reiner				Hofinger				Kohlert a)			Selmer a)			Gaillard a)		
no	function		d_H	l_H	h	l_G	d_H	l_H	h	l_G	d_H	l_H	h	l_G	d_H	l_H	l_G	d_H	l_H	l_G	d_H	l_H	l_G
	emb. {		10.3 12.2	5	=	0	10.4 12.2	5.7	=	0	10.2 12.2	4.3	=	0	10.6 12.0	5	0	10.5 12.5	4.5	0	10.3 12.2	?	0
16			7.7	2	1.1	199.0	7.2	2.2	1.5	196.7	7.8	2	2.5	190.9	7.3	2	195.9	7.3	1.5	200.1	7.7	2	199.5
15			7.7	2	1.1	215.0	8.0	2.0	1.5	211.1	7.8	2	2.5	206.1	7.3	2	212.4	7.3	1.5	215.9	7.7	2	216.6
14A			-	-	-	-	8.0	2.0	2	228.9	-	-	-	-	-	-	-	-	-	-	-	-	-
14	C - C#		7.5	2	1.7	234.0	7.2	2.0	1.5	231.4	7.2	2	3	229.2	6.9	2	230.2	6.7	2	233.9	7.0	2	233.0
13	B - C		13.6	3	2.7	265.0	12.7	1.6	2.8	261.5	12.4	3	3	258.8	13.8	3	262.4	13.1	3	265.9	12.5	3	262.0
12	A# - B		13.8	3	1.8	285.0	13.6	1.4	2.8	282.4	13.8	3	2	280.4	13.4	2	283.9	13.1	3	285.8	13.0	3	284.5
11	A - A#		13.8	3	1.8	305.5	13.6	1.4	2.8	302.9	13.8	3	2	301.2	13.4	3	302.9	13.1	3	307.1	13.0	3	305.2
10	+8	G - A	13.8	3	2.1	328.5	13.6	1.4	2.8	325.9	13.2	3	3	323.8	13.3	3	326.4	13.1	3	329.1	13.0	3	328.5
9		G - G#	13.8	3	2.1	351.0	13.4	1.4	1.8	348.3	12.8	3	2.5	344.4	13.2	3	353.5	12.5	3	349.5			
8			13.8	3	2.1	351.0	13.6	1.4	2.8	348.4	13.2	3	3	347.4	13.3	3	348.9	13.1	3	353.5	13.0	3	352.0
7	+4	F# - G	14.4	3	2.2	376.0	14.0	1.4	3.7	372.7	13.8	3	2.5	370.7	14.0	3	378.2	14.1	3	378.2	14.0	3	374.0
6	F - F#		14.4	3	2.2	401.5	14.0	1.4	3.7	397.7	13.8	3	3	397.6	14.0	3	399.7	14.0	3	403.0	14.0	3	401.5
5	E - F		14.4	3	2.2	428.5	14.0	1.4	3.7	425.0	13.8	3	3.2	426.2	14.0	3	425.2	14.1	3	431.2	14.0	3	430.5
4	D# - E		14.4	3	2.2	458.0	14.0	1.4	3.7	455.2	13.8	3	3	453.6	14.0	3	455.2	14.1	3	460.5	14.0	3	458.0
3	D - D#		15.3	3.5	1.7	492.0	15.2	1.5	2.8	486.2	15.5	5	3.8	487.8	14.8	3.5	489.7	15.1	3	493.4	15.5	3.5	492.0
2	C# - D		15.3	3.5	3	526.0	15.3	1.5	3.5	519.6	15.4	4.5	3.5	518.8	14.8	3.5	522.2	15.1	3	525.9	15.5	3.5	523.5
1	C - C#		15.3	3.5	2	560.5	15.3	1.5	3.5	553.3	15.4	3.5	3.5	553.2	14.8	3.5	557.2	15.1	3	560.6	15.5	3.5	558.0

a) h was not measured

hole			Hammig			
no			d_H	l_H	h	l_G
		emb {	8.6 10.3	5	=	0
15			4.7	3.0	2.2	96.1
14			4.7	2.8	2.2	105.9
13		C - C#	4.2	3.1	2.0	111.2
12	+11	B - C	4.2	2.8	1.5	122.1
11			4.3	2.7	1.5	132.2
10		A# - B	5.0	2.7	1.8	132.1
9		A - A#	5.8	2.6	1.8	143.7
8	+7	G - A	6.1	2.6	2.1	156.0
7		'	6.0	2.5	2.1	166.7
6		G - G#	6.0	2.4	2.1	167.6
5	+2	F# - G	6.5	2.2	1.8	179.5
4		F - F#	6.6	2.1	1.8	191.6
3		E - F	7.0	2.0	1.8	207.1
2		D# - E	7.0	1.6	2.0	223.0
1		D - D# {	7.8 8.2	1.3	1.8	236.1

hole			old piccolo			
no			d_H	l_H	h	l_G
		emb {	8.6 9.7	4.5	=	0
13			4.8	3.8	3	87.9
12		B - C#	4.8	4.3	=	115.3
11		B - C	3.9*	4.0	2	122.3
10		A - B	5.0	4.5	=	132.3
9		A - A#	4.0*	4.0	2.5	140.3
8		G - A	4.5	4.6	=	148.8
7		G - G#	3.8	4.0	1.7	162.1
6		F# - G	4.7	4.5	=	175.5
5		F - F#	5.0	4.4	=	192.5
4		E - F	4.5	4.0	2.5	202.5
3		E - F	4.5	4.0	2.5	202.5
2		D - E	4.4	4.7	=	212.8
1		D - D#	5.0	3.7	2.5	235.3

hole		old flute		
no		d_H	l_H b)	l_G
	emb {	10.9 12.2	?	0
13	B - C#	7.1	4.3	220
12	B - C	6.1	4.3	235
11	A - B	9.1	4.3	253
10	A - A#	4.8	4.3	270
9	E - A	7.1	4.3	288
8	G - E#	4.6	4.3	312
7	F# - G	7.6	4.3	349
6	F - F#	10.2	4.3	382
5	E - F	7.6	'4.3	400
4	D - E	5.6	4.3	420
3	D - D#	11.7	4.3	474
2	C# - D	11.2	4.3	505
1	C - C#	10.2	4.3	540

b) estimated

B. CLARINETS

	Dolnet				S.M.L.			
d_I	l_G	d_I	l_G	d_I	l_G	d_I	l_G	
mouth- a)		18.0	550	mouth- b)		16.0	503
piece		19.0	559	piece		16.5	516
		20.0	566			17.0	527
(0)	0	21.0	570	(0)	0	18.0	543
14.0	44.1	22.0	573	13.5	36	20.0	563
14.25	47.6	21.5	577	14	39.5	22.0	575
14.5	66.6	22.0	580	14.25	59.5	24.0	582
14.75	84.6	24.0	588	14.75	76.5	26.0	590
15.0	89.6	26.0	595	15.0	83.7	28.0	597
tube		28.0	601	15.1	88.5	30.0	609
1·.8	89.6	30.0	607	tube		34.0	614
14.8	450	32.0	613			36.0	619
15.0	473	34.0	618	15.1	88.5	38.0	624
15.25	486	38.0	627	15.1	430	40.0	629
15.5	498	40.0	632	15.25	467	42.0	634
15.75	510	46.0	645	15.5	487	49.0	649
16.0	522	53.0	650	15.75	496	58.0	666
17.0	539	59.0	663				
17.5	546	60.0	664				

a) mouthpiece volume = 10.5 ± 0.1 cm³
b) mouthpiece volume = 11.0 ± 0.1 cm³

hole			Dolnet				S.M.L.			
no			d_H	l_H	h	l_G	d_H	l_H	h	l_G
24		G – G#	3.0	12.5	1.8	155	3.1	12.5	3.2	155.0
23		G# – A	4.5+	7.0	2.2	169	5.3	6.5	3	167.0
22		G – G#	6.2+	6.5	2	194	5.9	6.4	1.5	194.8
21		F# – G	5.3+	7.0	2	204	5.5	6.7	2.5	203.5
20		F – F#	5.0+	7.0	2.7	215	5.4	6.5	5	214.5
19	+18	D# – F	4.6+	5.5	2.3	231	5.2	5.0	2.8	230.8
18		D – E	7.8	10.5	=	238.5	7.7	11.0	=	241.0
17		D# – E	5.0+	7.0	2.0	243	5.4	6.7	3	243.5
16		D – D#	5.0+	9.3	=	253	5.4	8.4	=	254.2
15	+14	C – D	5.0+	7.0	2	272	5.4	6.8	2.8	271.8
14	+11	G# – C#	6.4++	9.3	=	286	7.0	8.2	=	287.0
13		C – C#	6.0	7.0	2.5	288.5	6.0	6.6	2.8	288.8
12		C – C#	6.0	6.5	2	290	6.0	6.6	2.2	288.8
11		A# – C	7.1++	7.3	=	308	8.3	6.8	=	309.0
10		A# – B	5.1++	7.3	3	321.5	5.3	6.5	3	320.0
9	+ 8	G# – A#	7.8+	6.3	2	347	8.5	6.0	3.1	350.2
8		G – A	8.7+	9.0	=	363	8.7	8.0	=	366.0
7		G# – A	8.0+	6.3	2	369	8.0	6.5	3	368.5
6		G – G#	7.8+	9.0	=	387	8.7	7.7	=	391.5
5		F – G	9.1+	9.0	=	410	9.3	7.7	=	414.0
4		F – F#	10.0+	5.3	3.2	442	11.4	5.5	3	445.2
3		E – F	12.4+	5.3	3	470	12.2	5.5	3	470.0
2		D# – E	11.0+	5.3	4	502	12.4	5.0	3.5	503.5
1		D – D#	12.3+	5.0	4	540	11.4	4.8	3.5	537.5

C. OBOES

			Mönnig					
d_I	l_G	d_I	l_G	d_I	l_G	d_I	l_G
reed +		5.0	99.6	10.5	311.8	16.25	537.0
staple c)		5.25	109.5	10.75	325.0	16.5	537.9
(0.75)	0	5.5	118.4	11.0	366.2	16.75	539.8
(2.4)	24.0	5.75	128.0	11.25	345.5	17.0	541.5
3.3	37.5	6.0	138.2	11.5	356.8	18.0	546.4
3.5	40.5	6.5	157.3	12.0	377.5	20.0	554.5
3.7	44.9	7.0	175.6	12.5	398.2	22.0	563.2
4.0	49.0	7.5	195.6	13.0	418.0	24.0	570.2
4.2	53.6	8.0	215.2	13.5	437.5	26.0	579.8
4.5	58.2	8.5	238.5	14.0	457.8	28.0	588.4
4.8	66.0	9.0	260.5	14.5	477.0	30.0	596.5
tube		9.25	271.8	15.0	506.5	32.0	606.0
4.0	66.0	9.5	282.0	15.25	528.0	34.0	615.2
4.2	74.0	9.75	288.5	15.5	531.1	36.0	623.5
4.5	82.2	10.0	294.5	15.75	533.6	38.0	630.8
4.75	92.2	10.25	301.8	16.0	535.6	38.1	632.0

			Buffet					
d_I	l_G	d_I	l_G	d_I	l_G	d_I	l_G
reed +		4.75	91.8	10.25	299.6	15.8	534.6
stapel c)		5.0	98.0	10.5	307.4	16.25	547.1
(0.75)	0	5.25	106.0	10.75	320.8	16.5	552.4
2.4	24.0	5.5	114.8	11.0	333.1	16.75	555.2
3.3	37.5	5.75	124.2	11.25	344.6	17.0	557.9
3.5	40.5	6.0	133.0	11.5	355.8	18.0	564.6
3.7	44.9	6.5	151.0	12.0	377.2	19.0	570.1
4.0	49.0	7.0	171.7	12.5	400.2	20.0	574.4
4.2	53.6	7.5	193.6	13.0	419.6	22.0	581.9
4.5	58.2	8.0	214.2	13.5	440.7	24.0	588.1
4.8	66.0	8.5	237.5	14.0	460.8	26.0	596.1
tube		9.0	257.7	14.5	480.8	28.0	603.1
4.0	66.0	9.25	270.0	15.0	498.7	30.0	611.7
4.2	75.0	9.5	282.8	15.25	509.4	32.0	620.3
4.5	84.0	9.75	291.6	15.5	522.4	34.0	629.5
		10.0	294.6	15.75	529.2	37.0	644.3

c) volume of reed + staple = 580 ± 30 mm³

hole			Mönnig			
no			d_H	l_H	h	l_G
22			0.3	7?	1	73
21			0.3	7?	1	129
20		C – D	3.1	6	1	158
19		B – C#	3.0	6	1	170
18			4.2	6	?	182
17	+ 16	A# – C	3.6	6	1	201
16		A – B	4.8	8.5	=	213
15	+ 13	F# – A#	4.2	6	1.3	230
14		A – A#	4.2	6	3	230
13		G – A	4.7	8.5	=	246
12		G – G#	5.0+	6	1.7	275
11		F# – G	7.0+	5.5	1.5	304
10	+ 9	E – F#	4.6	6	1.5	321
9		D# – F	5.6+	6	=	337
8		E – F	7.3+	6	1.5	351
7		D – E	6.7+	8.5	=	365
6		D – D#	7.6	5.5	1.5	401
5		(D – D#)	8.5++	4.8	1.7?	403
4		C – D	9.7	4.5	1.7	431
3		C – C#	7.6+	5.4	1.5	463
2		B – C	9.8	4.5	1.5	499
1		A# – B	10.8	4.5	1.6	539

hole			Buffet							
			hole in key		outside		inside			
no			d_{H1}	l_{H1}	d_{H2}	l_{H2}	d_{H3}	l_{H3}	h	l_G
22					0.5	7?			1	74
21					0.5	7?			1	130
20		C – D			3.2	7.2			1	161.8
19		B – C#			3.2	7.2			1	171.8
18			2	4	6	2	2.7	4.5	2	181.9
17	+ 16	A# – C			2.8	7.0			1.1	199.3
16		A – B	3	4	6.2	2	3.8	3.8	1.2	212.4
15	+ 14	F# – A#			3.8	6.4			1.2	229.3
14		G – A	2.5	4	6.4	2	3.6	4.4	1.4	246.1
13		G – G#			4.8	7.0			1.7	275.9
12		F# – G			8.4	2	6.2	4.2	2.2	303.6
11	+ 10	E – F#			3.7	5.5			1.5	319.5
10		D# – F			8.4	1.8	5.8	4.4	2.5	337.2
9		E – F			6.4	6.6			1.5	349.7
8		D – E	4.8	7.5	8.4	1.8	5.9	4.6	1.2	368.6
7		D – D#			5.7	6.4			3.5	404.3
6		(D – D#)			7.2	6.8			2.0	405.3
5		C – D			9.7	5.7			2.2	435.8
4		C – C#			7.1	6.3			2	469.2
3		B – C			10.4	5.4			2.5	502.3
2	– 1	A# – B			11.3	5			2.2	544.2
1		A#			4.4	6.8			1.5	568.4

key wall bore d_{H1} l_{H1} l_{H2} l_{H3} d_{H2} d_{H3}

D. SAXOPHONES

Schenkelaars tenor (a)

d_1	l_G	d_1	l_G
mouthpiece a)		38.0	542
		39.5	570
(3)	0	40.4	586
12.75	50.5	41.8	615
17	64	42.5	623
17.5	102.5	44.2	663
17.7	117	45.2	673
		46.7	707
crook		47.8	725
12.0	72	49.6	758
12.3	97	50.1	769
13.5	122	52.1	809
15.3	147	53.6	834
17.3	173	55.3	866
19.4	197	56.4	887
21.4	222	59.1	932
23.5	247	60.3	945
24.6	276	62.1	995
26.0	300	63.9	1035 b
26.0	325	66.1	1080
tube		67.2	1146
26.5	325	69.6	1173
28.0	361	72.5	1220
29.8	488	74.1	1245
30.0	399	80.1	1298
31.1	416	82.5	1326
32.0	430	86.3	1358
34.0	466	89	1388
35.2	488	93	1423
36.0	504	151	1441

Racso tenor (c)

d_1	l_G	d_1	l_G
mouthpiece c)		35.6	498
		38.2	546
(3.5)	0	40.1	572
(16.4)	50	42.1	620
16.25	55	45.1	672
16.5	70.5	48.8	732
16.75	94.5	50.4	762
16.8	100.5	53.8	834
		55.1	872
crook		59.0	940
13.0	64	59.6	965
14.7	120	65.1	1045
16.6	150	65.6	1075
19.2	188	67.1	1100
21.6	228	68.6	1150
25.1	268	71.1	1218
25.7	300	74.6	1280
25.7	323	81.6	1328
tube		87.6	1378
26.6	323	91.6	1408
27.1	336	108.6	1448
28.4	369	164.0	1467
31.8	430		
33.6	462		

Schenkelaars alto (e)

d_1	l_G	d_1	l_G
mouthpiece e)		29.0	364
		30.0	382
(8)	0	31.0	399
12.0	44.3	32.0	416
15.5	48.9	33.0	434
15.75	59.7	34.0	452
16.0	68.7	35.0	469
16.25	75.4	36.0	487
16.5	84.7	37.0	503
16.75	92.3	38.0	522
17.0	99.5	40.0	557
		42.0	592
		42.7	608
crook		44.4	639
11.8	70	45.0	646
12.0	93	47.8	690
13.1	110	47.0	692
14.5	130	49.4	732
16.6	154	51.6	770
18.3	178	53.6	802
20.4	202	58.0	859
22.0	227	57.7	864
22.0	248	59.6	907
tube		60.6	921
22.4	248	65.4	967
23.0	258	68.4	996
24.0	276	70.4	1021
25.0	293	80.0	1043
26.0	314	81.6	1046
27.0	329	123.0	1062
28.0	347		

Selmer soprano (g)

d_1	l_G	d_1	l_G
mouthpiece g)		24.0	277
		25.0	294
(8)	0	26.0	311
8.0	33	27.0	327
13.3	33	28.0	344
16.5	57.5	29.0	360
13.5	71	30.0	373
tube		31.0	393
9.2	46	32.0	408
9.2	61.5	33.0	422
10.0	61.5	34.0	437
12.5	100	35.0	452
13.0	108	36.0	468
13.5	117	38.0	500
14.0	125	40.0	534
14.5	135	42.0	565
15.0	143	39.6	527
15.0	147	40.6	543
16.0	151	42.6	569
19.0	193	44.6	599
20.0	209	46.6	641
21.0	225	48.6	665
22.0	247	50.0	671
23.0	259	90.0	689

Schenkelaars soprano (h)

d_1	l_G	d_1	l_G
mouthpiece h)			
(1.6)	0	25.0	299
14.5	27	26.0	314
14.5	61	27.0	332.5
tube		28.0	344.5
6.8	36	29.0	358.5
6.8	53	30.0	374
10.2	53	31.0	388
11.7	66.5	32.0	402.5
13.0	83	33.0	418.5
13.5	92	34.0	432
14.0	100	35.0	447
14.5	108	36.0	463
15.0	121	37.0	477
15.6	134	38.0	491.5
16.4	147.5	39.0	508.5
17.2	156	40.0	522
18.0	175.5	42.0	555
19.0	190.5	44.6	589
20.0	208.5	47.1	627
21.0	226.5	50.6	656
22.0	243.5	54.0	656
23.0	259	64.0	678
24.0	282	101.4	686

Solotone soprano (j)

d_1	l_G	d_1	l_G
mouthpiece i)		26.0	294
		27.0	310
(8)	0	28.0	328
10.3	41	29.0	346
14.0	43	30.0	365
14.2	61	31.0	383
14.3	66	32.0	400
		33.0	418
		34.0	436
9.5	54	35.0	453
11.4	76	36.0	471
13.0	100	37.0	485
15.0	124	38.0	501
16.5	144	39.0	519
18.5	174	40.0	536
19.0	183	42.0	560
20.0	198	46.5	598
21.0	214	51.5	629
22.0	230	52.0	633
23.0	245	93.0	651
24.0	260		
25.0	277		

a) volume = 20.4 ± 0.1 cm³. c) volume = 16.0 ± 0.1 cm³. e) volume = 14.9 ± 0.1 cm³. g) volume = 7.0 ± 0.1 cm³. h) volume = 7.4 ± 0.1 cm³. j) volume = 6.7 ± 0.1 cm³.
b) R_0 = 48 mm. d) R_0 = 45 mm. f) R_0 = 42 mm.

hole			tenor								soprano k)													
			Schenkelaars				Racso				Selmer				Schenkelaars				Solotone					
no			d_H	l_H	h	l_G	d_H	l_H	h	l_G	d_H	l_H	h	l_G	d_H	l_H	h	l_G	d_H	l_H	h	l_G		
24			2.5+	-	2	177	1.7+	3.7	3	164	1.3+	5	3	93	1.6+	5.5	5	72	1.5+	6	2	84.5		
23			3.0+	9	2	363	2.3+	4.7	2	342	2.2+	6	2	174	2.3+	6.4	1.2	157	1.5+	6	3.5	169		
22		D–D#	12.5	2.2	2.5	354	15.0	3.2	4	360	6.5	2	3	172	5.5	2.5	2	153	–	–	–	–		
21		C#–D	13.0	2.2	4.5	380	15.0	2.7	3	386	6.5	2	3	183	5.4	2.5	3	164	–	–	–	–		
20		C–C#	13.5	2.2	4	408	15.2	3.2	4	417	6.5	2	3	194	5.5	2.5	2	175	5.1	2.8	3.5	188		
19		B–C	15.5	2.2	3	444	17.8	3.6	4	448	6.5	2	3	205	5.5	3	2	187.5	5.1	2.8	3.5	199		
18	+17	A–B	11.5	2.2	5	465	12.5	2.5	3	471	8.0	1.7	4	218	5.2	2.5	3.5	197.5	6.5	3	3	210		
17		G–A#	24.4	2.2	5	506	26.0	2.5	3	513	12.8	1.7	4.8	234	12.0	2.5	3.5	215	12.0	3	3	227		
16		A–A#	23.1	2.2	3	525	25.0	4	4	533	10.8	1.8	3	242.5	11.0	2.5	4	224.5	9.0	3	3	230		
15	+14	G–A	21.8	2.2	5	558	25.0	2.5	3	559	9.2	1.6	3.5	256.5	8.3	2.5	3.5	236	11.0	3	3	247.5		
14	+12	E–G#	23.5	2.5	5	601	23.8	2.2	5	603	10.8	1.7	4	276.5	12.0	2.5	4	257	–	–	–	–		
13		G–G#	21.0	2.5	4	600	22.0	2.8	4	602	10.8	1.8	3	279.5	11.0	2.5	4	263.5	11.0	3	3.5	273.5		
12		F–G	30.2	2.5	5	645	32.4	2.5	4	652	19.0	1.8	4.5	306.5	18.0	2.5	4	288	16.0	3	4	299		
11		F–F#	25.0	2.5	4	693	24.6	3.7	3	695	14.3	1.8	5	328	14.0	1.5	3.5	311	14.0	3	3	323		
10	+9	D#–F	25.0	2.5	5	744	24.8	2.7	3	745	19.5	1.8	5	352	14.2	2.5	3.5	335.5	14.8	3	4	347.5		
9		D–E	33.6	2.6	5	791	33.5	2.7	3	792	22.0	1.8	5	379	21.3	2.5	3.5	363.5	20.5	3	4	377		
8		D#–E	25.4	2.5	5	786	–	–	–	–	17.2	2	3.5	362.5	16.3	3.5	4	362.5	–	–	–	–		
7		D–D#	26.4	2.6	5	850	30.5	3	4	851	20.0	1.9	5	408	18.5	2.5	4	391.5	18.8	3	4.5	403.5		
6		C–D	39.5	2.6	5	910	38.0	2.5	4	912	24.5	2	5	439.5	24.3	2.5	4	421	25.0	3	4.5	433.5		
5		C–C#	30.6	3.5	5	967	29.5	3.5	4	980	20.5	2	4	474	19.8	3.5	4.5	454.5	21.0	3	3.5	468.5		
4		A#–C	36.8	3.0	9	1032	34.0	4.5	6	1028	29.0	2	4.5	508	27.4	3.5	3.5	489.5	27.0	3	4	502.5		
3		A#–B	33.1	3.0	3	1118	35.0	4	5	1127	28.0	2	5	542	25.0	3.5	3.5	527.5	25.0	3	3	540.5		
2		A–A#	42.0	3.5	7	1197	43.4	5	10	1204	31.5	2.7	6	582	29.0	3.2	3	570	29.0	3	4	580		
1		G#–A	41.3	3.5	7	1269	43.2	5	10	1283	31.5	2.7	8	624	30.6	3	3	612.5	–	–	–	–		

hole			Schenkelaars			
			alto			
no			d_H	l_H	h	l_G
24			2.5+	4.9	2	131
23			2.5+	7.4	2	265
22		G–G#	12.3	2.3	4	276
21		F#–G	12.2	2.3	5	291
20		F–F#	12.2	2.3	3	305
19		E–F	12.2	2.3	2.5	324
18	+17	D–E	9.3	2.3	4	344
17		C–D#	20.2	2.3	4	364
16		D–D#	18.8	2.3	2	375.5
15	+14	C–D	14.8	2.3	4.5	398.5
14	+12	A–C#	20.9	2.3	4.5	434.5
13		C–C#	19.0	2.3	3	437.5
12		A#–C	25.0	2.3	4	468.5
11		A#–B	20.9	2.3	3.5	503.5
10	+9	G#–A#	21.0	2.3	4.5	537.5
9		G–A	29.6	2.3	4.5	576
8		G#–A	19.3	2.3	4	569
7		G–G#	25.0	2.3	4.5	623.5
6		F–G	34.8	2.3	5	667.5
5		F–F#	31.8	2.5	4	712
4		D#–F	34.1	2.5	9	757
3		D#–E	30.7	2.5	4	835
2		D–D#	38.2	2.2	8.5	886
1		C#–D	39.0	2.2	8.5	944

k) On soprano saxophones, the key mechanism is such that high B on the second register is formed with hole 18 *closed*, holes 16 and 17 being open. On the Selmer, besides that, the key on hole 18 is perforated with a hole of diameter 4 mm and length 6 mm; the last hole can be closed on low register by a second key hanging 4 mm above the perforated first key.

E. BASSOONS

Heckel

d_1	l_G	d_1	l_G	d_1	l_G
reed a)		12.5	641	25.0	1527
(1.2)	0	13.0	679	25.5	1570
5.2	49	13.5	713	25.7	1570
5.2	58	14.0	747	26.5	1638
		14.5	780	27.0	1669
crook		15.0	817	27.5	1707
4.0	49	15.5	863	28.0	1745
4.35	74	15.8	866	28.5	1781
4.8	99	15.3	866	29.0	1820
5.15	124	15.5	880	29.5	1858
5.4	149	16.0	915	30.0	1890
6.0	174	16.5	950	30.5	1936
6.49	199	17.0	988	31.0	1957
6.8	224	17.5	1025	31.5	1998
7.1	249	18.0	1060	32.0	2039
7.6	274	18.5	1096	32.5	2077
7.67	299	19.0	1129	33.0	2119
7.95	324	19.5	1167	33.5	2154
8.3	344	20.0	1209	34.0	2215
8.6	377	20.5 | b	1209	34.5	2236
tube		20.8) b	1257	35.0	2243
8.8	377	21.0	1257	35.3	2247
9.0	393	21.5	1277	35.7	2247
9.5	439	22.0	1308	36.0	2287
10.0	466	22.5	1342	37.0	2374
10.5	497	23.0	1376	38.0	2454
11.0	534	23.5	1414	39.0	2526
11.5	570	24.0	1448	40.0	2556
12.0	604	24.5	1487	40.4	2560

Riedl

d_1	l_G	d_1	l_G	d_1	l_G
reed a)		12.5	630	25.5	1580
(1.2)	0	13.0	664	25.6	1587
5.2	49	13.5	700	26.1	1587
5.2	58	14.0	736	26.0	1618
		14.5	775	26.5	1653
crook		15.0	811	27.0	1683
3.9	49	15.5	845	27.5	1730
4.5	74	15.8	854	28.0	1764
5.0	99	16.6	854	28.5	1796
5.6	124	16.8	883	29.0	1830
5.95	149	17.0	907	29.5	1868
6.45	174	17.5	945	30.0	1903
6.7	199	18.0	987	30.5	1940
7.15	224	18.5	1033	31.0	1974
7.35	249	19.0	1078	31.5	2010
7.55	274	19.5	1128	32.0	2042
7.8	299	20.0	1195	32.5	2074
8.0	314	20.3	1196	33.0	2105
8.15	329	20.1	1196 } c	33.5	2142
8.5	369	20.3	1250 }	34.0	2174
tube		20.5	1250	34.5	2209
8.8	369	21.0	1267	35.0	2226
9.0	377	21.5	1291	35.0	2226
9.5	415	22.0	1329	35.5	2267
10.0	452	22.5	1350	36.0	2304
10.5	484	23.0	1392	37.0	2377
11.0	524	23.5	1437	38.0	2445
11.5	559	24.0	1473	39.0	2494
12.0	592	24.5	1502	40.0	2539
		25.0	1535	40.1	2542

Kohlert

d_1	l_G	d_1	l_G	d_1	l_G
reed a)		13.0	669	25.5	1620
(1.2)	0	13.5	702	26.0	1655
5.2	49	14.0	753	26.5	1691
5.2	58	14.5	790	27.0	1721
		15.0	823	27.5	1764
crook		15.5	861	28.0	1808
4.2	49	14.9	861	28.5	1837
4.8	69	15.0	874	29.0	1863
5.2	89	15.25	895	29.5	1895
5.5	109	15.5	912	30.0	1926
5.9	129	15.75	931	30.5	1964
6.2	149	16.0	948	31.0	2009
6.5	169	16.25	971	31.5	2044
6.8	189	16.5	1005	32.0	2073
7.0	209	16.75	1026	32.5	2108
7.4	229	17.0	1043	33.0	2142
7.6	249	17.5	1081	33.5	2156
7.9	269	18.0	1133	33.8	2161
8.2	289	18.5	1165	31.7	2161
8.4	309	19.0	1192	31.0	2189
8.7	329	?	1192	31.0	2239
9.2	357	?	1239 } d	31.0	2280
9.3	375	20.5	1239	31.5	2340
tube		21.0	1277	32.0	2372
8.5	375	21.5	1303	32.5	2405
9.0	405	22.0	1333	33.0	2453
9.5	422	22.5	1397	33.5	2475
10.0	446	23.0	1422	34.0	2483
10.5	491	23.5	1448	36.0	2492
11.0	529	24.0	1486	38.0	2498
11.5	569	24.5	1550	40.0	2504
12.0	605	25.0	1578	42.0	2507
12.5	633	25.0	1578	50.0	2513

a) Volume of reed = 675 ± 25 mm³, b) R_0 = 14 mm, c) R_0 = 15 mm, d) $R_0 \approx$ 13 mm.

Heckel / Riedl holes

no	hole		d_H out	d_H in	l_H	h	l_G	d_H	l_H	h	l_G
29			0.85		5.0		328	0.85	5		338
28			–	–	–	–	–	1.7+	12	4	418
27				1.9	11.0		430	3.2	12	4	473
26				3.2	12.2		486	4.8	15.5	3	571
25		E–F	4.7	4.1	32.0		593	4.4	31	=	580
24		D–E	6.8	6.0	36.2	=	672	7.1	32	=	657
23		C–D	5.0	4.6	36.0	=	711	4.7	31	=	698
22	+23	C#–D#		3.7	13.5		776	4.0	14	3	782
21		C–C#	4.3		25.0		829	4.2	24	4	811
20				4.8	12.5		875	4.8	11		865
19		B–C	5.0	4.5	25.0	=	877	5.3	27	=	867
18			4.5	4.4	22.0		924	3.9	23	2	914
17		A–B	6.8	6.6	24.0	=	948	6.6	23	=	937
16	+9+8	A–A#		6.7	30.5		1020	6.8	27	2	1005
15	+14	G–A	12.7	8.5	14.5		1168	8.5 } 12.5 }	14	4	1155
14				3.0	20.0		1293	1.8	29	4	1263
13		G–G#		11.7	14.2		1294	12.5	16	3.5	1283
12		F–G		13.5	16.3		1362	14.6	15	3	1345
11		(F–F#)		7.0	13.0		1430	6.9	14	4	1415
10		F–F#		7.7	14.0		1434	8.8	11		1423
9				4.6	13.2		1459	4.6	10	2	1449
8				4.6	13.2		1466	4.6	10	2	1456
7		E–F		14.8	23.0		1554	14.6	20	3.5	1536
6		D–E		14.8	3.0		1679	16.0	3.2	3	1602
5		D–D#		13.5	4.2		1792	13.4	4.3	3.5	1777
4		C–D		14.5	3.0		1895	15.0	4.0	5	1879
3		C–C#		14.9	4.3		2048	15.0	4.3	5	2031
2		B–C		17.9	4.6		2179	17.0	4.3	5	2162
1		A#–B		15.2	3.8		2329	15.1	5	5	2308

Kohlert holes

no	hole		d_H out	d_H in	l_H	h	l_G
30			0.85		5		334
29				2.5			377
28				2.2	12		390
27				2.2	12		435
26				3.4	10		531
25				4.8	18		551
24		E–F	4.8	4.1	39	=	560
23	+22		5.5	4.8	18		572
22			5.7	4.8	18		599
21	+17	D–E	6.2	5.8	34	=	635
20		C–D	6.2	5.6	35	=	678
19		D–D#	4.6	4.2	18		686
18		C–C#	3.6	3.2	32		720
17				2.1	9		803
16				7.3	9		868
15		B–C	6.2	5.6	22	=	896
14	+13	A–B	3.2	3.1	22		949
13				6.0	5.7	20	=	964
12		A–A#	6.1	5.6	19		1043
11		G–A	6.8	6.3	19		1073
10		G–G#		10.0	12		1257
9		F–G		9.2	12		1287
8		F–F#	6.5	6.3	14		1332
7		E–F		7.8	14	=	1486
6		D–E		13.3	5.5		1644
5		D–D#		7.2	7		1714
4		C–D		11.7	7		1856
3		C–C#		8.7	6.7		1989
2		B–C		10.6	6		2094
1		A#–B		11.7	7.5		2290

Table 4. Data on Musical Scales.

A. Frequency of musical notes, expressed in hertz (number of complete oscillations per second)

European notation		C''	C'	C	c	c'	c''	c'''	c''''	c'''''
American notation		C_0	C_1	C_2	C_3	C_4	C_5	C_6	C_7	C_8
	C	16.3516	32.7032	65.4064	130.813	261.626	523.251	1046.50	2093.00	4186.01
		17.3239	34.6478	69.2957	138.591	277.183	554.365	1108.73	2217.46	4434.92
	D	18.3540	36.7081	73.4162	146.832	293.665	587.330	1174.66	2349.32	4698.64
		19.4454	38.8909	77.7817	155.564	311.127	622.254	1244.51	2489.02	4978.03
	E	20.6017	41.2034	82.4069	164.814	329.628	659.255	1318.51	2637.02	5274.04
	F	21.8268	43.6535	87.3071	174.614	349.228	698.457	1396.91	2793.83	5587.65
		23.1247	46.2493	92.4986	184.997	369.994	739.989	1479.98	2959.96	5919.91
	G	24.4997	48.9994	97.9989	195.998	391.995	783.991	1567.98	3135.96	6271.93
		25.9565	51.9131	103.8262	207.652	415.305	830.609	1661.22	3322.44	6644.88
	A	27.5000	55.0000	110.0000	220.000	440.000	880.000	1760.00	3520.00	7040.00
		29.1352	58.2705	116.5409	233.082	466.164	932.328	1864.66	3729.31	7458.62
	B	30.8677	61.7354	123.4708	246.942	493.883	987.767	1975.53	3951.07	7902.13

B. Period or reciprocal of frequency, in millisecond

		C_0	C_1	C_2	C_3	C_4	C_5	C_6	C_7	C_8
	C	61.1561	30.5781	15.2890	7.64451	3.82226	1.91113	0.955564	0.477782	0.238891
		57.7237	28.8618	14.4309	7.21546	3.60773	1.80386	0.901932	0.450966	0.225483
	D	54.4839	27.2419	13.6210	6.81049	3.40524	1.70262	0.851311	0.425655	0.212828
		51.4259	25.7130	12.8565	6.42824	3.21412	1.60706	0.803530	0.401765	0.200883
	E	48.5396	24.2698	12.1349	6.06745	3.03373	1.51686	0.758432	0.379216	0.189608
	F	45.8153	22.9077	11.4538	5.72691	2.86346	1.43173	0.715864	0.357932	0.178966
		43.2439	21.6219	10.8110	5.40549	2.70274	1.35137	0.675686	0.337843	0.168922
	G	40.8168	20.4084	10.2042	5.10210	2.55105	1.27553	0.637763	0.318881	0.159441
		38.5259	19.2630	9.6315	4.81574	2.40787	1.20394	0.601968	0.300984	0.150492
	A	36.3636	18.1818	9.0909	4.54545	2.27273	1.13636	0.568182	0.284091	0.142046
		34.3227	17.1614	8.5807	4.29034	2.14517	1.07258	0.536292	0.268146	0.134073
	B	32.3963	16.1982	8.0991	4.04954	2.02477	1.01238	0.506193	0.253096	0.126548

C. Acoustical length for a sound velocity of 346 m/s (in mm)

Clarinets		C_0	C_1	C_2	C_3	C_4	C_5	C_6	C_7	C_8
Others		C_1	C_2	C_3	C_4	C_5	C_6	C_7	C_8	C_9
	C	5290.00	2645.00	1322.50	661.250	330.625	165.313	82.6563	41.3281	20.6641
		4993.10	2496.55	1248.27	624.137	312.069	156.034	78.0172	39.0086	19.5043
	D	4712.86	2356.43	1178.21	589.107	294.554	147.277	73.6384	36.8192	18.4096
		4448.34	2224.17	1112.09	556.043	278.022	139.011	69.5054	34.7527	17.3763
	E	4198.68	2099.34	1049.67	524.835	262.417	131.209	65.6043	32.8022	16.4011
	F	3963.02	1981.51	990.76	495.378	247.689	123.845	61.9223	30.9611	15.4806
		3740.60	1870.30	935.15	467.575	233.787	116.894	58.4468	29.2234	14.6117
	G	3530.65	1765.33	882.66	441.332	220.666	110.333	55.1665	27.5832	13.7916
		3332.49	1666.25	833.12	416.562	208.281	104.140	52.0702	26.0351	13.0176
	A	3145.45	1572.73	786.36	393.182	196.591	98.296	49.1477	24.7739	12.2869
		2968.91	1484.46	742.23	371.114	185.557	92.779	46.3893	23.1946	11.5973
	B	2802.28	1401.14	700.57	350.285	175.143	87.571	43.7856	21.8928	10.9464

Table 5.

Relative frequency shift $g = \Delta f / f$ as a function of the number of semitones ν.

ν	g	ν	g
−1	−0.056126	1	0.059463
−2	−0.109101	2	0.122462
−3	−0.159104	3	0.189207
−4	−0.206299	4	0.259921
−5	−0.250846	5	0.334840
−6	−0.292893	6	0.414214
−7	−0.332580	7	0.498307
−8	−0.370040	8	0.587401
−9	−0.405396	9	0.681793
−10	−0.438769	10	0.781797
−11	−0.470268	11	0.887749
−12	−0.500000	12	1.000000

Table 6. Data of closed side-holes

Co-ordinates (L_a, y_a) and (L_b, y_b) of the terminal points of the best straight line through the points $y = \Sigma V_H/S_1$ as a function of the acoustical length L.

Dimensions in mm. ϵ is the penetration factor.

	y_a	L_a	y_b	L_b	ϵ
flute	0	310	20.8	650	0.5
piccolo	0	150	18	290	0.11
clarinet	0	200	40	580	0.13
tenor sax	0	580	32	1666	0.5
alto sax	0	440	34	1248	0.5
soprano sax	0	320	25	833	0.5
oboe	0	275	44	730	0.07
bassoon	0	925	62	2140	0.2
	62	2140	68	3100	0.04

addendum
developments since 1969

A1. Introduction

This addendum is included to update the original book and also to draw attention to some aspects of woodwind acoustics which are, in my opinion, underexposed. It supplements excellent books by, for example, Benade (1976), Campbell and Greated (1987) and Fletcher and Rossing (1991).*

A woodwind instrument can be considered to consist of a number of coupled resonators: the air column, the excitation mechanism, the mouth of the player and the vibrating wall enclosing the air column. A complete description taking all interactions into account, for example as a set of equations, is not possible with the present state of knowledge. Even if this could be accomplished, solving the equations would be a formidable, if impossible, task. However, solutions can be obtained after sensible simplifications, leading to understanding and practical applications.

For the calculation of the resonance frequencies of a woodwind, a useful simplification is dealing only with the most important coupling, namely that of air column and excitation. A further simplification is assuming linear behavior, i.e. the ratio of pressure and velocity (the impedance) is independent of the amplitude. This leads to a very useful condition for the steady state: impedances of tube and excitation must match.

A general description of the excitation interacting with the resonating air column is given in Section A2. The resonating air column is described as a passive network of tubes, each having an impedance with a resistive and a reactive part. In Section A3 some recent increases in knowledge on the reactive part are presented. Section A4 deals with the resistive part of the tube input impedance, in particular with its non-

linear aspects. Section A5 describes additions to the descriptions of the excitation mechanisms. Section A6 shows how the knowledge can be applied in practice, for example for design and tuning.

As in the original book, most of the attention in the new text focuses on the interaction of excitation and air column. Section A7 deals with the remaining interactions and some new insights in that area.

A2. The air column and its excitation

In this and in the next four sections, the interactions of the resonating systems are restricted to those between the air column and its excitation. The lesser damped resonator of a system of two coupled resonators plays an important role in determining the resonance frequency. In a wind instrument, under normal playing conditions, this should be the air column, so the excitation must be sufficiently damped. On a clarinet, the reed is damped by the player's lip. Without this lip contact the reed goes into resonance resulting in the well-known squeal. On conical instruments (saxophone, oboe and bassoon), lip damping appears not to be necessary. Apparently the reed itself is more heavily damped than the tube; the instrument can be blown without the lips contacting the reed, although the note may be somewhat out of tune due to the absence of a correction related to lip position on the reed. For a saxophone, the much wider bore apparently brings the tube damping below that of the free reed. For double-reed instruments (oboe, bassoon), the damping of the relatively narrow bore will be large, but the double reed enclosing a small cavity with narrow openings will be damped more than the tube. Hirschberg (1995) remarks that the small tube entrance in conical double-reed instruments constitutes a Bernoulli-type resistance in series with the reed. This opening is comparable to that of the slit between the reeds when in open position.

Air oscillations in musical instruments can be

---

* References to the literature in the original book, listed on pages 98–102, are given in square brackets: []; references to new literature are given with the author's name and the publication year in parentheses: ().

studied in the frequency or in the time domain. The frequency domain gives information on the steady state, for sinusoidal signals, but also for other wave forms. The time domain is important when studying transient signals. For steady-state signals the results can be transformed from one domain into the other, using the fast Fourier transform (FFT) or its reciprocal.

A quick way to find the steady state resonance frequency, as done in Chapter 3, is to neglect losses and set the passive input impedance to zero or to infinity at the excitation, applying corrections thereafter. More information is obtained by calculating both real and imaginary parts of the input impedance of a woodwind over its entire frequency range (Plitnik and Strong 1979). This also allows for taking into account resonances in the tube sections between holes and in long holes (bassoon), which were neglected in Chapter 3.

A simplified but useful model of a woodwind instrument is a network of tube pieces (see Fig. A2.1). At position A, the acoustical admittance at the exit of the previous tube 3, $Y_{3,\text{out}}$, equals the sum of the input admittances of tube piece 1 and hole 2.

$$Y_{3,\text{out}} = Y_{1,\text{in}} + Y_{2,\text{in}}. \tag{A2.1}$$

The next step is to determine the input admittance of tube 3, $Y_{3,\text{in}}$, from its output admittance, $Y_{3,\text{out}}$, and its dimensions. Then for position B the procedure is re-

peated for tube piece 3 and hole 4. In this way we move up to the top of the instrument. Diameter variations in the bore can be accounted for in the same way: the hole is left out by setting its admittance to zero.

The effective acoustic dimensions of the tube pieces to be used in this model may differ somewhat from the geometrical dimensions. Although the changes in the reactive parts of the impedances are small, they cause perceptible changes in the resonance frequency of the combination. The differences can be accounted for in corrections, usually applied to the lengths. At least at low frequencies, these corrections are independent of frequency. To obtain the pertinent geometrical dimensions, the instruments have to be measured as accurately as possible, which may mean taking them apart. The accuracy and extent to which the dimensions and corrections need to be known depend on the required accuracy, determined by the (very sensitive) human ear. The human ear can detect frequency changes of approximately 0.2%, or 3 cents (Wier et al. 1977). This corresponds to a hole-length change of 7% (see Section 32e), which amounts to 0.5 mm for a hole of 8 mm length. The difference in end correction between a fully or zero flanged open end is 0.2 x 4 = 0.8 mm (cf. Fig. 38.2), which would generally correspond to a detectable difference in frequency. This shows that an accurate knowledge of geometric corrections is necessary for accurate frequency calculations. It can be expected to be one of the causes of the large scatter in the results in Chapter 4.

The next section reports on some of the recent advances in knowledge on the part of the geometrical corrections.

A3. The reactive component of the impedance

As was shown in Section 36, deviations of an ideal cylindrical or conical bore can be dealt with by describing the bore as a succession of cylinders and cones. Smooth bore perturbations can also be consid-

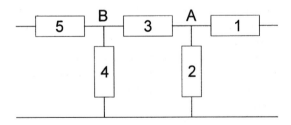

Fig. A2.1. Network representation of a woodwind with holes.

ered as local changes in compressibility and inertance of the ideal tube (Section 35; [98]). The effects are usually described as length corrections to the tube which are proportional to the volume of the perturbation. For abrupt changes in the bore, such as sudden diameter changes and side holes, this method fails. The changes in the compressibility remain accurately described by the volume change, but the inertance changes are less than proportional to the volume change since the flow does not fully penetrate the cavity or follow the diameter jump. Therefore, investigations of these perturbations mainly concern the magnitude of the inertance change. In most cases the Helmholtz number He (the length over which the perturbation has an influence on the sound field divided by the wavelength) is small compared to unity, at least at low frequencies. This simplifies the task of finding a solution, since the flow can be approximated by a conservative flow (a flow only caused by a potential difference) for which a Laplace equation is valid.

a. Corrections at and due to side holes

Where the hole joins the bore, two impedance corrections can be distinguished, one due to the local widening of the bore and one due to the adaptation of

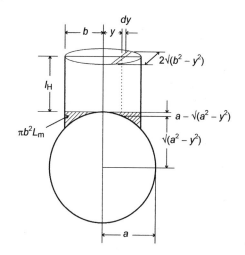

Fig. A3.2. Dimension definitions for a side hole in a cylindrical tube.

the flow from the bore into the hole entrance (internal "radiation"). The original asymmetrical model of Fig. 35.2 was improved by Keefe (1982a) by making it symmetrical; see Fig. A3.1 in which the extra impedances are shown enclosed in a rectangle.

As Keefe (1990) observed, the hole length l_H has to be corrected since its inner end is curved where it joins the bore (see Fig. A3.2). Denoting the bore radius by a and the hole radius by b, the extra length L_m due to this mismatch is found by integrating the hatched area over the hole width:

$$L_m = \frac{1}{\pi b^2} \int_{-b}^{+b} 2\sqrt{b^2 - y^2} \left(a - \sqrt{a^2 - y^2} \right) dy.$$

$$(A3.1)$$

The integral can be evaluated numerically; the results are plotted in Fig. A3.3. The fitting formula proposed by Keefe can be modified slightly to make it accurate to within ± 0.001:

$$L_m/b = (1 + 0.207 b^3/a^3) b/8a. \qquad (A3.2)$$

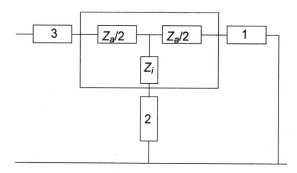

Fig. A3.1. Additional impedances in the more detailed side hole model, shown in the rectangle.

112

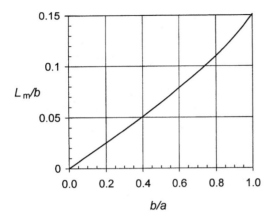

Fig. A3.3. Length correction coefficient L_m/b at the inside of the side hole due to the mismatch of the two cylinders.

The series impedance Z_a determines the effects due to the flow entering the side hole at a velocity antinode. In Section 35 a penetration factor ε was introduced, representing that part of the hole volume effectively used by the flow. Such a factor can be distinguished for a closed as well as an open hole; the values may not be the same.

In 1969, the knowledge on the correction impedances was limited to preliminary experimental results. Since then, Keefe published theory (1982a) and measurements (1982b). Coltman (1979) measured the total inertance of flute holes.

Keefe calculated Z_a and Z_i, using modal decomposition in three dimensions. The sum of a plain-wave mode and a number of evanescent modes were fitted into the tube and in the side tube. At both sides of the common boundary of the two fields, the pressure and the pressure gradient are the same. Some simplifications made in this common-boundary condition and a limited number of terms restricted the accuracy of Keefe's calculations. However, recently Dubos et al. (1998) repeated and extended this investigation.

Recently, the magnitude of the corrections was in-vestigated in two alternative ways (Nederveen et al. 1998). The first approach was approximating the three-dimensional flow by a stratified flow field consisting of thin two-dimensional flow slices in parallel. Calculations on two-dimensional flow are easy and very accurate. Conformal transformation (Schwarz-Christoffel) can be applied analytically or by using computer programs. Since cross-flow between the slices is neglected, the inertance thus obtained will be too high (Pierce 1989).

The second approach was dividing the inner space into small cubes and solving the Laplace equation by a finite difference method. The accuracy obtained is determined by the number of nodes in the network.

From both calculations it appeared that the length correction due to Z_a could be expressed as the product of a term with the cube of b/a and a coefficient F. This coefficient can be interpreted as that part of the radius of the hole that the flow effectively penetrates.

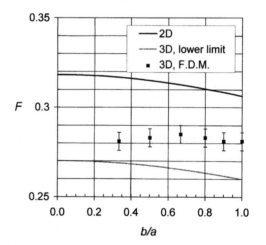

Fig. A3.4. Penetration coefficient F for a long side hole as a function of b/a for the two-dimensional case, the three-dimensional lower limit obtained from a stratified flow approximation and the three-dimensional values obtained by a finite difference calculation.

In Fig. A3.4 some results are plotted for F as a function of b/a, for a two-dimensional flow, for three-dimensional flow obtained from the stratified-flow approximation and by the finite difference method. The uncertainty of the latter method is indicated by error bars. It is caused by the limitation in the number of points (here 200000) due to the limitation of computer capacity at the time the investigations were carried out. A reasonable approximation for F is 0.282 over the whole range. Accuracy is insufficient to estimate the magnitude of a possible b/a dependence.

With this result, the length correction L_a to be applied to the tube length can be expressed as

$$L_a/a = -F(b/a)^3\cos^2 kL_R, \text{ where } F = 0.282 \pm 0.01 \,,$$
(A3.3)

where L_R is the distance to the open end or to a velocity antinode (see Section 35). The present penetration factor ε is 40% larger than the value used in eq.(35.4).

The results obtained for the internal length correction L_i to the hole where it joins the main tube are given in Fig. A3.5 as a function of b/a. Shown are results of the three-dimensional finite difference method. Making use of the fact that the limiting value of L_i for a small hole is the one for an infinite flange, the following formula fits the results reasonably well:

$$L_i/b = E_i = 0.82 - 1.4(b/a)^2 + 0.75(b/a)^{2.7} \,.$$
(A3.4)

The formula for E_i obtained by Benade from experimental data, eq.(38.3), appears to give somewhat higher values than eq.(A3.4).

Holes are sometimes undercut (see Fig. A3.6), a practice used for fine-tuning and (supposedly) reducing vortex losses at the sharp edges. This will cause modifications to the values given here. Indications of the effects of undercutting on tuning can be obtained by calculating the inertance assuming the flow to be stratified (see above) and by comparing the answers

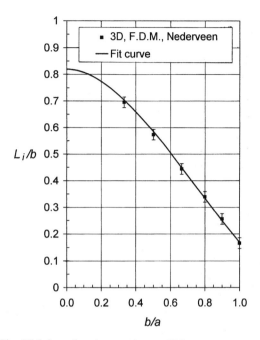

Fig. A3.5. Inner length correction coefficient L_i/b for a long side hole as a function of b/a obtained by a finite difference method, and an empirical fit-curve drawn through the points.

with the same approximation for straight holes. Instrument builders claim that the frequency ratios of successive modes shrink when the upstream side of the hole is undercut and stretch when the opposite is done. Upstream undercutting means displacing the flow splitting point upstream, which increases the length of the tube piece downstream of the splitting

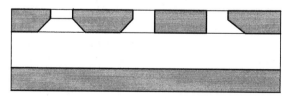

Fig. A3.6. Undercutting of holes, symmetrical (left), upstream (middle) or downstream (right).

point. Due to this, the acoustic length of this tube piece at higher modes will increase relative to that of the fundamental, as the tangent function in the tube impedance will deviate more strongly from its first-term approximation. This will raise the frequencies of the higher modes less than that of the fundamental. From calculations (carried out by the author but not described here) these effects appear to be small, but they might be significant for accurate tuning.

When the holes are short, as on flutes and saxophones, some simplifying assumptions are no longer valid. For a short open hole the inside and outside fields are influencing each other which modifies the shunt impedance. A short hole will be penetrated to a larger part: the penetration factor ε will be larger. This effect has been studied for a closed hole in two dimensions, applying two-dimensional conformal transformations. In Fig. A3.7 the dependence of F on the hole shape $l_H/2b$ (l_H = hole height or depth) for a closed hole is plotted. It can be observed that for very shallow holes the penetration approaches that of a smooth perturbation, for which $\varepsilon = 1$ (Rayleigh's formula [98]; see Section 35). The dashed line is a simple fitting formula, applicable for any hole size:

$$F \approx (2l_H/\pi b)\arctan(b/2l_H). \qquad (A3.5)$$

When holes are close together they may influence each other by mutual distortion of their near fields. The theoretical article on woodwind finger holes of Leppington (1982) formally considers mutual influences of two finger holes, but no applications are given. The effect was experimentally investigated by Keefe (1983), who found it to be negligible when the hole spacing d was larger than 1.5 times the hole diameter $2b$. A separate method for estimating the magnitude of internal interaction applies the two-dimensional conformal transformation, from which the author found that internal interactions are negligible when the holes are at mutual distances greater than the tube diameter.

When holes are very close together, for example when they are opposite each other in a tube, there could be an interaction. Its magnitude is estimated for two holes, either both open or both closed, of equal size opposite each other in a tube. For reasons of symmetry, the sound field will be symmetrical with respect to the center of the main tube. This can be considered as an effective reduction of the main tube diameter. An estimate of the effect of this reduction

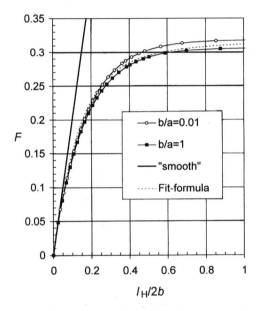

Fig. A3.7. Penetration coefficient F for a closed side hole as a function of the depth/width ratio $l_H/2b$, for two diameter/bore ratios. The dashed line is a fit-formula (see text). The straight line indicates the fictitious value for a perfectly smooth perturbation.

on the correction terms can be obtained from looking at the dependence of these terms on b/a. The penetration coefficient F, appearing in the series impedance, is hardly dependent on b/a (Fig. A3.4); no effects are expected here. The internal length correction L_i, however, is strongly dependent on b/a (Fig. A3.5). Assuming the dependency to be similar to the sloping part of the curve shown in Fig. A3.5, a halving of b/a increases the internal length correction by approximately $0.4b$. For an (open) flute hole this may add 25% to its effective length, which may amount to a tuning change of 12 cents (see Section 32e), which is sufficiently large to be perceptible.

For estimating the interaction of the external fields we use Pritchard's (1960) calculation of the radiation impedance Z_1 of a disk 1 in a rigid plane due to a vibrating disk 2. Both disks have the same radius b and their mutual distance is d. The radiation impedance of disk 1 is

$$Z_1 = Z_{11} + Z_{12}(u_2/u_1), \qquad (A3.6)$$

where

$$Z_{11} = R_{11} + jX_{11} = (\rho c/S)(k^2 b^2/2 + j0.82kb),$$

$$Z_{12} = (R_{11}/kd)(\sin kd + j\cos kd),$$

and

u_2/u_1 = ratio of disk velocities.

According to Pritchard, the expression for Z_{12} is an approximation valid for $kd < 1$ and $b/d < 1$. For low frequencies, $kd \ll 1$, so $Z_{12} = R_{11}(1+j/kd)$. Inserting this into the expression for Z_1 and considering only the reactive terms, which are responsible for the length correction, we find

$$\mathrm{Im}(Z_1) = X_1 = [1 + (b/1.6d)u_2/u_1]X_{11}. \qquad (A3.7)$$

In practice, d/b will seldom be smaller than 3, u_2/u_1 is about one-fourth, so the maximum value of the term between square brackets is 1.05. In this case the end correction change will be 5%, which may cause a length correction of the hole of 2%, which corresponds to a frequency change of 1 cent (0.06%), negligible in practice. We conclude that in nearly all realistic situations in woodwind instruments, the external mutual influences of holes can be neglected.

b. Flanges

At the open ends of tubes and holes, energy is radiated into the surroundings. The radiation impedance depends on size and shape of the flanging. Exact figures are available only for flat circular flanges and then only for one of zero size and one of infinite size. Most flanges on musical instruments are in between these extremes; besides, they are usually not flat. Section 38 describes the state of the art in 1969. Since then, additional work has been done. Ando (1969/1970) analytically investigated circular flanges in the range of the ratio of tube and flange radius, a/b, from 0.7 to 1. The accuracies of the results are restricted due to the limited number of terms in his expansion. Later, Bernard and Denardo (1996) checked the calculations and found an error for the value for $a/b = 0.85$. Triangles in Fig. A3.8 show the end correction coefficient E_f as a function of the diameter ratio, after fixing the error. Plotted in the same diagram are the coefficient according to Benade and Murday [21], eq.(38.2), and measurements by Peters et al. (1993). From measurements with flanged resonators with $a/b \approx 0.33$, Denardo and Bernard (1996) concluded that E_f probably is close to 0.82. Recent calculations by the author using a finite difference method are shown with circles, to which the following formula can be fitted:

$$E_f = L_f/a = 0.821 - 0.135(a/b) - 0.073(a/b)^4. \qquad (A3.8)$$

A key hanging above the hole gives an extra length correction Δl_d, for which Benade and Murday [21] experimentally obtained an expression (eq. 38.6). The coefficient $E_d = \Delta l_d/b$ is plotted in Fig.

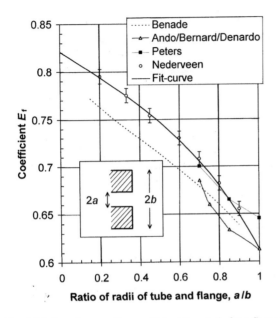

Fig. A3.8. Length correction coefficient $E_f = L_f/a$ for a flange as a function of the tube/flange diameter ratio. Results from various sources.

A3.9, together with measurements by Coltman (1979) and finite difference calculations by the author. Coltman's data were fitted vertically since values without key are not available. The approximate geometry of the holes is sketched in Fig. A3.9; the same geometry was used for Benade's and the author's calculations. As can be concluded, the results from these three sources are not contradictory. Historical measurements reported by Bouasse ([28], page 238, reprint 1986 by Blanchard, Paris) also fit reasonably well.

The author applied the same finite difference method to a perforated key. The coefficient E_d to be used in this situation is plotted in Fig. A3.10. Coltman's measurements (1979) correspond to these results.

The flange correction coefficient for a hole ending in a cylindrical surface, without a flattened end face, is given in Fig. A3.11, according to the experimental expression eq.(38.4) and according to results from the

finite difference method by the author. Note that the correction is to be applied to the farthest hole end, so the length l_H in Fig. 38.1 is incorrectly indicated.

Peters et al. (1993) report that end corrections increase at high acoustic velocities and decrease when a high, steady flow is superimposed on the acoustic flow. These effects may become important at high sound levels in wind instruments and may influence the tuning.

c. Total of open hole corrections

To recapitulate, the total effective (or acoustic) length of an open hole of geometrical length l_H is

$$L_H = l_H + L_i + L_m + L_r. \qquad (A3.9)$$

L_r is the length correction due to radiation, which may consist of the correction for a circular or cylindrical flange and for a key.

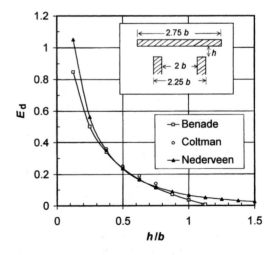

Fig. A3.9. Length correction coefficient $E_d = \Delta l_d/b$ due to a key hanging a distance h above a hole of diameter $2b$. Shown are experimental results of Benade and Coltman and theoretical results by Nederveen obtained with a finite difference method.

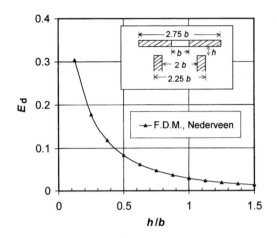

Fig. A3.10. Same as Fig. A3.9 for a *perforated* key.

For very short holes, inside and outside fields influence each other; the expressions are no longer exactly valid. However, errors may be within acceptable limits. This appears from applying the formulas to the (short) flute holes for which Coltman (1979) did measurements: it appears that eq.(A3.9) predicts the effective lengths measured by Coltman to within ± 5%.

d. Diameter jumps

At discontinuities in the bore, apart from the correction due to changes in the diameter (see Section 36), an extra inertance occurs at the diameter jump. The substitution circuit is equal to that of Fig. A3.1, without the hole impedance 2. The effects are largest at a velocity antinode, where the flow is highest. In the extreme case of a narrow tube passing into a very wide one, the correction will be equal to the end correction for a flanged tube. When the diameter ratio tends to unity, this "internal radiation" correction gradually reduces to zero. The magnitude of the extra inertia was calculated by Karal [64] for the "plane piston" approximation. Kergomard and Gar-

cia (1987) removed this restriction and obtained results for the real situation. As expected (Pierce 1989), their numbers are somewhat lower than Karal's numbers. The results are expressed in polynomials of the a/b (the ratio of the radii) and of the wave number, making them valid for high frequencies too. For low frequencies the following formula for the length correction L_J is useful:

$$L_J/a = E_J \cos^2 kL_R, \qquad (A3.10)$$

$$E_J = 0.82 - 1.1\,(a/b) + 0.28\,(a/b)^{3.5},$$

where L_R is the distance to the open end or to a velocity antinode and a and b are the radii of the small and the large tube, respectively. In Fig. A3.12 both the Kergomard and Garcia results for low frequencies and the fit-formula are plotted as a function of a/b. The curves coincide closely enough for practical purposes.

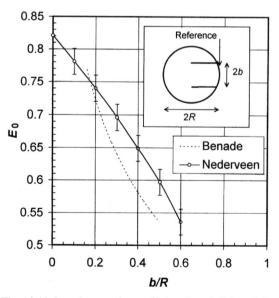

Fig. A3.11. Length correction coefficient $E_0 = L_0/b$ for a hole ending in a cylindrical flange.

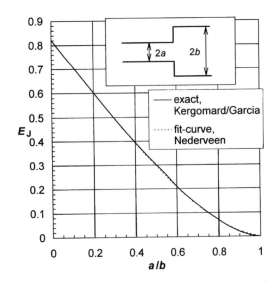

Fig. A3.12. Length correction coefficient $E_J = L_J/a$ in a velocity antinode for a diameter jump, as a function of the ratio a/b of the tube radii. Exact curve according to Kergomard and Garcia (1987).

The expression can also be used when calculating the inertance of a hole covered by a perforated key. The coverage consists of two cylindrical holes with different diameters in series.

e. Toroidal bends

Various studies have appeared as a result of the correction proposed in Section 37 to the inertance in a toroidal bend, among others Rostafinski (1972), Brindley (1973), Cummings (1974) and Keefe and Benade (1983). Keefe and Benade remarked that the transition of torus to cylinder causes an additional inertia. Reported measurements of the effects, though roughly confirming theory, are insufficiently accurate to verify details.

Nederveen has reported on differences and correspondences of these studies (1996) and will publish this in more detail (Nederveen 1998). Calculations were carried out along the same lines as was done for the side holes, first using two-dimensional conformal transformation, then mimicking the three-dimensional flow field by two-dimensional slices and finally by finite difference approximations in three dimensions. All earlier theoretical results on the torus were confirmed. The magnitude of the length correction in a velocity antinode due to the extra inertia at the transition of cylinder to torus, as obtained from the various calculations, is plotted in Fig. A3.13. The correction is given as a fraction of the bore radius, as a function of the bend curvature parameter $B = r_0/R_0$. Keefe and Benade's measurement is also inserted. Considering the difficulties of measuring this small high-order effect, the correspondence with theory is not unsatisfactory.

Coltman (1984) and Laszewski and Murray (1984) investigated the effects on the sound power and tone color of a flute with a "recurved" head (see Fig.

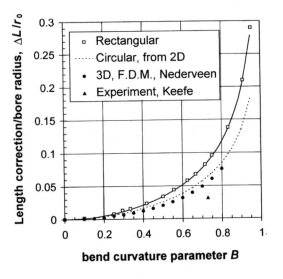

Fig. A3.13. Correction for the tore-to-cylinder transition in a velocity antinode, for various geometries and methods of determination.

A3.14). The inside sound pressure did not change by replacing a straight head by a recurved one. The radiated sound underwent changes due to a greater proximity of the two sound sources of the instrument (the embouchure hole and the tone hole), which may reinforce or weaken each other, depending on the mode. This effect was calculated as well as measured. The changes were on the order of ± 3 dB and were quite perceptible in listening experiments.

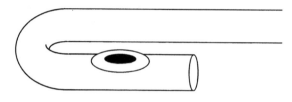

Fig. A3.14. Sketch of a "recurved" head joint of the flute, where a toroidal part connects two cylinders.

f. The ideal bore

The effects of all sorts of deviations from the simple bore have been studied. An important question is, which bore gives the ideal tuning? At first sight, the best bores to give pure harmonics are the ones closest to the purely cylindrical or conical; in modern instruments a trend toward this can be observed. However, some bore deviations appear to be functional. The slightly widened upper part of the clarinet stretches the frequency spacing of modes, thereby compensating for "mode shrinkage" due to closed holes (cf. D_V in Fig. 44.12). In flutes and piccolos, "mode stretching" results from the reduced bore in the upper part of the instrument (cf. D_{bore} in Fig. 44.5). A cylindrical flute has a conical head, a conical flute a cylindrical head. The reduced bore compensates the mode shrinkage due to increasing coverage of the mouth hole with frequency (Coltman 1990). Coltman found the bore-induced stretch to be larger on conical pic-

colos than on cylindrical ones, which explains differences in ease of playing and tone quality of the two types of piccolo. Lower notes are easier to play on a conical instrument, higher notes easier on a cylindrical one.

On the oboe, near the top, we sometimes find that the cone angle in the upper part of the instrument is slightly increased, in the way sketched in Fig. A3.15. Kergomard (1988) and Dalmont et al. (1995) have shown that this modification helps the higher resonances to remain harmonic up to higher frequencies. This can be understood as follows. In the resonance condition eq.(27.2) the term containing the mouthpiece volume V approximately compensates the second term in the power series expansion of $\tan(w_0 - W_0)$. The increased cone angle near the top introduces a term which compensates the third term in this expansion.

The bores of baroque instruments seem to mock the mathematically dictated preference for a simple bore. Their ragged bores seem to be the product of sloppy workmanship. However, when an instrument builder tries to rationalize it or is faced with the task of building a similar instrument in another key, the seemingly meaningless irregularities appear to be important for tuning and blowing the instrument. To my

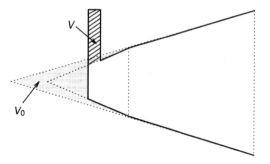

Fig. A3.15. Succession of cones giving improved mode purity in a conical instrument.

120

knowledge there are no studies which have unveiled a possible concept behind those irregular bores.

Apparently, the simplest bore is not the only solution to a pure tuning. There are other solutions delivering harmonically tuned resonances. This is proved by a peculiar design for conical instruments (Dalmont and Kergomard 1994): the cone is replaced by a series of n cylinders with increasing diameter according to a certain pattern (Fig. A3.16). Theory and measurements show that this combination has a series of

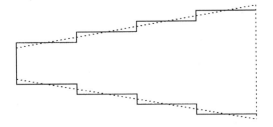

Fig. A3.16. Saxophone made of successive cylinders.

harmonically tuned resonances, except that "harmonic" number $n + 1$, and multiples thereof, are missing. Note that the clarinet, where $n = 1$, fits in this picture: the clarinet has no even harmonics. A model of this "Dalmontphone", built by J.-P. Dalmont, with a cylindrical-lattice bore having the mean conicity of a saxophone can be blown with a regular saxophone mouthpiece and sounds like a saxophone.

A4. The resistive component of the impedance

For a smooth cylindrical tube, the theoretical magnitude of the damping term (in SI units) at room temperature is $\alpha' = 0.21 \times 10^{-3} k^{-1/2} a^{-1}$ (see Section 22); this value has been verified by measurements on smooth tubes and low sound levels [44, 106, 111]. For noncylindrical tubes, thermal and viscous losses have to be kept separated, for example as was done for conical tubes in Section 23. Kergomard (1981) and Caussé

et al. (1984) also considered other shapes and experimentally verified the theory for these shapes.

At sharp edges of holes, reeds and mouthpieces and at sharp entrances of narrow tubes, vortices can form. These cause extra damping (Benade 1976). Rounding the edges reduces the losses. Rounding of reed edges in double-reed instruments and of edges of narrow tube entrances has been found to influence playing: such smoothing reduces the contraction of the free jet and consequently the turbulent dissipation losses (Hirschberg et al. 1994). In Section 22, the extra losses, although nonlinear, were accounted for as a 60% increase in the damping term α' for all situations and instruments. This is a simplification. Backus [7] and Nederveen et al. (1995) reported the damping to be dependent on a superimposed steady air flow. Coltman [38] found the losses to be dependent on the sound pressure level: at a typical level in a flute of the root-mean-square pressure $p_{rms} = 210$ Pa [or $20 \log(p_{rms}/20\mu\text{Pa}) = 140$ dB] the increase was 50%. Coltman ascribed this to nonlinear losses as observed by Ingard and Ising [55] for a series diaphragm. Taking $\alpha' kl = 0.06$ (Section 22), the velocity in a velocity antinode is $u = p/\rho c \alpha' kl = 9$ m/s. In the embouchure hole, which is smaller than the bore, the particle velocity will be higher.

In reed-blown instruments the sound level can be much higher than in the flute. At a blowing pressure of 4 kPa (40 cm water gauge) and with a beating reed, p_{rms} in the tube will be approximately 2 kPa, or 160 dB. The velocity in a velocity antinode then is 90 m/s. At these high velocities, the acoustical boundary layer will be turbulent, giving nonlinear damping (Stuhlträger and Thomann 1986). The dynamic air velocity in the reed slit, as calculated from the Bernoulli expression $\Delta p = \rho u^2/2$, may be as high as $\sqrt{(2\Delta p/\rho)} \approx 60$ m/s; the steady component of this velocity is spread out over the much wider bore of the instrument, resulting in a steady velocity of about 1 m/s in the tube.

The pressure drop over a constriction is given by $\Delta p = \rho u^2/2$. Ingard and Ising [55] performed measurements for a series constriction and found this to be approximately true, also for dynamically varying flows. The in-phase part of the ratio of pressure and velocity, or the resistive term of the specific acoustic impedance, for sinusoidal pressure fluctuations is about ρu. For a side hole, similar effects can be expected. For a hole of length $H = 10$ mm, the resistive term becomes comparable to the reactive one ($= \omega \rho H$) at velocities of 10 m/s, which corresponds to the above-mentioned value experimentally found by Coltman. It means that at much higher sound levels the resistive term due to flow acceleration in a hole is larger than the reactive term. As mentioned above, rounding the edges (undercutting, see Fig. A3.6) smoothes the transition and can reduce the losses, to the benefit of the instrument.

Ingard and Ising also investigated the situation where a steady flow is superimposed over an oscillative one. They found that a satisfactory description of the phenomena is obtained by assuming a quasi-static approximation for the resistance; this means that the resistance at every moment is determined by the Bernoulli pressure drop.

To estimate the influence of the pressure-dependent term in the impedance of a woodwind, we calculated the real part of the input impedance and the resonance frequency as a function of the resistive term of a side hole for a model clarinet according to Fig.

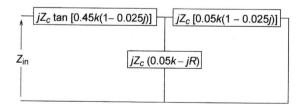

Fig. A4.1. Model used for calculating the influence of the non-linear resistive term of the side hole impedance.

A4.1. Its tube is approximately 50 cm long, and a hole is situated at about 5 cm from the open end. For simplicity, the right hand tube piece and the hole are assumed to be short with respect to the wavelength and to have the same reactance. Fig. A4.2 shows the real part of the input impedance and the resonance frequency when the resistive part R of the side hole is varied over 5 decades. The impedance goes through a minimum, whereas the resonance frequency gradually decreases. At very high R the tube behaves as if the hole were closed.

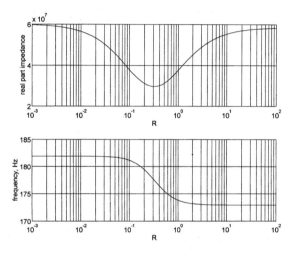

Fig. A4.2. Real part of the input impedance and resonance frequency as a function of the real part R of the side-hole impedance, calculated with the model of Fig. A4.1.

This may explain peculiar phenomena observed with very small holes. For instance, opening the tiny hole on the crook of a bassoon changes the spectrum considerably, as determined by theoretical calculations as well as by measurements of the input impedance. When playing, however, there is no change when the hole is opened (Cronin and Keefe 1996). A similar phenomenon can be observed for a specially built clarinet-like tube with unusually short and small holes, but such that the input impedances (calculated as well as measured) are the same as those of the normal holes (Keefe 1983). With the holes open, this clarinet sounds very softly. However, when blown very forcefully, the holes act as if closed. This corresponds to the predictions from Fig. A4.2. The behavior of the pipe can be changed by changing the excitation impedance. For instance, it can be lowered by using a weaker reed, with the result that the maximum sound level for soft blowing has increased.

One can wonder whether the great loudness difference between a saxophone and a clarinet could be explained by the larger losses in the smaller clarinet holes. For example, in the smallest of the saxophone family, the sopranino, a loudness difference of 8 to 10 dB is observed. Inner wall area, mouthpiece, reed, reed slit and blowing pressure in both instruments are approximately the same (Fig. A4.3). Different are only bore shapes and hole sizes: a clarinet is cylindrical, a saxophone conical, the holes of a saxophone are shorter and wider than those of a clarinet. However, as will be shown in Section A5, the bore shape can explain most of the observed loudness difference.

Inside the instrument steady and oscillating flows may interact. Analogous to the oscillating jet flow which excites a flute, a downstream steady flow in the pipe can oscillate across a side hole entrance and can be coupled to air oscillations in the tube. This will occur when the phase shift has the proper value, which is the case when the Strouhal number ($St = fL/u$, f = frequency, L = characteristic length, u = velocity) is around 0.3 (Ingard and Singhal 1976; Bruggeman 1987; Kriesels et al. 1995). This effect is probably not very important in a woodwind; for at a typical steady velocity u of 1 m/s and for a hole diameter (or length) of 7 mm the interaction would occur at a frequency of 40 Hz, which is outside the playing range.

Although the explanation of the anomalous behavior of small holes as given here seems qualitatively acceptable, particulars and details need to be verified by measurements on realistic geometries. Introductory investigations were reported by Nederveen et al. (1995).

A5. The excitation mechanism

a. Flute excitation

Many authors have studied the interaction between the sound field in the pipe and the air jet under various assumptions. Without being exhaustive, the list given in Section 24 may be extended with Coltman (1976 and 1992b), Fletcher (1976), Schumacher (1978a), Schlosser (1979), Yoshikawa and Saneyoshi (1980), Thwaites and Fletcher (1980 and 1982),

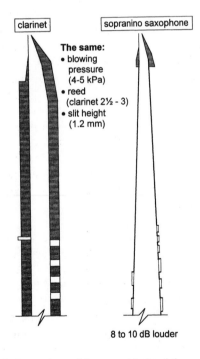

Fig. A4.3. Comparison of the geometrical and the acoustical properties of two similar instruments.

Fletcher and Rossing (1991), Nolle and Finch (1992), Verge et al. (1994), and Hirschberg (1995). Despite much theoretical and experimental effort there still is no satisfactory quantitative description of the flute excitation. Such a description is far from simple: in principle, it should encompass all the interactions of the sound field with the jet during its entire travel across the mouth hole. Some semi-empirical formulas are moderately successful. Apparently, further research is necessary.

In the description of the flute excitation given in Section 24, the transverse acceleration of the moving jet particles was ascribed to an (oscillating) pressure gradient of the acoustic field. This gives the jet a sinusoidal shape of constant amplitude propagating in the direction of the labium with a velocity equal to the jet particle velocity. With the proper time delay the jet enters the tube, compensating for the losses of the oscillation. However, this insufficiently describes reality: experiments show that the lateral displacement is amplified during its travel, propagates with approximately half the air particle speed and may be accompanied by vortices (Cremer and Ising [41]; Fabre et al. 1996). This type of motion is better described with models of the propagation of jet disturbances. Powell [95] states that "it is generally agreed by experimenters that the stream disturbances of jets originate at the nozzle". Conforming to this observation, such models consider the jet deflection after interaction with a single acoustic parameter at the position where the flow exits the flue slit ("nozzle").

The interacting parameter can be the displacement, the particle velocity, the pressure gradient or a combination of these. The parameter determines a distortion of the jet at its origin; this distortion is amplified when it travels toward the downstream edge with about half the velocity of the jet particle. During this travel the phase of the acoustic oscillation in the pipe shifts with respect to that of the distortion. At least part of the injected flow must be in phase with the oscillations in the tube to compensate for the losses in the tube. Out-of-phase flow shifts the tube resonance up or down. Coltman (1992a) remarked that the three types of drive show marked differences in magnitudes, phases and frequency dependencies of the impedances. When the particle velocity is u, the acoustic displacement is $u/j\omega$ and the pressure gradient $j\omega\rho u$.

Experiments have been indecisive. From measurements, Coltman (1992b) concluded that either the pressure gradient or the velocity was to be preferred, depending on what aspect of the coupling was considered. Fletcher and Rossing (1991) and Verge et al. (1994) favored a displacement-coupling model.

The impedance generated by the flute excitation has a certain value. This value can be approximately calculated for a simplified displacement-controlled model — resembling the one described by Powell [95] and Fletcher and Rossing (1991) — which is in fact based on Rayleigh's description of jet behavior ([98], volume 2, page 376). In this model, the amplitude of the displacement of the jet arriving at the labium, due to a disturbance at the flue slit, is assumed to be G times the absolute value of the acoustic displacement at the flue slit, $u_E/j\omega$, in which u_E is the particle velocity, assumed to be equal to the mean particle velocity over the area of the embouchure hole. This particle velocity is related to the pressure p_E by $u_E = p_E/S_E Z_E$, where Z_E is the mouth hole impedance and S_E the mouth hole area. It is assumed that the jet displacement has the proper phase when it reaches the labium. The real part of the jet flow, injected into the tube, is given by $U_j' = VBGu_E/\omega$, where V is the jet speed and B the width of the flue slit. Combining the formulas, the jet admittance is found to be $Y_j' = U_j'/p_E = VBG/\omega S_E Z_E$. The mouth impedance is $Z_E = j\omega\rho\Delta L/S_E$, where ΔL denotes the end correction of the mouth hole. This end correction is taken by Fletcher (1976) to be $1.3\,r_E$, where r_E is the effective radius of the mouth hole.

The factor 1.3 is a value for a flue pipe; it will be different for a flute, but it suffices for a qualitative treatment. Using this end correction, the real part of the jet admittance is

$$Y'_j = \frac{VBG}{\rho\omega^2 1.3 r_E} . \qquad (A5.1)$$

Inserting the following typical numerical values, $V = 10$ m/s, $B = 5$ mm, $\omega = 2000$ s^{-1}, $r_E = 5$ mm, $G = 10$, the real part of the jet admittance becomes 1.6×10^{-5} m^{4}s/kg, which is within the range of passive input impedances of a flute (cf. Fig. A6.3). By adjusting V, B and r_E, the jet admittance can be adjusted to that of the tube. The range of the adjustment determines the range of admittances which can be excited.

Linearized models are adequate for a qualitative description and an approximate prediction of the frequency. There is, however, more to a musical instrument than this stable-amplitude, mono-frequency generator system. The character of a musical instrument is determined by its harmonic composition, its initial transient (important for its recognition [108, 109]) and its non-stabilities (fluctuations in amplitude, frequency and harmonic content). Some of these aspects are partly at the control of the player, but they also are partly chaotic, because of the large number of variables interacting.

Conclusions or numerical values obtained with a sinusoidal signal cannot be expected to be realistic because in actual playing the signals are far from sinusoidal. For example, at the mouth hole, the pressure wave form is nearly a square and the velocity wave form nearly a triangular function of time (Coltman 1976). There are mathematical models and simulations explaining this (Schlosser 1979; McIntyre et al. 1983; Coltman 1992a).

The initial transient is important not only for its influence on the character of an instrument but also for its practical role; in some instruments certain notes are difficult to start, though the note may be very stable once started. This may be related to a difference in the excitation conditions of initial transient and steady state.

For jet-excited instruments the rise time of the blowing pressure has an important influence on the harmonic composition of the attack transient. Experiments of Nolle and Finch (1992) on flue organ pipes have shown that for a very short, fast-rising blowing pressure (rise time less than one period of the fundamental oscillations) and for a long and smoothly rising pressure (10 periods or more), the fundamental dominates the attack. For in-between rise times, the second mode (the second harmonic for an open, or the third harmonic for a closed pipe) tends to dominate the attack. This was confirmed by computer simulations. Verge (1995, page 201) found similar behavior. The higher modes (above the second) as present in the 'precursor' (a brief oscillation which may proceed the remainder of the attack transient) Nolle and Finch ascribe to oscillations in the cross dimension of the pipe near the mouth.

From measurements on organ pipes, Angster and Miklos (1992) found that the harmonics composition of the attack transient depended on the (cross) dimensions of the pipe. When harmonics fitted in the cross dimension, they were influenced.

Under certain conditions, it is possible to start a flue pipe in its third mode instead of its first, as reported by Kokkelmans (1995) and Kokkelmans and Wijnands (1996) for the peculiarly shaped Rohrfloete (or reed-flute; see [50], page 206). This flute is a closed organ pipe with a small doubly open chimney in its closed cap (Fig. A5.1). The chimney is tuned to the fifth harmonic. In the lower part of the figure, measurements are shown of the signal outside the pipe with the chimney in the middle position. The blowing pressure rose gradually over about 5 periods of the steady state mode. The initial transient can be seen to contain mainly the fifth harmonic. When the

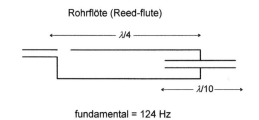

Rohrflöte (Reed-flute)

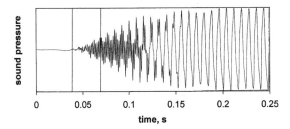

fundamental = 124 Hz

Fig. A5.1. Sketch of the Rohrfloete and its pressure signal, outside the tube.

chimney is positioned in or out of the cap, this effect disappears: then the fundamental dominates in the attack transient.

Coltman (1992a), using a time domain simulation for a flute, observed that the amount of stretching of the 'harmonics' had a significant influence on the harmonic content of the signal and the blowing pressure at which the instrument switches into a higher vibrational mode.

b. Reed excitation

An amendment has to be made to the description of the reed slit resistance as given in Section 25. Extensive measurements by Gilbert (1991) did not confirm Backus' results [6] that the velocity dependence of the pressure drop in the slit followed a power of 1.5 rather than 2. Gilbert found the pressure drop through the slit of a single reed (within the measurement accuracy) to be dependent on the velocity in the same way as that of a double reed; namely, it also

followed Bernoulli's law, i.e. $\Delta p = \rho u^2/2$. This simplifies the algebra, making it identical for both single and double reed(s). Setting $q = 2$ and $E = \rho/2$ and neglecting correction factors due to geometry, the equation for the real part of the "excitation" impedance (obtained from eq. 25.12) can be rewritten, using eqs. (25.7) and (25.8) to eliminate h_0 and U_0, into

$$Z'_E = \frac{\sqrt{2\rho P}}{B(2C_t P - H)}.$$ (A5.2)

Experiments by Wilson and Beavers (1974) have shown this rather simple theoretical expression to be approximately correct. In Fig. A5.2 the excitation impedances, as calculated with eq.(A5.2), are plotted as a function of mouth pressure P for various sets of

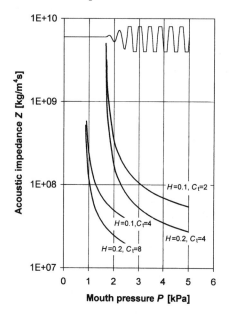

Fig. A5.2. Impedance generated by a 12 mm wide reed as a function of blowing pressure at various values of slit height H (in mm) and reed compliance C_t (in 10^{-8} m/Pa). The corresponding typical reed displacement is indicated at the top of the diagram.

parameters H and C_t for a B = 12 mm wide reed. For reeds of other widths, the vertical scale must be adapted. The diagram shows the possibilities of adjusting the excitation impedance to that of a (cylindrical) tube. The reed moves "sinusoidally" at mouth pressures between one-third and one-half of the maximum pressure; "beating" starts at pressures larger than one-half the maximum value (Kergomard 1995). When beating, the reed closes the aperture (although it will not suddenly stop, it will bend inward), and a transition toward square waves occurs. The upper curve in Fig. A5.2 schematically visualizes the reed motion in the two regimes.

Worman (1971, Appendix A) calculates the magnitude of the Bernoulli forces which supposedly influence the balance of forces on the reed. In a single reed, with its relatively short slit, these forces are negligible, but in a double reed, with its relatively long and narrow slit, they would have to be dealt with. Schumacher (1981) and Barjau and Agullo (1989) included these forces in their models. However, Hirschberg et al. (1990) argued that the magnitude of Bernoulli forces on the walls is unknown and questionable, and if they are present they even could have the opposite sign as proposed by Worman.

The description of double-reed action on narrowbored instruments such as the oboe and bassoon is complicated by the additional pressure drop which will occur at the neck at the narrow entrance of the tube (Hirschberg 1995; Wijnands and Hirschberg 1995). The effect can be substantial: the area of this neck can be smaller than the area between the open reed tips.

Sketched in Fig. A5.3 is the shape of the reed pressure (or the displacement, which is approximately alike) as measured as a function of time (Backus [3]; Rocaboy 1989; Dalmont and Kergomard 1995; Gokhshtein 1982 and 1995) for cylindrical and conical instruments at large amplitudes. On a clarinet, the beating reed closes the aperture for about 50% of the

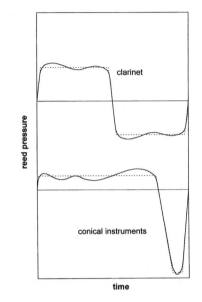

Fig. A5.3. Pressure across the reed for a beating clarinet reed (above) and a reed on conical instruments (below).

time. On conical instruments (single as well as double reed) the closing percentage is less than 50%, in fact approximately equal to the relative truncation of the cone: r_0/R_1 (r_0 = truncation length, R_1 = length of the tube to the apex). Explanations are given by Rockaboy (1989) and Gokhshtein (1982 and 1995). The reasoning is as follows.

First consider the reed action on the cylindrical clarinet tube. When the reed is open, a compression pulse travels down the tube. At the open end it is reflected as a rarefaction, which closes the reed when it returns. Reflected at the now closed end as a rarefaction, it returns as a compression and reopens the reed. This makes the total traveling distance 4 times the tube length, which corresponds to a quarter wavelength. In a conical tube, the time a compression needs to return as a rarefaction is the same as in a clarinet, also two times the tube length. When the reed is closed, a resonator is formed, composed of the compliance of the cavity in the mouthpiece and the impedance of the conical tube. The tube impedance is calculated from the ratio of the pressure of an outgoing propagating wave in the cone $p = (1/r)\exp(j\omega t - jkr)$ and the volume velocity calculated from the pressure by $U = S(-j/\omega\rho)\partial p/\partial r$. The value of this impedance at the tube entrance, where $r = r_0$, is

$$Z_0 = (\rho c/S_0)/(1 + 1/jkr_0) , \qquad (A5.3)$$

where S_0 is the cross-sectional area at the tube entrance. For a long tube, the truncation r_0 is small, $1/kr_0$ is large as compared to unity and the expression for the input impedance can be approximated by $Z = j\omega L$, where $L = \rho r_0/S_0$ is an inertance. The optimum volume of the mouthpiece cavity for a cone was shown in Section 27 to be $S_0 r_0/3$, which has a compliance of $C = S_0 r_0/3\rho c^2$. The resonance frequency of the inertance/compliance combination then is

$$f = (1/2\pi)(1/LC)^{1/2} = (\sqrt{3}/2\pi)c/r_0 \approx c/4r_0 . \qquad (A5.4)$$

After a half-oscillation, the rarefaction has become a compression which reopens the reed. The time for a half-oscillation is $2r_0/c$, which equals the time a pulse would need to travel to the fictitious apex and back. So the ratio between closing and opening time of the reed equals the ratio of truncation to tube length.

As was mentioned in Section 54, the saxophone is much louder than the clarinet. It can be shown that differences in bore and in reed behavior can offer an explanation.

When the dimensions of the radiating open end of a wind instrument are small with respect to the wavelength, it can be approximated by an oscillating sphere. The volume velocity produced by a sphere, U_s, causes a pressure level p_{far} at a distance r_{far} proportional to the volume velocity (Pierce 1989, page 155):

$$p_{far} = \rho\omega U_s/4\pi r_{far} . \qquad (A5.5)$$

Therefore, comparing loudnesses boils down to comparing radiated volume velocities. The radiated volume velocity is related by the acoustic pressure in the top of the instrument, p_E, through the so-called transfer admittance $Y_T = U_s/p_E$. For a cylinder this admittance is obtained from eq.(13.10), setting $kx = m\pi/2$ (m odd) and eq.(13.11), setting $kx = 0$, and $\psi = 0$ in both equations. This gives the expression

$$|Y_T| = \pi a_s^2/\rho c , \qquad (A5.6)$$

where a_s is the radius of the tube where it radiates into the surroundings. For a conical tube, from eqs. (23.1), (23.5) and (23.10) it is found

$$|Y_T| = \pi a_E a_s/\rho c \sin kL_1 , \qquad (A5.7)$$

where a_E is the tube radius at the embouchure. Note that the formula reduces to the one for the clarinet, eq. (55.6), after setting $a_E = a_s$ and $\sin kL_1 = 1$. Note that losses do not appear in the expressions. The quantity $a_E a_s$ may be called the "logarithmic mean" section of the cone. When cone and cylinder have the same logarithmic mean section, the difference in transfer admittance is determined by $\sin kL_1$. For example, for a cone where $r_0/R_1 = 0.2$, its value is approximately 0.3, which means a difference in transfer admittance of $20 \log(1/0.3) = 10$ dB. For other notes this difference will take on another value because the truncation and the logarithmic mean diameter are different. Measurements have confirmed that the expression is essentially correct (Dalmont and Nederveen 1997).

Another cause of difference is the power produced in the mouthpiece of the instrument which depends on the local acoustic pressure p_E. The source of this acoustic pressure is the mouth pressure P (supposed constant). Consider the case of high level sound production, where the mouthpiece pressure waveform is close to rectangular. The pressure alternates between a positive value p_+ and a negative value p_-. The duration of the two states are the same for clarinet, but for a saxophone the positive state is (L_1/r_0) as long as the negative state (Fig. A5.3). Since the mean value of the pressure is zero, for a clarinet, $p_- = -p_+$, but for a saxophone, $p_- = -(L_1/r_0)p_+$. This means that the power produced in the mouthpiece is proportional to p_+^2 for the clarinet and $(L_1/r_0)p_+^2$ for the saxophone. For the same cone as above, this is a difference of $10 \log 4 = 6$ dB. This is confirmed by measurements by Dalmont and Nederveen (1997), where values of 4 ± 2 dB were found, for both clarinet and saxophone. In the same study, p_+ was found less than the mouth pressure P by about 4 ± 2 dB. The latter figure also can be deduced from results in theoretical studies (Gilbert et al. 1989; Schumacher 1978b; Kergomard 1995).

As anybody who has once observed pressures in woodwinds will know, pressure signals in woodwind instruments can take any shape. They are seldom purely sinusoidal or purely rectangular; in conical instruments the closure-open cycle can even be inverted. Consequently these calculations are only indicative. They indicate that the total loudness difference between a saxophone and a clarinet is $10 + 4 = 14$ dB. This will only be a rough estimate, but it approximately corresponds to the experimental findings.

When we want to investigate the initial transient and the harmonic composition we have to use more elaborate models of the reed excitation. A set of three equations has to be solved. They will be given here in a simplified form. The first equation is the equation of motion of the reed, eq.(25.1). It is completed with a term for the reed mass m, h_0 is left out and eq.(25.15) is used to introduce P_{max}. This gives the expression

$$C_t(p - P + P_{max}) = h + \tau\, dh/dt + m\, d^2h/dt^2. \quad \text{(A5.8)}$$

The equation for the slit entering the tube consists of the slit flow U_{sl} and the reed motion flow U_r. The length correction caused by the reed motion flow is estimated in Section 26 to be between 6 and 9 mm. This corresponds quite well with the experimentally obtained values of between 5 and 13 mm by Dalmont et al. (1995). The slit flow is found from eq.(25.2), simplified by disregarding M, h_0 and U_0, taking $q = 2$ and $E = \rho/2$ and introducing h from eq.(A5.8), neglecting τ and m. Benade (1976) confirmed this expression by static measurements. The flow entering the tube is

$$U = U_{sl} + U_r = BC_t(p - P + P_{max})[2(P - p)/\rho]^{0.5} - S_r\, dh/dt. $$

$$\text{(A5.9)}$$

Most studies assume a position-independent reed stiffness, which is an oversimplification at higher amplitudes. However, the errors induced may be restricted: measurements of Boutillon and Gibiat (1996) showed that the stiffness during playing is not very different from the value statically measured.

For studies in the frequency domain, the tube properties are defined from the input impedance $Z(\omega) = p(\omega)/U(\omega)$. For studies in the time domain one can use

$$p(t) = G(t) * U(t) = \int_0^\infty G(t')U(t - t')dt', \quad \text{(A5.10)}$$

where $*$ stands for the convolution operation and $G(t)$ is the impulse response function, the inverse Fourier transform of the input impedance of the tube in which the reed is replaced by a closed wall. Alternatively, an expression containing the reflection function $r(t)$ may be used. The reflection function formalism is based on the impulse response of the pipe anechoically terminated at the excitation side (McIntyre et al. 1983).

For studies in the frequency domain, the various functions can be expanded in power series, resulting in conditions for the amplitudes and phase angles of the harmonic components (Worman 1971; Schumacher 1978b; Gilbert et al. 1989; Worman et al. 1990; Kergomard 1995; and Grand et al. 1997). All authors restrict the analysis to three harmonics, which seems to be a practical limit. Since a beating reed generates many higher harmonics, the applications of this method seem limited. Gilbert et al. (1989) showed that the method they employ ("harmonic balance") is accurately predicting steady-state frequencies with a sampling frequency (reciprocal of time domain resolution) rate of only 8 kHz.

In the time domain, the set of differential equations is approximated by difference equations which are solved advancing in the time with sufficiently small steps. A clear overview is given in the tutorial paper by McIntyre et al. (1983). The input impedance can be calculated from the dimensions or obtained from measurements. Sometimes, computational time can be saved by using the reflection function instead of the impulse response function. Keefe (1996) and Sharp et al. (1996) reported the direct measurement of the impulse response function.

Various authors have carried out modeling, using various procedures to solve the equations and studying various aspects: Stewart and Strong (1980), Schumacher (1978b and 1981), McIntyre et al. (1983), Sommerfeldt and Strong (1988), Gazengel et al. (1995) and Ayers (1996). Barjau and Agulló (1989) modeled a double reed on a cone, using a deformation-dependent reed stiffness and including the reed mass and Bernoulli forces on the inner area of the reed.

All the obtained results realistically predict the shape of the initial transient, sinusoidal signals at low blowing pressure and trapezoidal-shaped signals at high blowing pressure. Sampling frequencies of the modeling varied between 8 and 400 kHz. Gazengel et al. (1995) showed that for sampling frequencies below 44 kHz, the steady-state frequency of the pressure may be ± 5 cent in error.

In all these studies the tube is supposed to be a passive linear element. In the previous section it was mentioned that the impedance is amplitude-dependent. It would be interesting to include this fact in the descriptions and to investigate the influence on the oscillations.

Because of the great number of variables interacting, non-periodic and chaotic behavior can occur. Normally, a musician tries to avoid this, but he may use it for special effects. Quasi-periodic oscillations, multiphonics (two or more frequencies together) and subharmonic generation (period doubling) have been observed and explained [Benade (1976), Backus (1978), Maganza et al. (1986), Gibiat (1988), Dalmont et al. (1995), Gazengel and Gilbert (1995), Kobata and Idogawa (1995), Idogawa et al. (1993), Rihs et al. (1995), and Kergomard (1995)]. Kergomard (1995) found that chaotic phenomena are more likely to occur at "loose" embouchure (great rest height, low lip pressure) which corresponds to the experience of the player: the looser the embouchure, the greater the chance of obtaining odd sounds.

A6. Applications of input impedance spectra

For reed-blown instruments with short holes and a sufficiently strong fundamental in the spectrum, it has been shown that the input impedances determined by calculations closely correspond to those "passively" (without blowing) measured and those actually blown, the latter by either an artificial mouth or a musician or by both (this book, Chapter 4; Dalmont et al. 1995; Coltman 1979). An exception forms very small holes, as discussed in Section A4.

At low sound levels the excitation may produce a pure sine, controlled by a single resonance of the tube. At larger amplitudes the excitation mechanism becomes nonlinear and generates higher harmonics. If the tube has only a single resonance (a Helmholtz resonator or bottle), a nonlinear excitation produces only this resonance. However, when the tube has more resonances they will compete with each other. Those resonances with the lowest damping have the best chances of being excited. If the resonances are nearly harmonic, they will cooperate. Nonlinear processes cause locking the modes into harmonic relationships (Fletcher 1978). In practice, the resonances usually are not exactly harmonic. In that case the excitation will settle for a situation of maximum energy. This means that a strong resonance at a frequency which is not an exact harmonic may shift the fundamental frequency of the tube. When the fundamental is weak and there are strong non-harmonic higher resonances, it is possible that the latter cluster as harmonics of a fundamental which is very different from that of the real fundamental. These notes are known as pedal or privileged notes (Benade [18]; Campbell and Greated 1987); they are occasionally used on trombones. A reed or a mouth resonance may also provide a missing harmonic in the cluster. This may explain reported observations on a bassoon, where a particular reed could shift the intended note a semitone or more into another (stable) frequency. The player circumvents these embarrassments by selecting a proper reed, without knowing which parameter causes the trouble.

Wogram (1972) proposed employing a "sum function"

$$S(f) = \frac{1}{n} \sum_{1}^{n} Z'(nf), \qquad (A6.1)$$

where $Z'(nf)$ is the real part of the impedance at frequency nf. The maxima of this sum function should indicate the frequencies the tube will sound. This assumes an excitation consisting of a spectrum of n peaks of the same height. For other excitations weight factors may have to be introduced related to the peak height in the excitation spectrum (Wogram 1996).

As they applied this to trombones, Elliot and Bowsher (1982) found that the sum function reliably predicted the played frequencies, although Pratt and Bowsher (1979) were less enthusiastic. Dudley and Strong (1990) showed that a similar function, called the mouthpiece pressure response, is useful for brass instruments. It would be worthwhile to investigate the usefulness of such functions, attractive because of their simplicity, for woodwind instruments.

To illustrate the method, Fig. A6.1 shows a (calculated) impedance spectrum for a cylindrical tube (clarinet) with wall damping only (radiation losses at the open end were neglected; they appear hardly to influence the spectrum). The wall damping factor α' is proportional to $k^{-1/2}$ (eq. 22.9); it decreases with frequency. Since α' slightly lowers the wave number, the modes are not exactly harmonic; they are stretched somewhat. The peak heights, inversely proportional to $\alpha'k$, also decrease (eq. 22.27). The width of a resonance peak between its half-power points (Pierce 1989) is $f/Q = 2 f\alpha' \sim \sqrt{k}$, so it increases on a linear frequency scale. The three effects can be seen in Fig. A6.1. In reality, this simple pattern is modified due to the intricate geometry of the pipe. At

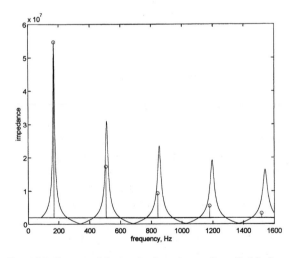

Fig. A6.1. Spectra of the passive impedance of a cylindrical pipe (drawn line) and that of the impedance generated by the reed (circles).

higher frequencies, for which the tube pieces are no longer short with respect to the wavelength, resonances can occur in these tube pieces. The spectrum loses its character of well-defined isolated peaks. The frequency where this occurs, the so-called cut-off frequency f_{co}, has been calculated by Benade ([17]; see also Benade [1976], page 449) for a tube with a row of identical and equally spaced holes as

$$f_{co} = 0.11c(b/a)(sL_H)^{-1/2}, \tag{A6.2}$$

where c = sound speed, a, b = tube, hole radius, L_H = effective hole length, and $2s$ = spacing between holes.

The Fourier spectrum of a clarinet reed, producing the trapezoidal shape shown with a dashed line as in Fig. A5.3, is plotted in Fig. A6.1 with circles. This spectrum has odd harmonics only. It closely resembles that of a square wave where the peaks of the successive odd harmonics are in the ratio $1:\frac{1}{3}:\frac{1}{5}:\frac{1}{7}$, and so forth. The excitation spectrum is shown locked in on the first mode, due to which it is not perfectly locked in on the higher harmonics. The spectrum shapes of tube and generator are more or less similar. It can be expected that for both sinusoidal or trapezoidal excitation the impedances can be made to fit reasonably well. Due to the relatively strong first mode, the influence of higher modes on the resonance frequency will be limited. Since the reed displacement is a result of responses from the tube and is dependent on sound level, the procedure looks simpler than it probably is, but it would be worthwhile to compare its frequency prediction with that of time-consuming calculations in the time domain (see previous section).

To investigate the fit of the spectra for conical instruments, the spectrum of the conical tube is first calculated with the expression for the input admittance given by eq.(23.30) and then modified by adding a mouthpiece cavity term, which leads to the expression

$$Y = \frac{-jS_0}{\rho c}\left[\frac{1}{w} - \frac{V_m w}{3V_0} - 2\beta g - \frac{\beta \varepsilon_v}{w^2}\right.$$
$$\left. - \left(1 + 2\beta f - \frac{2\beta \varepsilon_v}{w}\right)\cot B\right], \tag{A6.3}$$

where B is given by eq.(23.35). Radiation at the open end was neglected. With this expression, the admittance is calculated for a tube with an entrance radius of 4 mm, a length to the apex of 1 m, a relative truncation of $w/W_1 = 0.1$ and $V_m/V_0 = 1.2$. This is plotted in Fig. A6.2. This spectrum is very similar to measured spectra up to the cut-off frequency, just as in the case of a cylinder. A typical property for a cone is the first peak being smaller than the higher frequency peaks. The peaks can be seen close to harmonic, due to the "overcompensated" mouthpiece cavity, which tends to lower the higher modes (cf. Fig. 27.4). The spectrum of the motion of a reed on a cone (Fig. A5.3) is shown in Fig. A6.2 with circles, the first mode locked in on

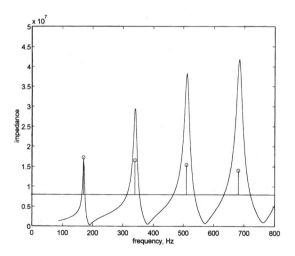

Fig. A6.2. Spectra of the passive impedance of a conical pipe (drawn line) and that of the impedance generated by the reed (circles).

that of the tube. It is close to that of a spiked signal, in which all harmonics are of equal strength. This makes a better fit to the cone spectrum than a clarinet reed spectrum would. Even so, the mismatch is larger than that for a cylinder. This will have consequences for the lowest notes, for which the lowest peak is the fundamental. These will be more difficult to excite both for low (sinusoidal) levels, where a low impedance is necessary, and for higher levels, where the added higher modes demand larger impedances. This will put a greater demand on adjustments of the excitation, which may explain why these low notes on conical instruments (saxophone, oboe, bassoon) are difficult to play softly. This also corresponds with the observation that reeds on conical instruments seldom oscillate sinusoidally.

It may be possible to change the damping in the instrument by changing the losses at the holes through modifying their dimensions. An experiment with an alto saxophone, on which the chimneys of the two lowest holes were lengthened to a value equal to the diameter, proved to enhance the attack of the lowest notes (Postma 1996). It is worthwhile to investigate this further.

Observing the impedance spectrum is simple and of practical use, as Cronin and Keefe (1995) have shown in their study on the ease of blowing for various bassoon fingerings. They found that blowing could be enhanced when higher resonances were brought in line with the fundamental by changing the fingerings.

The necessary adjustment of the excitation impedance to that of the tube can be achieved by varying the parameters appearing in eqs.(A5.1) or (A5.2). We already mentioned the limits for reed-blown instruments. On flutes, the parameters can be changed by changing the jet velocity and the mouth hole coverage. But in practice there are also limits to this. This appears from blowing the well-known fork fingering (● ● ○ ● ●) on an old-model flute for A-sharp on the high register, in which three holes are closed below

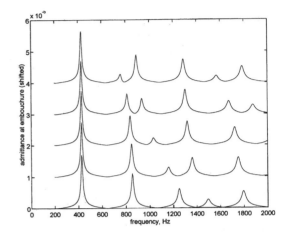

Fig. A6.3. Admittance spectra of a flute with one open hole, where the right-hand tube piece length L_R is stepwise increased in length, starting with 0.1 m and stepping up with 0.025m. Left-hand tube piece length L_L is 0.379 m, hole radius is 9.5 mm, and (transformed) hole length λ_H is 22 mm. The plots are shifted vertically for better visibility.

the one opened for sounding the A. In the low register, closing these three holes lowers the note somewhat, but in the second register the note goes up a semitone (a similar phenomenon can be observed on a modern Boehm flute). An explanation is found from studying the spectrum (Coltman 1996b). Fig. A6.3 shows admittance spectra, calculated for a flute with one open hole, where the length of the right hand tube piece L_R is increased stepwise up to the value for the fork fingering. The curves are shifted vertically to separate them. At short L_R, the peaks approximately form a harmonic series. At greater L_R, the second peak progressively moves to lower frequencies and diminishes in height, which corresponds to actual playing experience: it becomes difficult to play the note. At the same time the third mode shifts downwards, its amplitude first decreases, later increases and finally becomes larger than the second mode. At a certain L_R its level apparently is sufficiently high for the player to sound it, whereas the second mode cannot be sounded any more. Coltman (1996b) suggests to use the graphical determination of the frequency as given in Fig. 4 of his 1976 paper: it may be impossible to get the jet-phase-shift line to intersect with a resonance peak lying in the shadow of a high peak at a lower frequency.

A7. Mouth, reed and wall vibrations

In the normal way of operating, the air column vibrations are excited by the flow controlled by the air column pressures. 'Other' resonances, of the vocal tract (mouth), the reed or the tube wall may be involved. They can be coupled to the excitation or to air column vibrations and have either a positive or a negative contribution. Their effects may be inaudible to the listener while still helping or hindering the player, an aspect which indirectly can be detected by the listener. They may add to the character of the instrument, but they should not be too prominent as to interfere with the normal operation of the instrument.

A beating clarinet reed mainly generates odd harmonics, which benefits the resonances in the fundamental mode but is not optimal for those in a high register. To support other resonances it can be imagined that there is help from the 'other' resonances. It is also possible that these resonances play a role in the initial transient (Hoekje 1993).

The vocal tract is not a chamber with a constant pressure. It also is a resonator, though at the upstream end of the excitation. For reed-type excitations the reed(s) can be considered to be located between two resonators and to be coupled to both. Backus (1985) concluded that the influence on the instrument tone is negligible. Coltman (1973) observed frequency shifts and increased losses in flutes due to mouth resonances. Clinch et al. (1982) found influences of vocal tract resonances on clarinet and saxophone sound. Hoekje (1986) and Sommerfeldt and Strong (1988)

have shown how a mouth resonance can support the reed motion, despite the fact that there is hardly a difference in the frequency spectrum of the radiated sound, so the listener does not hear a difference. The player, however, may feel the difference in the ease of playing. Johnston et al. (1987) carried out computer simulations for a clarinet and showed that the vocal tract can take over the function of the instrument, provided the damping is low enough. The frequency can be pulled down quite substantially. Clarinet players will confirm this: by lip/mouth manipulations the frequency can be pulled down several tones below that of the tube. Wilson (1996) confirmed this by measurements.

Smith and Mercer (1974) suggest that reed resonances contribute to the formant (an area in the frequency spectrum of strong overtones) of a reed-blown instrument. Thompson (1979) observed that an experienced player tends to adjust the reed resonance to one of the signal harmonics, to ease playing. Although the lip pressure already is in use for the adjustment of the slit height, the reed resonances are complicated (Hoekje 1996a), and it can be imagined that by shaping the lips and/or the teeth the resonance frequency can be adjusted somewhat while keeping the slit height the same. If this effect were important, it would mean that some slit heights give more stable notes than others.

Still a hot item is the possible influence of wall vibrations on the sound quality. As was measured by Backus [8], the walls of a clarinet vibrate with an amplitude of about 1 μm, but radiation from the walls due to this vibration is at least 40 dB below the air signal. Some exploratory measurements (carried out by the author in Le Mans, France, in cooperation with Jean-Pierre Dalmont) have confirmed that vibrations of clarinets and flutes are of flexural type with amplitudes in the range of 1μm. From listening experiments, Coltman (1971) found no effect of material on flute tone quality.

Wall vibrations can be excited by internal pressures since the tube is not an exact cylinder; the holes make it asymmetrical. Also, the reaction forces of the excitation transfer energy. The reed bending causes forces of about 1 N per mm deflection. Forces from vortices swaying across the labium of flutes probably are smaller than those due to a moving reed. Powell [96] calculated the force F of a jet of width B with mean velocity u oscillating across an edge of width d as

$$F < 5\rho u^2 Bd .\qquad\qquad (A7.1)$$

For typical values of $\rho = 1.2$ kg/m^3, $u = 10$ m/s, $B = 10$ mm, and $d = 1$ mm, $F < 0.006$ N. Fabre measured the lateral forces on the labium of an organ flue pipe (28 cm long, square cross-section 2 cm x 2 cm, flue channel height 1 mm, flue exit to labium 4 mm) and found values between 0.01 and 0.1 N (Fabre 1996).

Once excited, wall vibrations may interact with the excitation. For example, a flute is supported rather weakly by the lip and fingers; its head can freely move up and down, thereby intercepting a varying amount of the jet flow and/or deforming the lower lip, varying the slit height (see Fig. A7.1). For a jet emerging from a slit of height 1 mm which deforms or changes its direction 1 μm, changes in the flow will be of the order of 1%, or 40 dB below the signal and hardly detectable. Due to amplification of the jet instability, however, the effects will be larger.

Similar conclusions can be drawn for the single reed. Since the mouthpiece of a single-reed instrument is held between the teeth, it may seem immovable here. However, explorative measurements during the blowing of a clarinet, done with Thomas Rossing at Northern Illinois University, showed that at a reed amplitude of about 100 μm, the top of the mouthpiece near the teeth vibrated with an amplitude of 3 μm. This corresponds to a 30 dB difference. A re-

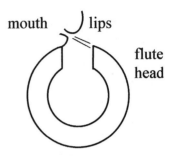

Fig. A7.1. Flute embouchure and its support by the lower lip.

markable finding was that the frequency of the tube vibration could be different from that of the reed. In some cases the mouthpiece vibrated in a frequency twice that of the reed.

For a double reed, which is held between the lips, similar reasoning leads to the conclusion that its vibrations may be coupled to those of the instrument walls. For example, the bassoon crook (bocal), when hit like a tuning fork, vibrates at about 400 Hz. This is in the same range as the first formant of the instrument. It is tempting to see a relationship here, particularly as many bassoon players and builders are convinced that shape and material of the crook are of paramount importance. Could there be a connection with the resonance frequency and/or damping of the crook?

The enigmatic loudness increase during the breaking-in period of high-quality recorders could be related to changes in the wall roughness and porosity, but the following observation about descant recorders indicates that vibrations of the recorder bodies can be a factor. A manufacturer claimed that the amount of paraffin absorption during the manufacturing process influenced the sound level. This was verified by weighing and blowing 18 recorders randomly taken from the production. The lowest note of those recorders which were 4 g heavier than the mean of 80 g appeared to be 3 dB louder. From a separate investigation of the flexural vibrations of the recorders as a freely suspended bar, it was found that the lowest resonance frequency approximately coincided with the lowest blown note and that the quality factor of the flexural resonance of the heavier recorder was 1.5 times that of the light one (Nederveen 1973).*

There are other stories about wall influence on playing properties. Gibiat (1993) reports that a saxophone builder had problems blowing the instrument when the production process of the bell was changed, supposedly due to wall vibrations. Phenomena of this type could well be studied by determining playing properties as a function of the wall vibration amplitude, the latter artificially adjusted by an external excitation (Fletcher 1996).

While the radiation from thick-walled instruments was found to be negligible, this may not be the case for thin-walled metal instruments like the saxophone. This follows from studies on thin-walled lip-blown instruments such as the trumpet, French horn and trombone by Smith (1978), Pyle (1981), Watkinson and Bowsher (1982), Lawson and Lawson (1985), Campbell and Greated (1987) and Hoekje (1996b). The bell can vibrate at a great number of frequencies, closely spaced in the audio range. Changing the wall material, applying metal layers, or coating the bell with lacquer could change the radiated power and/or that of the higher spectral components by 3 dB or more. This is probably noticeable by listeners: Coltman (1996a) found that most listeners can detect differences of 3 dB in the harmonic composition.

---

* Recent investigations by the author have shown that the most likely explanation is a porosity difference due to a difference in impregnation. The measured input impedance peaks of the recorders were some 10 dB below the theoretical values. This can be explained by the high porosity of the walls, which corresponds to microscopic observations. The peaks of a light recorder are 2 to 3 dB lower than those of a heavy one, for which a higher damping due to a larger porosity offers an explanation.

A8. Conclusions

As is stipulated at several places in this chapter, the knowledge on woodwind instruments has increased tremendously in the past 25 years, but many questions remain unanswered.

Linear acoustics (low sound level) is very useful for predicting the tuning. There is a need for increasing the accuracy of predicting the resonance frequencies from the geometry. With the present state of computing power combined with sophisticated measurement facilities this gap of knowledge can be expected to be filled in the near future.

At high sound levels the linear description fails. Losses can increase up to the level where they interfere with the air resonances. The loudness of instruments seems to be related to the hole size. With certain hole sizes instruments cannot be blown anymore, presumably due to high losses. Sometimes small holes act as if closed. There is insufficient knowledge of the magnitude of these losses and which parameters they depend on. The occurrence of vortices and the absence of basic knowledge obstruct a theoretical approach. Experiments may indeed be difficult, but they seem the only sensible approach to obtain basic insight.

Although the mathematical aspects of simulation are well-defined and convenient to apply, the parameters are hardly defined. In particular the double-reed parameters and those of the flute excitation are badly known, rendering many sophisticated simulations into exercises in programming. Thorough physical investigations of the excitation parameters need to come first.

Input impedance spectra appear to be a promising tool for judging the quality of woodwinds. At present, these spectra can be obtained theoretically and experimentally without too much effort. Simple notions as the "sum function" appear to be useful for improving tuning and ease of blowing.

It is clear that there is or can be an influence of mouth, reed and wall vibrations on the functioning of woodwinds, but many questions are unanswered here.

To summarize, the following proposals for investigations on woodwind instruments are made:

1. Linear acoustics: determine theoretically all corrections due to deviations from the ideal geometrical model. Verify these experimentally.
2. Determine to what extent the sum function (or any similar function) is useful for predicting accuracy of tuning, ease of blowing and harmonic content.
3. Determine if the irregular bore of baroque woodwinds serves any function and, if so, how this bore can be predicted or improved.
4. Determine the losses at holes as a function of their shape, acoustic velocity and steady flow.
5. Determine all energy flows and losses in various instruments, notably at holes of various dimensions, and compare these with the energy supplied by the excitation.
6. Investigate influences on blowing properties and frequency spectrum of the resonances of the vocal tract, reed and wall by systematically (artificially) changing the magnitude of these effects with respect to the air oscillations.

The results of the above-proposed investigations presumably will indicate how to optimize bore and hole dimensions to better match energy demand and supply, leading to instruments with a greater flexibility and dynamic range.

references to the addendum

Y. Ando (1969/1970). On the sound radiation from semi-infinite circular pipe of certain wall thickness. Acustica 22, 219–225.

J. Angster, A. Miklos (1992). Transient sound spectra of a variable length organ pipe. Int. Symp. Mus. Acoust., Tokyo, Japan, 159–162.

R.D. Ayers (1996). Impulse response for feedback to the driver of a musical wind instrument. JASA 100, 1190–1198.

J. Backus (1978). Multiphonic tones in woodwind instruments. JASA 63, 591–599.

———— (1985). The effect of the player's vocal tract on woodwind instrument tone. JASA 78, 17–20.

A. Barjau, J. Agullo (1989). Calculation of the starting transients of a double-reed conical woodwind. Acustica 69, 204–210.

A.H. Benade (1976). Fundamentals of Musical Acoustics. Oxford University Press, New York.

M. Bernard, B. Denardo (1996). Re-computation of Ando's approximation of the end correction for a radiating semi-infinite circular pipe. Acustica 82, 670–671.

X. Boutillon, V. Gibiat (1996). Evaluation of the acoustical stiffness of saxophone reeds under playing conditions by using the reactive power approach. JASA 100, 1178–1189.

G.S. Brindley (1973). Speed of sound in bent tubes and the design of wind instruments. Nature 246, 479–480.

J.C. Bruggeman (1987). Flow induced pulsations in pipe systems. Ph.D. thesis, Eindhoven, The Netherlands.

D.M. Campbell, C.A. Greated (1987). The Musician's Guide to Acoustics. Dent, London. American edition (1988) by Schirmer Books, New York.

R. Caussé, J. Kergomard, X. Lurton (1984). Input impedance of brass musical instruments - Comparison between experiment and numerical methods. JASA 75, 241–254.

P.G. Clinch, G.J. Troup, L. Harris (1982). The importance of vocal tract resonance in clarinet and saxophone performance, a preliminary account. Acustica 50, 280–284.

J.W. Coltman (1971). Effect of material on flute tone quality. JASA 49, 520–523.

———— (1973). Mouth resonance effects in the flute. JASA 54, 417–420.

———— (1976). Jet drive mechanisms in edge tones and organ pipes. JASA 60, 725–733.

———— (1979). Acoustical analysis of the Boehm flute. JASA 65, 499–506.

———— (1984). Enhanced sound power from a recurved flute. JASA 75, 1642–1643.

———— (1990). Mode stretching and harmonic generation in the flute. JASA 88, 2070–2073.

———— (1992a). Time-domain simulation of the flute. JASA 92, 69–73.

———— (1992b). Jet behavior in the flute. JASA 92, 74–83.

———— (1996a). Just noticeable differences in timbre of the flute. CASJ Series II, Vol 3:1, 26–33.

———— (1996b). Personal communication.

R.H. Cronin, D.H. Keefe (1996). Understanding the operation of auxiliary fingerings on double-reed instruments. JASA 99, 2456 (abstract).

A. Cummings (1974). Sound transmission in curved duct bends. J. Sound Vib. 35, 451–477.

J.P. Dalmont, B. Gazengel, J. Gilbert, J. Kergomard (1995). Some aspects of tuning and clean intonation in reed instruments. Applied Acoustics 46, 19–60.

J.P. Dalmont, J. Kergomard (1994). Lattices of sound tubes with harmonically related eigenfrequencies. Acta Acustica 2, 421–430.

———— (1995). Elementary model and experiments for the Helmholtz motion of single reed wind instruments. Proceedings of the International Symposium on Musical Acoustics, Dourdan, France, 115–120.

138

J.P. Dalmont, C.J. Nederveen (1997). Why is a saxophone louder than a clarinet? International Symposium on Musical Acoustics, Edinburgh. Proceedings of the Institute of Acoustics, Vol. 19, Pt. 5, 267–272.

B. Denardo, M. Bernard (1996). Design and measurement of variably nonuniform acoustic resonators. Am. J. Phys. 64(6), 745–751.

V. Dubos, J. Kergomard, A. Khettabi, D.H. Keefe, J.P. Dalmont, C.J. Nederveen (1998). Theory of a tube branched on a duct using modal decomposition. Submitted for publication in Acustica.

J.D. Dudley, W.J. Strong (1990). A computer study of the effects of harmonicity in a brass wind instrument: impedance curve, impulse response and mouthpiece pressure with a hypothetical periodic input. Applied Acoustics 30, 117–132.

S.J. Elliot, J.M. Bowsher (1982). Regeneration in brass wind instruments. J. Sound Vib. 83, 181–217.

B. Fabre (1996). Personal communication.

B. Fabre, A. Hirschberg, A.P.J. Wijnands (1996). Vortex shedding in steady oscillation of a flue organ pipe. Acustica 82, 863–877.

N.H. Fletcher (1976). Sound production by organ flue pipes. JASA 60, 926–936.

——— (1978). Mode locking in nonlinearly excited inharmonic musical oscillators. JASA 64, 1566–1569.

——— (1996). Personal communication.

N.H. Fletcher, T.D. Rossing (1991). The Physics of Musical Instruments. Springer Verlag, New York.

B. Gazengel, J. Gilbert (1995). From the measured input impedance to the synthesized pressure signal: application to the saxophone. Proceedings of the International Symposium on Musical Acoustics, Dourdan, France, 1995, 484–489.

B. Gazengel, J. Gilbert, N. Amir (1995). Time domain simulation of single reed wind instrument. From the measured input signal to the synthesis

signal. Where are the traps? Acta Acustica 3, 445–472.

V. Gibiat (1988). Phase space representations of acoustical musical signals. J. Sound Vib. 123, 529–536.

——— (1993). Personal communication.

J. Gilbert (1991). Etude des instruments de musique à anche simple. Ph.D. thesis, Le Mans, France.

J. Gilbert, J. Kergomard, E. Ngoya (1989). Calculation of the steady-state oscillations of a clarinet using the harmonic balance technique. JASA 86, 35–41.

A.Y. Gokhshtein (1982). Role of air flow modulator in the excitation of sound in wind instruments. Sov. Phys. Dokl. 26, 954–956.

——— (1995). New conception and improvement of sound generation in conical woodwinds. Proceedings of the International Symposium on Musical Acoustics, Dourdan, France, 1995, 121–128.

N. Grand, J. Gilbert, F. Laloé (1997). Oscillation threshold of woodwind instruments. Acustica/Acta Acustica 83, 137–151.

A. Hirschberg (1995). Aero-acoustics of wind instruments. In Mechanics of Musical Instruments. Springer, New York.

A. Hirschberg, J. Gilbert, A.P.J. Wijnands, A.M.C. Valkering (1994). Musical aero-acoustics of the clarinet. J. de Physique IV, Vol. 4, Colloque C5, C5-559–568.

A. Hirschberg, R.W.A. van de Laar, J.P. Marrou-Maurières, A.P.J. Wijnands, H.J. Dane, S.G. Kruijswijk, A.J.M. Houtsma (1990). A quasi-stationary model of air flow in the reed channel of single-reed woodwind instruments. Acustica 70, 146–154.

P.L. Hoekje (1986). Intercomponent exchange and upstream/downstream symmetry in nonlinear self-sustained oscillations of reed instruments. Ph.D. thesis, Case Western Reserve University, Cleveland, Ohio.

——— (1993). Transient behavior of time-domain wind instrument models. JASA 94, 1833 (abstract).

——— (1996a). Observed vibrational patterns of clarinet reeds. JASA 99, 2462 (abstract).

——— (1996b). Personal communication.

T. Idogawa, T. Kobata, K. Komuro, M. Iwaki (1993). Nonlinear vibrations in the air column of a clarinet artificially blown. JASA 93, 540–551.

U. Ingard, V.K. Singhal (1976). Flow excitation and coupling of acoustic modes of a side branch cavity in a duct. JASA 60, 1213–1215.

R. Johnston, P.G. Clinch, G.J. Troup (1987). The role of vocal tract resonance in clarinet playing. Acoustics Australia 14:3, 67–69.

D.H. Keefe (1982a). Theory of the single woodwind tonehole. JASA 72, 676–687.

——— (1982b). Experiments on the single woodwind tonehole. JASA 72, 688–699.

——— (1983). Acoustic streaming, dimensional analysis of nonlinearities, and tone hole mutual interactions in woodwinds. JASA 73, 1804–1820.

——— (1990). Woodwind air column models. JASA 88, 35–51.

——— (1996). Wind-instrument reflection function measurements in the time domain. JASA 99, 2370–2381.

D.H. Keefe, A.H. Benade (1983). Wave propagation in strongly curved ducts. JASA 74, 320–332.

J. Kergomard (1981). Quasi-stationary waves in horns with visco-thermal losses at the walls, calculated from the impedance. Acustica 48, 31–43 (in French).

——— (1988). General equivalent electric circuits for acoustic horns. J. Audio Eng. Soc. 36, 948–955.

——— (1995). Elementary considerations on reed-instrument oscillations. In Mechanics of Musical Instruments, Hirschberg et al., editors, Springer, New York.

J. Kergomard, A. Garcia (1987). Simple discontinuities in acoustic waveguides at low frequencies: critical analysis and formulae. J. Sound Vib. 114(3), 465–479.

T. Kobata, T. Idogawa (1995). A study on clarinet-equations of Schumacher. Proceedings of the International Symposium on Musical Acoustics, Dourdan, France, 170–176.

J. J. M. F. Kokkelmans (1995). Properties of the Reed-flute. Report of a stage on the University of Eindhoven, The Netherlands (in Dutch).

J. J. M. F. Kokkelmans, B.P.J. Wijnands (1996). Influence of chimney length and position on the sound production of the rohrflöte. Submitted for publication to JASA.

P.C. Kriesels, M.C.A.M. Peters, A. Hirschberg, A.P.J. Wijnands, A Iafrati, G. Riccardi, R. Piva, J.C. Bruggeman (1995). High amplitude vortex-induced pulsations in a gas transport system. J. Sound Vib. 184, 343–368.

R.M. Laszewski, A.D. Murray (1984). Some observations on tone color in the recurved flute. JASA 75, 1643–1644.

B. Lawson, W. Lawson (1985). Acoustical characteristics of annealed French horn bell flares. JASA 77, 1913–1916.

F.G. Leppington (1982). On the theory of woodwind finger holes. J. Sound Vib. 83, 521–532.

C. Maganza, R. Caussé, F. Laloë (1986). Bifurcations, period doublings and chaos in clarinetlike systems. Europhys. Lett. 1, 295–302.

M.E. McIntyre, R.T. Schumacher, J. Woodhouse (1983). On the oscillations of musical instruments. JASA 74, 1325–1345.

C.J. Nederveen (1973). Blown, passive and calculated resonance frequencies of the flute. Acustica 28, 12–23.

——— (1996). Influences of sharp toroidal bends on the tuning of wind instruments. JASA 99, 2456 (abstract).

—— (1998). Influence of a toroidal bend on wind instrument tuning. Submitted for publication in JASA.

C.J. Nederveen, J.-P. Dalmont, H.J. Dane (1995). Influence of static flow on the input impedance of a woodwind instrument, or why a clarinet with tiny holes demands another reed or mouthpiece. International Conference on Musical Acoustics, Dourdan, France, 141–147.

C.J. Nederveen, J.K.M. Jansen, R.R. van Hassel (1998). Corrections for woodwind tone-hole calculations. Forthcoming in Acustica/Acta Acustica.

A.W. Nolle, T.L. Finch (1992). Starting transients of flue organ pipes in relation to pressure rise time. JASA 91, 2190–2202.

M.C.A.M. Peters, A. Hirschberg, A.J. Reijnen, A.P.J. Wijnands (1993). Damping and reflection measurements for an open pipe at low Mach and low Helmholtz numbers. J. Fluid Mech. 256, 499–534.

A.D. Pierce (1989). Acoustics. An Introduction to Its Physical Principles and Applications. Acoustical Society of America, New York. (Estimation of acoustic inertances, 341; definition of resonator quality, 120.)

G.R Plitnik, W.J. Strong (1979). Numerical method for calculating input impedances of the oboe. JASA 65, 816–825.

M. Postma (1996). Personal communication.

R.L. Pratt, J.M. Bowsher (1979). The objective assessment of trombone quality. J. Sound Vib. 65, 521–547.

R.L. Pritchard (1960). Mutual acoustic impedance between radiators in an infinite rigid plane. JASA 32, 730–737.

R.W. Pyle Jr. (1981). The effect of lacquer and silver plating on horn tone. Horn Call 11(2), 26–29.

N. Rihs, V. Gibiat, M. Castellengo (1995). Period doubling production on a bassoon. Proceedings of the International Symposium on Musical Acoustics, Dourdan, France, 184–188.

F. Rocaboy (1989). Proposed model for reed action in the bassoon. CAJS Series II, Vol. 1 (no. 4): 20–25.

W. Rostafinski (1972). On propagation of long waves in curved ducts. JASA 52, 1411–1420.

E.G. Schlosser (1979). Tonerzeugung und Toncharakteristika bei Labialpfeifen. Acustica 43, 177–187 (in German).

R.T. Schumacher (1978a). Self-sustained oscillations of organ flue pipes: an integral equation solution. Acustica 39, 225–238.

—— (1978b). Self-sustained oscillations of the clarinet: an integral equation solution. Acustica 40, 298–309.

—— (1981). Ab initio calculations of the oscillations of a clarinet. Acustica 48, 71–85.

D. Sharp, D.M. Campbell, A. Myers (1996). Pulse reflectometry as a method of leak detection in historical brass instruments. Paper at Forum Acousticum, Antwerp, Belgium.

R.A. Smith (1978). Recent developments in trumpet design. International Trumpet Guild Journal 3, 27–29.

R.A. Smith, D.M.A Mercer (1974). Possible causes of woodwind tone colour. J. Sound Vib. 32, 347–358.

S.D. Sommerfeldt, W.J. Strong (1988). Simulation of a player-clarinet system. JASA 83, 1908–1918.

S.E. Stewart, W.J. Strong (1980). Functional model of a simplified clarinet. JASA 68, 109–120.

E. Stuhlträger, H. Thomann (1986). Oscillations of a gas in an open-ended tube near resonance. J. Appl. Math. Phys. (ZAMP) 37, 155–175.

S.C. Thompson (1979). The effect of reed resonance on woodwind tone production. JASA 66, 1299–1307.

S. Thwaites, N.H. Fletcher (1980). Wave propagation on turbulent jets. Acustica 45, 175–179.

—— (1982). Wave propagation on turbulent jets II. Acustica 51, 44–49.

M.P. Verge (1995). Aeroacoustics of confined jets, with applications to the physical modeling of recorder-like instruments. Ph.D. thesis, Eindhoven, The Netherlands.

M.P. Verge, R. Caussé, B. Fabre, A. Hirschberg, A.P.J. Wijnands, A. van Steenbergen (1994). Jet oscillations and jet drive in recorder-like instruments. Acta Acustica 2, 403–419.

P.S. Watkinson, J.M. Bowsher (1982). Vibration characteristics of brass instrument bells. J. Sound Vib. 85, 1–17.

C.C. Wier, W. Jestead, D.M. Green (1977). Frequency discrimination as a function of frequency and sensation level. JASA 61, 178–184.

A.P.J. Wijnands, A. Hirschberg (1995). Effect of a pipe neck downstream of a double reed. Proceedings of the International Symposium on Musical Acoustics, Dourdan, France, 1995, 148–152.

T.A. Wilson, G.S. Beavers (1974). Operating modes of the clarinet. JASA 56, 653–658.

T.D. Wilson (1996). The measured upstream impedance for clarinet performance and its role in sound production. Ph.D. thesis, School of Music, University of Washington, Seattle, Washington. Abstract in JASA 102, 1250.

K. Wogram (1972). A contribution to the measurement of the intonation of brass instruments. Ph.D. thesis, Technical University of Braunschweig, Germany.

——— (1996). Personal communication.

W.E. Worman (1971). Self-sustained nonlinear oscillations of medium amplitude in clarinet-like systems. Ph.D. thesis, Case Western Reserve University, Cleveland, Ohio.

W.E. Worman, A.H. Benade, M. Vadnais (1990). A simplified model for a beating reed: preliminary results. CASJ Series II, Vol. 1 (no. 5), 17–22.

S. Yoshikawa, J. Saneyoshi (1980). Feedback excitation mechanisms in organ pipes. J. Acoust. Soc. Jpn (E) 1, 3, 175–191.

list of symbols

a	tube radius, m	p	sound pressure, N/m² or Pa
b	radius of joining tube or side hole, m	q	constant (p. 29)
B	function (p. 24)	Q	resonator quality
	slit width, m	r	fractional pressure of gas fraction of air (p. 17)
	bend curvature parameter		distance to apex (top) of conical tube, m
c	sound velocity, m/s	R	major radius of torus, m
C_p	heat capacity at constant pressure, J/kg°C or J/kgK	S	area, m²
C_t	reed compliance, m³/N	S_r	effective reed area, m² (p. 29)
D	relative frequency shift $= \Delta f/f$	St	Strouhal number
E	geometrical factor (p. 62)	t	time, s or sec
	constant (p. 29)	T	temperature, °C
f	frequency, Hz	u	particle velocity, m/s
	function (p. 23)	U	volume velocity, m³/s
F	penetration coefficient (p. 112)	V	jet speed, m/s (p. 123)
G	amplification factor of jet distortion (p. 123)	w	argument of trigoniometrical function $= kr$
g	function (p. 23)	x	place coordinate, m
	relative frequency shift when opening a hole $= \Delta f/f$	Y	acoustic admittance $= 1/Z$, m⁴s/kg
h	function (p. 23)	z	specific acoustic impedance, Ns/m³
	oscillating component of the slit height, m		factor used for calculating hole position (p. 48)
H	slit height in rest position with lip force applied, m	Z	acoustic impedance, kg/m⁴s
He	Helmholtz number = geometrical length divided by wavelength	α	wall damping influence factor (p. 16)
		β	function (p. 22)
		γ	ratio of specific heats
j	$\sqrt{(-1)}$	ε	penetration factor for side hole flow (p. 54)
k	wave number, m⁻¹	ε_v	constant (p. 22)
K	bulk (compression) modulus of air, N/m²	η	viscosity of air, Ns/m²
l	tube length, not corrected, m	λ	wavelength, m
L	tube length, corrected, m		thermal conductivity, W/mK
	length of reed slit, m	λ_H	transformed hole length, m
m	mass, kg	μ	10^{-6}
	mode number, 0.5, 1.5, 2.5, . . . for clarinet; 1, 2, 3, . . . for other instruments	θ	quantity used for imaginary part of end correction
M	acoustic mass of the air in the slit between reed and mouthpiece, kg/m⁴ (p. 29)	ρ	density of air, kg/m³
		ω	angular frequency $= 2\pi f$, s⁻¹
		ξ	quantity used in real part of end correction
n	integer	ψ	phase angle

index